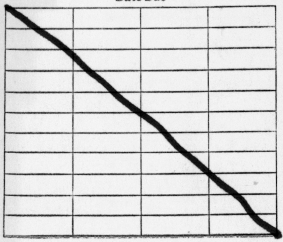

Faculty Unions and Collective Bargaining

E. D. Duryea, Robert S. Fisk, and Associates

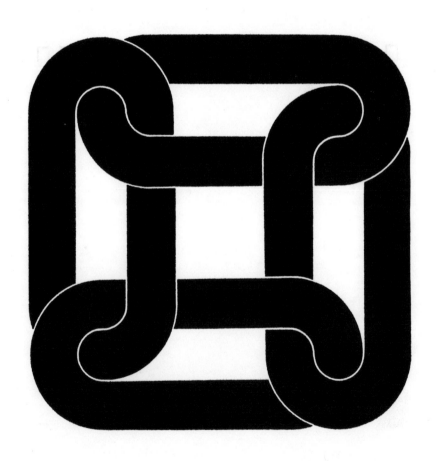

FACULTY UNIONS AND COLLECTIVE BARGAINING

Jossey-Bass Publishers

San Francisco • Washington • London • 1973

FACULTY UNIONS AND COLLECTIVE BARGAINING
by E. D. Duryea, Robert S. Fisk, and Associates

Copyright © 1973 by Jossey-Bass, Inc., Publishers

Published and copyrighted in Great Britain by
Jossey-Bass, Ltd., Publishers
3 Henrietta Street
London WC2E 8LU

Library of Congress Catalogue Card Number LC 72-11968

International Standard Book Number ISBN 0-87589-159-4

Manufactured in the United States of America

JACKET DESIGN BY WILLI BAUM

FIRST EDITION

Code 7302

The Jossey-Bass
Series in Higher Education

Preface

Only ten years ago, it would have been difficult to conceive the relevance of this book, much less its sophistication and depth of analysis. Faculty unionism was certainly then an anathema to faculty members oriented to the professional nature of teaching and research and its ideals of self-imposed professional standards. Yet, *Faculty Unions and Collective Bargaining* is one of an increasing number of publications devoted to the philosophy and policies as well as to the operational intricacies of organized academicians pitted against administrative colleagues, governing board members, and—in some public institutions—officials of state governments.

What is this change all about? Why has it taken place? What does it proffer for the future? Are we in the process of a dramatic shift in relationships that will relegate the role of professors and their nonteaching professional associates to that of employees who must organize to protect their welfare? Can unionism and professionalism exist side by side? Will academicians retain the dedication which ideally has made their classrooms their castles and their research and scholarship a reflection of scholarly commitment to disciplinary and professional areas and to the learning of students? Or will unionism lead to an extension into the campuses of a supervisory bureaucracy which will regulate the work of academicians as employees and establish hours for the classroom and office, the substance and method of courses, and the nature and extent of required scholarship? Does unionism threaten a schism in higher education separating faculty and other professional staff members from administrative colleagues in a manner that will destroy the unity of purpose associated with an academic community?

The ancillary question arises as to whether the unprecedented growth of academic unionism will continue, will slow down to become a gradual evolution, or will level off or even retrogress to constitute simply one more form of faculty representation limited to a majority of institutions. In a related dimension, will collective bargaining continue to be a meaningful resource for those unable to fend for themselves by other means?

No analysis written at this time can predict the answers to these questions. They present, however, a perspective for an examination of collective bargaining in higher education. Certainly, they identify the concerns which motivated us to think in some depth about this development and to seek the assistance of the authors of the chapters which follow in a survey of the situation in four-year colleges and universities.

Faculty Unions and Collective Bargaining falls logically into three parts. The first chapters introduce the nature of collective bargaining, the issues which have been raised, and the procedures involved. In the second part, the book moves from these broad, introductory insights to an examination of particular negotiations. In conclusion, we summarize in the Epilogue the previous chapters and return to a broad perspective—including a look at changes in the academic culture and in the nature of institutional governance —as well as suggesting some of the more immediate consequences of the introduction of collective bargaining into four-year colleges and universities. In the introductory note to each chapter we outline its relevance and the significance of the issues raised in it.

As all who are informed about higher education and the advent of professional unionism recognize, this phenomenon cannot be viewed perceptively outside of other developments which concurrently influence the academic enterprise. Yet, in a book such as this, one must focus primarily upon the one aspect. Therefore, we offer *Faculty Unions and Collective Bargaining* as an initial survey, a state-of-the-nation overview, one anticipating a growing body of literature which will contribute over time to increased understanding of the various conditions associated with bargaining in institutions encompassing the complex of functions associated with higher education.

Buffalo   E. D. DURYEA
January 1973   ROBERT S. FISK

Contents

Contributors

George W. Angell, *president, State University College at Plattsburgh, New York*

Neil S. Bucklew, *vice-provost, Central Michigan University*

E. D. Duryea, *professor, Department of Higher Education, State University of New York at Buffalo*

Matthew W. Finkin, *director of the northeastern regional office and acting counsel, American Association of University Professors*

Robert S. Fisk, *professor of educational studies and chairman of the Policy Studies Consortium, State University of New York at Buffalo*

Joseph W. Garbarino, *professor of business administration and director of the Institute of Business and Economic Research, University of California, Berkeley*

David L. Graham, *negotiations specialist, National Education Association*

Frederick E. Hueppe, *professor of modern foreign languages, St. John's University*

G. Gregory Lozier, *research associate, Office of Budget and Planning, Pennsylvania State University*

Kenneth P. Mortimer, *research associate, Center for the Study of Higher Education, and professor of higher education, Pennsylvania State University*

William C. Puffer, *graduate assistant, Survey Research Center, University of New York at Buffalo*

Donald E. Walters, *deputy director, Massachusetts State College System*

Donald H. Wollett, *professor of law, University of California, Davis*

Faculty Unions and Collective Bargaining

1

Emergence of
Collective Bargaining

Joseph W. Garbarino

As we review the advent of collective bargaining in higher educa-tion, we cannot avoid noting the change in perspective about the role of faculty. In 1967 a task force of academic leaders sponsored by the American Association for Higher Education enunciated a firm commitment to the concept of shared authority based upon recognition of the community of interest within which faculty mem-bers and administrators cooperate in governing colleges and uni-versities. This point of view culminated a long tradition spearheaded by the American Association of University Professors. It implied that professorial commitment to participation in academic policy-

*making implemented the sense of partnership in the higher educa-
tion enterprise.*

*Yet, today the possibility of professors on the picket line
phalanxed against the administration has become real. This demonstrates the impact unionism has had in little more than five years.
Why? An analysis of the nature of collective bargaining requires a
review of the causative factors.*

*Joseph W. Garbarino introduces the book with a perceptive
analysis of the influences which have supported the emerging faculty
commitment to unionism. Much of his analysis is drawn from a national study of collective bargaining which he recently conducted
and which was sponsored by the Carnegie Commission on the Future of Higher Education. He brings to his observations an extensive
experience in industrial relations and collective bargaining in business and government.*

*In his chapter he has probed beneath the surface to examine
a number of the more fundamental developments which have
affected the character of higher education. He has also identified
the major national associations which have taken the leadership in
pressing for unionism in colleges and universities.*

E. D. D. and R. S. F.

In the many theories that have been advanced to explain the growth
of the labor movement, two pervasive elements warrant special attention in terms of the unionization of higher education. One is the
desire of craft workers to control collectively the conditions under
which they exercise their skill. The other is the effects of large, complex, and bureaucratic organizational structures in depersonalizing
and rationalizing employer-employee relationships in general. Although developed in the context of a labor movement made up
predominantly of manual workers, these two factors appear to be
the most basic explanations of unionization among professionals in
higher education. At the same time, additional reasons account for
academic unionism at the particular times and locations in which it
has appeared.

From this perspective, academic unionism in the latter half

of the 1960s resulted from a combination of factors external and internal to the system of higher education.

These factors include the movement to extend legal encouragement for collective bargaining to public employees generally, the cycle of boom and quasibust that higher education has passed through in terms of enrollment and finances along with the concurrent shifts in public attitudes toward higher education, and finally changes in the institutional structure of higher education itself. In the next three sections I examine each of these elements in turn. In the fourth section I review the evolution of the organizations competing to represent faculty and other academic employees, leading finally into a review of the present status of the unionization movement.

Change in Legal Environment

The extension to government workers, particularly at the state level, of the right to organize for collective bargaining is the most important single reason for the present form and growth of academic unions. Compared with many of the industrialized countries of the world, the United States has been slow to extend to public employees the right to union representation guaranteed to employees in the private sector since 1935. Traditionally, in representing the interests of their members, associations of public employees engaged primarily in lobbying and political activity. They usually limited their membership to a single employing jurisdiction such as a state or county. At times they did include substantial numbers of members from education, but in addition, organizations based on particular occupational groups were formed to speak for the interests of particular constituencies. In education these included the local affiliates of the National Education Association (NEA), locals of the American Federation of Teachers (AFT), and independent associations of faculty members in some college and university systems.

However, in the 1950s the legal right to organize began to be extended to public employees in certain major metropolitan areas. State legislation for collective bargaining by state employees followed in the 1960s. By 1972, twenty-nine states had adopted laws permitting the formation of unions of state employees. In 1962 President John F. Kennedy, by executive order, introduced a limited system of representation for federal employees, and in 1969 the National Labor Relations Board (NLRB), the federal agency overseeing collective bargaining in the private sector, extended its jurisdiction and thereby the right to organize to the majority of private colleges and universities (those with incomes of a million or more dollars). But, since education is a function basically of the states, while the degree of encouragement among the states varies greatly, permissive state legislation is the key explanation for the burst of academic unionism in the late 1960s and early 1970s. (Some groups, such as AFT locals, were in special local circumstances which enabled them to win recognition as bargaining representatives without the aid of permissive legislation. For example, in Chicago, where the support of the general labor movement was strong, a formal bargaining relationship was gained in the City Colleges by means of the threat of sanctions in 1966 and has continued despite the absence of an Illinois law covering bargaining in higher education.)

State legislation supporting the right of faculties to negotiate falls into two broad categories which can be denoted for convenience as meet-and-confer and as collective bargaining laws. Typical meet-and-confer laws recognize the employees' right to organize and require employers to deal with employee organizations on a wide variety of matters but limit this requirement to "meeting and conferring." Usually they provide no administrative machinery for deciding representation questions, no exclusive bargaining rights, and no requirement that employers bargain collectively or sign written contracts. Perhaps most importantly, no impasse procedure is provided if agreement is not achieved. Collective bargaining laws include all or most of these omitted features and contain a requirement to bargain collectively "in good faith," a term that has acquired impressive legal meaning in private-sector bargaining over the years. The category into which an individual law falls is not always clear, but approximately one-fifth of the state statutes are meet-and-confer laws.

The significance of the distinction between the two laws is

demonstrated by the fact that thirty-six of the thiry-seven formal relationships established by the summer of 1972 in four-year colleges and universities were in states with collective bargaining laws. The one exception was Nebraska, where the NEA affiliate was recognized as the bargaining agent for the State College System under a meet-and-confer law described as permissive.

The most prominent of the meet-and-confer states is California. The status of collective negotiations on the eighteen state college campuses and the University of California's nine campuses illustrates the situation under this type of law. By 1966 interest in collective bargaining on some of the state college campuses was at a high level. Five potential representative organizations were campaigning for membership. Informal elections were held on four campuses, and a series of surveys were undertaken to reveal faculty attitudes on the question of bargaining. Two of these surveys conducted by the independent faculty association showed only 37 and 54 percent of faculty statewide favoring collective bargaining in principle. By 1969, with the other faculty organizations moving toward the AFT position of favoring collective bargaining, the proportion of faculty supporting bargaining rose to 61 percent. Throughout this period, the Board of Trustees refused to engage in collective bargaining, preferring to deal with the statewide academic senate in the traditional way while having the administrative staff meet and confer with separate employee organizations as provided for in state law (Haehn, 1970).

Faculty at the University of California have only recently begun to express serious interest in collective bargaining, but the effect of a meet-and-confer law is illustrated by the fact that, at the Berkeley campus forty different organizations purport to represent some portion of the employees. At least six of them claim to represent academic employees, although none can count more than a minor fraction of their respective constituencies as members. The Board of Regents has refused to authorize any formal process of bargaining. Under these circumstances the organizations have been limited to conducting a form of guerrilla bargaining by publicizing demands, issuing statements, pressing individual grievances, attacking administrative actions, and calling for the scheduling of meet-and-confer sessions. Under a collective bargaining law it is quite likely that in the state college system one of the competing organizations would have succeeded in winning formal bargaining rights.

As these facts of meet-and-confer laws and of guerrilla responses suggest, assessments of the extent of "bargaining" in higher education depend on the definition of this term. Most reviews of collective bargaining (including this one) use the criterion of formal recognition of one organization as an exclusive bargaining agent to identify bargaining situations. But beyond this unambiguous example, faculty-administration bargaining and negotiation range from the formal recognition of multiple faculty organizations to informal discussion with committees of faculty senates or associations. In short, bargaining may occur without formal organizations identified as unions and thus, as a process, is more prevalent than unionism. But the new and significant growth of formal, structured relationships with their potential for strikes or other forms of group conflict that has marked the past decade has depended in large measure on the support provided by public employee bargaining laws and procedures of the NLRB, and faculty organization has been encouraged by examples of successful collective action by other public employees. Faculty unionism at some junior colleges, for example, has grown out of a sense of identity with the lower schools and the success of teachers' unions in the public schools. A survey in Michigan in the late 1960's confirmed that seven of the ten highest-paying institutions of higher education in the state were junior colleges—"most of which had unions" (Boyd, 1971). A 1970 study of twenty-one community college collective bargaining contracts in New York State showed that the top of the faculty scale at sixteen colleges was $18,000 or more and that six of the sixteen paid maximums of from $20,000 to $26,075 (McHugh, 1971).[1] By comparison the top salary in the California State Colleges at that time was

[1] In this source the eight community colleges in the City University of New York (CUNY) system and the six agricultural and technical institutes that are part of the State University of New York (SUNY) are not included. The CUNY contract called for a maximum of $31,275 for community college professors with a doctorate as of October 1, 1971. See Chapter Five of this volume for additional community college data.

$19,224 for the academic year. Rightly or wrongly, a majority of the faculty in four-year colleges and universities undoubtedly interpret such information as a testimonial to the effectiveness of collective bargaining.

Boom or Bust in Labor Market

The late 1950s and virtually all the 1960s were prosperous years for the faculties in higher education in spite of the problems created after 1964 by student unrest. While faculties in many less prestigious colleges did not experience the same degree of prosperity enjoyed by their more favored brethren, on the whole it was a period of remarkable gains. The growth in the college-age population, the continued growth in the proportion of the relevant age group attending college, the international scientific and technological competition touched off by the successful Soviet satellite launching in 1958, and the competition among states to provide university centers to facilitate the growth of science-based industry combined to expand university budgets and—because of the relative shortage of experienced faculty—to expand salaries and perquisites.

By the end of the 1960s, however, the situation had changed dramatically. The rate of growth in student enrollment slowed, and the shift in social priorities signified by the war on poverty of the Johnson administration began to influence state financing. The new depression in higher education took form. The demand for new faculty fell off even though student enrollments continued to grow but at a slower rate.[2] At the same time that faculty demand softened,

[2] An exaggerated and oversimplified example of this point can be illustrated by assuming a stable total faculty population of a hundred thousand which is experiencing a withdrawal of three thousand persons annually. If student enrollments are increasing at an annual rate of 4 percent and student-faculty ratios are maintained, a total annual demand of seven thousand (three thousand for replacements and four thousand for additions) is generated. If the rate of growth in enrollments now slows to 2 percent, total demand for new entrants falls approximately five thousand for a decrease in new positions of two thousand, or 28 percent. An increase in the rate of growth has a magnified effect in the opposite direction, which helps to explain the feast-or-famine situation of the 1960s.

the supply of new doctorates continued o expand, having grown from less than ten thousand in 1959–1960 to more than twenty-six thousand in 1969–1970.

Financial support has begun to lag. While total budgetary support for higher education in both the public and the private sectors has not suffered an absolute decline, its rate of increase has declined and has not kept pace with continued growth in enrollments or increases in educational costs. According to some financial officers, the rate of increase in the costs of goods and services purchased by universities in the last half of the 1960s may have been nearly twice that of the consumer price index. Moreover, rising costs of providing financial aid to new groups of low-income students added to the financial pressures, as did the decline in overall research support from federal sources, particularly from the space and defense agencies, and the change in this support from technology and physical science to social, educational, and health areas. These research-and-development changes had little direct effect on most institutions, but they had a substantial impact on the visible and prestigious universities, which train the majority of new recruits to the academic profession. Insecure conditions there affected professional atttiudes and aspirations which permeate a large part of higher education.

This new situation in research and development had a secondary depressing effect on the labor market, not only in decreasing job opportunities in science and engineering in private industry and in nonprofit research corporations, but also in reducing demand in the labor markets of higher education as a whole and of individual institutions in particular. Although it had become commonplace in the postwar years to point out that faculty members were increasingly oriented to their disciplines while their ties to and their interest in their home institutions were weakened, in the new situation concern with institutional policies has risen rapidly. Employee mobility had served as a substitute for unionism, and the new situation reduced faculty mobility and bargaining power. Six of the ways in which the position of various groups of faculty have worsened are: (1) A substantial reduction in new positions limited the number of jobs for new entrants into the faculty labor market and the opportunities of established professors to advance by moving or threatening to move. (2) The rate of salary increase slowed as the need to raise entry levels in order to attract the best new graduates dwindled. Particularly in public institutions, the amount of compression in salary structures that was politically tenable was limited and the whole structure rose to accommodate competition for faculty at the bottom. As the need to raise entry levels disappeared, the whole structure lost its buoyancy. (3) The rate of advancement through the salary structure probably lagged. Although no hard evidence is available, this lag has certainly occurred, particularly in private colleges and universities. (4) The proportion of nontenured faculty acquiring tenure declined, although, again, no data lead directly to this conclusion. At one disciplinary association meeting in 1970, a major private university reported that all its assistant professors were available for new jobs. In many institutions in the 1960s, the acquisition of tenure was almost automatic for new faculty members (95 percent in one major state system). In selective institutions, the proportion of assistant professors promoted rose under the pressures of the market. As the prospects for new positions dimmed, the possibility of a top-heavy distribution of faculty caused the institutions to slow their rates of promotion. (5) Well-established faculty were threatened by pressures to change working conditions and practices —for example, attacks on tenure, attempts to increase teaching loads, to limit outside income from professional activity, to reduce the availability of sabbatical leaves, to encourage early retirement, and to reduce faculty control of the work environment. Senior faculty who feel they have reached their favorable position through long service and through consistent performance in competitive environments now find their favored status called into question. (6) Finally, several groups of professional employees lacking official faculty rank found their positions less secure. Part time and temporary faculty faced the threat of layoff if teaching requirements declined. Professional research staff members were threatened by the decline or the shift in application of university and extramural research funds. Administrative professionals servicing the diverse functions of the university that expanded under the benign environment of the times found their jobs threatened.

Probably few institutions have not felt these effects to some degree. A substantial number have experienced all of them. As a result, in many colleges and universities support for aggressive and active representation of faculty interests exists among the various segments of the academic labor market. The subgroups of professional personnel who are insecure in the current unsettled situation see new strength in union organization.

So far nothing has been said about subjective factors such as the decline in popular esteem of the institutions and their faculties (and students) in the eyes of the public or the threat of educational "reform" measures. To the extent that they exist, they exacerbate the general feeling of professional unease.

Structural Change and Faculty Response

I treat structural changes in the higher education system as distinct from external influences arising from sources such as demographic change and financial stringency. The sheer magnitude of the expansion in higher education has led to conditions which increase the likelihood that faculty and other professional staff will feel the necessity for new types of representation. Over the ten-year period 1959–1969 total enrollment in degree credit courses rose from 3.4 to 7.3 million students, an annual rate of increase in excess of 8 percent. The number of professional staff (excluding graduate students) increased at a somewhat lower rate of about 7 percent annually, reaching a total of more than six hundred thousand full-time and part-time members (U.S. Department of Health, Education, and Welfare, 1970). Changes of this magnitude in the educational establishment brought changes in the scale and the structure of the systems of higher education. Virtually all the changes removed the faculty and other professional staff from the locus of decision-making and made it difficult for them to influence institutional affairs through the relatively informal mechanisms of institutional governance associated with the old relationships.

There are numerous examples of faculty organizations in small, single-campus units, but the most important organizations in terms of numbers of faculty involved and impact on policies are in the complex, multicampus institutions. Leading examples are SUNY and CUNY, with twenty-six and sixteen campuses and 13,500 and 16,000 individuals in their bargaining units, respectively. These two systems account for 40 percent of all the staff covered by collective bargaining negotiations.

The effect of institutional complexity on the move to organization is seen in the community colleges as well, although it is less pronounced at this level. The multicampus Chicago City Colleges have a militant, well-established bargaining unit. In California the AFT has had its significant impact only in the large, mature Los Angeles community college system.

However, anyone evaluating the effect of structural change on the tendency of faculty to opt for union organization faces a paradox. Two apparently conflicting trends were evident in the 1960s. First, a trend toward decentralization (in, for example, California, Michigan, and New Jersey) has removed systems of state teachers colleges from the jurisdiction of state departments of education and given them independent boards of their own either singly or as a group. Second, a trend toward centralization (in, for example, New York and Wisconsin) has combined separate segments of higher education into a single system under one governing board. In both these situations, faculties have either organized for collective bargaining or launched attempts to gain recognition of bargaining agents.

The most important force at work in these instances is the concept of the emerging university. The conversion of teachers colleges to state universities provides the best example of such a favorable climate. From the standpoint of the growth of unionism the important new element is not the change in the locus or the form of administrative control, but the broadening of educational function and the accompanying change in the composition of the faculties and in their professional self-image. In their original centralized form the special-purpose institutions were subject to a high degree of administrative control and a correspondingly low degree of faculty influence in educational and administrative decisions. As their mission changed and new departments and colleges were created, the new faculty recruited for these units had high expectations of professional independence and of professional influence over institutional policy.

The conversion to the prestigious university status also legitimized high expectations among the old faculty. However, the administrators and established faculty leadership of some of the new systems were slow to adopt the forms of governance and faculty power associated with universities, at least in the opinion of some of their faculty constituents, and unionism appeared as a device to hasten the process.

Even where an emerging institution attempted to anticipate some of the problems of internal governance associated with its new status and provided for expansion of faculty participation, other tensions developed. Sometimes the new, young, academically oriented faculty felt that the governance machinery, dominated by the entrenched faculty, was being operated to the detriment of the institution or themselves, and unionism was viewed as a means to a different distribution of power. On occasion, the original faculty felt that the new additions to their ranks were favored in terms of salary, rank, teaching load, or other academic perquisites, and unionism seemed to be the best way to obtain fair treatment. Even under conditions of expansion, changing the character of an organization generates stresses among the organizational members. In some cases a new organization was introduced so that one or more interest groups could influence how changes would be implemented.

The pressures and opportunities produced by structural change also provide an explanation of the development of unionism in the systems that were centralizing. In a sense SUNY was an emerging university in that its statewide operation was relatively recent, although some of its units enjoyed a considerable reputation for a long time. Since SUNY includes eleven teachers colleges that have been converted into general-purpose colleges, the analysis above applies to this segment of the system. In addition, SUNY contains sixteen units, four of which were university centers. One had been functioning under the traditional form of university governance as a private institution, and the others soon subscribed to this form although two were new and the third a transformed teachers' college. The integration of the twenty-six campuses into a single administrative unit threatened to impose increased standardization on the separate campuses. (An additional arts and science college was established recently to make a current total of twelve in the general purpose category.) In addition, the centralization of administration promised to shift the locus of decision-making to distant headquarters in Albany, making the decision-makers less accessible to local interest groups. A universitywide academic senate was established, but the heterogeneous collection of faculty and professional groups in the system chose unionism as the best way of gaining direct impact on administrative decisions and redistributing power within the system. The AAUP organization at Rutgers was viewed as a means to preserve institutional independence against pressures to develop an integrated system for all public higher education in New Jersey.

In brief, changes in the structure and the functions of systems of higher education create new conflicts of interests among groups and reveal the existence of conflicts already present. As the system moves to a new power equilibrium, organization to advance collective interests appears to be a logical move to some groups, while to others organization is necessary to retain present advantages. This analysis does not imply that unionization solves the problem of the appropriate balance of power among interest groups or that it assures satisfactory access to the centers of administrative power. This explanation is designed to illustrate the forces behind the movement, but it does not permit a prediction of the outcome.

All systems of higher education faced with the problem of adapting to structural change have not generated unionism as a faculty response. A key factor in the evolution is a strong collective bargaining law that precipitates organizing campaigns and the establishment of a bargaining system. The steady spread of unionization from the public higher education systems of New York through those of New Jersey, Massachusetts, Michigan, Pennsylvania, and Nebraska testifies to the tie between structural change and a favorable legal environment in the formation of academic unions.

Bargaining and Bargainers

Turning to an analysis of the bargainers, I remind the reader that bargaining can be carried on in the absence of a formally recognized bargaining agent. Faculty salary committees functioning in organizations such as faculty senates or associations have been involved in negotiations with administrations and governing boards in some institutions for years. One study by the NEA reported that during 1969–1970, 43 percent of 1141 four-year institutions responding to a survey had arrangements whereby the governing board conferred with faculty representatives on salary or welfare (National Education Association, 1970a, p. 32). Another 2.7 percent reported that they negotiated with representatives of their faculties. Among two-year institutions the proportions were higher, particularly with respect to the prevalence of negotiations. Of the 650 units that reported, 46 percent described their relationship as conferring, while 12.5 percent reported that they negotiated with the faculty (National Education Association, 1970a, p. 75). Overall, in 1969–1970 about half the 1800-plus institutions participating in the survey had some formal procedure for consultation between the governing board and the faculty over economic matters, but only a small fraction of these would be classed as formal collective bargaining arrangements as the term is used in this chapter.

The great bulk of the formal procedures reported to the NEA involved internal representation by committees of faculty bodies whose membership was limited to the staff of the particular institution under the guise of an academic senate or a faculty association. In some colleges and universities where formal bargaining relationships have been established, these internal organizations have acquired the status of official faculty representatives. But, as of mid-1972, no more than 13 of the 158 bargaining agents with official standing as exclusive bargaining agents were independent or internal organizations not affiliated with an external organization. (See Table 1.)

The paucity of instances in which an independent internal organization held official bargaining status is due to the difficulties

Table 1

INSTITUTIONS WITH RECOGNIZED BARGAINING AGENTS, June 1972

	Units	NEA	AFT	AAUP	Other
Two year	119	72	38	1	10
Four year	39	11	14	11	3
Total	158	83	52	12	13

Sources: Compiled from various sources including reports of the AFT, AAUP, and NEA. Two units have dual representation; each organization has been credited with the unit.

experienced in functioning as effective representatives. In a substantial number of institutions internal associations that have been in existence for a long time have merged or affiliated with one of the external organizations during an organizing campaign or after winning recognition as a bargaining agent. The most prominent of these are the Legislative Conference of CUNY, an internal faculty organization which affiliated with the New York State Teachers Association (NEA) after more than thirty years of separate existence and after winning an election as the exclusive bargaining agent for the faculty of the system, and the Senate Professional Association of SUNY, an organization with roots in the statewide Faculty Senate that allied itself with the same group during the organization campaign in that university (see Chapter Seven).

An independent internal organization finds it hard to provide the services that a full-fledged bargaining relationship requires. The resources needed for full-time staff to lobby in state capitals, to function in lengthy and often technical negotiation sessions, to undertake legal representation before administrative boards and in the courts, to conduct grievance hearings and arbitrations, to press membership drives and carry on election campaigns, and to service the membership after a contract has been negotiated cannot be commanded by the independent institutional representatives in the usual case. Ten of the thirteen existing independent agents are found in public community colleges where the activities are manageable with limited resources.

The most active external organizations are the college and university divisions of the AFT—affiliated with the American Federation of Labor-Congress of Industrial Organizations (AFL-CIO)—the state affiliates of the NEA, and the chapters of the AAUP. (In several states the civil service employee associations have competed in elections for the right to represent faculty, but they have not been successful.) Previously it would have been meaningful to discuss the differences in philosophy, goals, and tactics of these separate organizations. Under the pressure of organizational competition in bargaining elections however, the differences have been reduced almost to the vanishing point. The AFT locals, which derive most of their power from alliances with organized labor, have always taken a forthright adversary position in their bargaining relationships, stressing conflict of interests, exclusion of supervisors, a broad membership base, formal contracts, third-party resolution of disputes, and acceptance of the strike as the ultimate form of sanction. As has been the pattern in the public schools, the NEA groups, which are the dominant faculty organizations at present, have moved from a stance which emphasized professional relationships to a position virtually identical with that of the AFT. As a result, mergers between units of the NEA and the AFT have begun to occur, the most notable example being the merger of the Legislative Conference and the AFT local in the CUNY system in 1972.

At the national level the AAUP, with almost a hundred thousand members, still views itself as a professional association in the traditional pattern. At the local level important vestiges of professionalism remain, but their continued existence is questionable. The AAUP chapters stress community of interest and respect for the role of faculty senates somewhat more than their competitors do. They have, however, continuously broadened their base of membership to correspond more closely to the composition of the bargaining units that have been established by public employment relations boards and the NLRB. They emphasize the traditional concepts of academic freedom and tenure somewhat more than their rivals do and try to maintain the informal, internal, peer review approach to dispute settlement with greater insistence. At the 1972 convention of the AAUP, the delegates voted to expand their efforts to function as bargaining agents on individual campuses in spite of warnings that they would be endangering their unique, hard-won, traditional status as a professional investigatory body. Whether the AAUP can be successful in providing a model of bargaining relationships that preserves some of the cooperative characteristics of faculty governance mechanisms or whether it becomes just one more faculty bargaining organization remains to be seen. A real danger is that its present split personality will be a transitional phase. It will be difficult for it to continue to serve as a mutually acceptable intervener in academic disputes in situations where a substantial portion of the institutions are engaged in formal collective bargaining with other organizations holding exclusive rights to represent faculty.

The general public has a tendency to overestimate the degree of central control that unions exercise over their constituent local bodies, particularly for organizations in education. A high degree of local autonomy exists in all three major national organizations, especially for the local units which originally organized independently of the external organizations and which negotiated the terms of their affiliation as a unit. The internal distribution of function and power within national union organizations tends to parallel that of the employing organizations with which they deal. In this respect the educational unions are much closer to decentralized unions like those of the construction workers or the musicians than to those the steel or the automobile workers, where the bargaining structures match the size of the companies. Local contracts in education differ and reflect local conditions in the bargaining units. In spite of national affiliations, this diversity will continue for a long time, although pattern following will probably develop in respect to broad economic issues. Faculty unionism in public institutions, like public employee unionism generally, will gain its strength through a complex process combining direct bargaining, appeal to professional traditions, networks of alliances with other organizations, and old-fashioned lobbying and electoral politics.

Status Report

As collective bargaining spreads through institutions and states, presenting an accurate picture becomes complex. The data reported in various sources have different, sometimes inconsistent, bases of measurement. A clear picture of the growth of unionism is difficult to obtain. The biggest source of confusion has been the question of how multicampus institutions are to be accounted for. For example, the large multicampuses SUNY and CUNY occur as single units in much of the tabulated data, along with single-campus units which sometimes have fewer than a hundred members. The problem of getting an accurate count of individuals is even less tractable.

Although the composition of bargaining units is diverse and some of them include substantial numbers of nonteaching professionals, a rough guess of how many individuals are covered by collective bargaining in higher education can be made on the basis of the number of faculty reported for the institutions—there are about seventy thousand individuals.

Even counting the giant CUNY and SUNY systems as only two bargaining units, New York leads the states with thirty-nine units, followed by Michigan with thirty-two units, almost all of which are single-campus units. The approximately 29,500 persons in the two big New York systems account for almost 40 percent of the national total.

Some speculation on the future of collective bargaining among faculties may be useful here. Approximately 2500 institutions of higher education exist in the United States, and these employ over 600,000 professional staff, including part-time teachers, researchers, and other professional instructional staff, but excluding graduate students who teach part-time. From June 1971 to June 1972 about thirty-three new units acquired representation status by my definition. The pace of expansion to date has been slowed by the lengthy process of holding hearings to determine the composition of bargaining units and of conducting representation elections. The recent rejection of organization at Michigan State may have a dampening effect. Because of the peculiarities of the academic calendar, elections cannot be held during the three or four summer months. Only about one-third of the states have effective collective bargaining laws at this time, and the NLRB has begun only recently to function actively in private institutions. Most important, the external faculty organizations have limited staff and finances to devote to organizing campaigns. As precedent decisions are made, as more states pass laws that stimulate the representation process, as the organizations move toward combined campaigns through mergers or otherwise improve their financial position, the pace of organization will quicken. Even allowing for these factors, it will be many years before a majority of colleges and universities are organized. However, academic unionism is well-established, and, unless something unforeseen happens, it will continue to expand.

Faculty unions may or may not turn out to be the vehicle to enhance faculty power that their proponents expect them to be, but they will be given a trial in some sectors of higher education. On the basis of developments to date, most of the unions will be established in public institutions, where, like other public employee unions, their success will depend on a mixture of bargaining power, cooperative alliances with other parts of the union movement and with other pressure groups in education and in state employment, lobbying power in the legislative process, and the endorsement and support of individual candidates.

2

Issues
at Stake

Donald H. Wollett

However it is viewed, the advent of faculty unionism presents us with two primary questions: Will it become a major means for handling decision-making relationships within institutions and systems of higher education? How will it affect the nature of the institutions in which it does gain acceptance?

Garbarino's analysis has suggested the possibility of an affirmative response to the first question but concludes with the judgment that even if the use of collective bargaining continues to spread, it will be many years before a majority of the colleges and universities are organized. In this chapter, Donald H. Wollett continues the analysis with a realistic and at times skeptical review of the nature of this process as it has taken form. Fundamentally, he notes, we must consider whether the process is a viable and sensible answer to the problems confronting faculties. This perspective serves as the backdrop to his discussion of how the move to unionism will affect the nature of higher education.

Wollett writes from the base of rich experience as both a legal practitioner and a scholar. His legal practice has included representation for the National Education Association and many of its state and local affiliates.

Wollett focuses, here, upon the interrelated concerns of with whom and for whom the academic unions bargain and about what. He notes the most evident issues and concludes with a number of searching questions of importance to both faculty and administrators. Not the least of these is his final concern about the impact of bargaining upon the quality of life in our colleges and universities.

E. D. D. and R.S. F.

Although collective bargaining has gained a substantial beachhead in higher education, becoming a reality at about 158 accredited colleges or universities between 1969 and 1972, the following prediction is probably an exaggeration: "The 1960s were the era of explosive growth of collective negotiations in the elementary and secondary schools. The decade ahead seems destined to be recorded as the era when collective bargaining arrived as the primary vehicle for faculty participation in the governance of institutions of higher learning. One of the better bets of 1970 is that (circa 1980) some graduate student in some industrial relations school will write a doctoral dissertation entitled: 'Poets on the Picket Line: The Day the United Association of Liberal Arts Professors Socialized the Medical School's Differential Salary Schedule: A Normative Response;' or (short title): 'Why Local 751 Hit the Bricks' " (Wollett, 1970). A more accurate prognostication would be that collective bargaining will arrive as a dominant rather than as the primary instrument for faculty participation in institutional decision-making.

The most critical point of differentiation between higher education and public school K-12 education is the extraordinary amount of variation among the former. Approximately three hundred fifty thousand full-time equivalent college and university teachers of differing educational backgrounds are distributed among more than two thousand institutions characterized by diversity in number of students, in mission, in emphasis, in number of campuses under centralized administration, in number of years and types of curricular and programatic offerings, in source of funds, and in traditions in respect to the degree and form of faculty participation in institutional decision-making.

Amid this diversity, talking about the issues at stake in collective bargaining is not realistic. The various problems which vex faculties, administrators, governing boards, and students; the form and structure of the bargaining process; the extent to which it is adversarial rather than collegial; the delineation of bargaining units; the subject matter of bargaining; the incidence and effectiveness of strikes and other sanctions; the impact of an egalitarian process on the so-called star system, which permits a core of elitist faculty to enjoy advantages; and the effect on the functioning of academic or faculty senates suggest many different issues. This is not to imply that the obstacles are insurmountable—they are not. Collective bargaining has occurred in complex university systems such as the State University of New York (suny) and the City University of New York (cuny), in single campus public universities such as Rutgers, and in private universities such as St. John's.

The development of collective bargaining and unionization in higher education will probably be uneven—neither a wave nor a ripple—but something in between, reflecting the diversity in institutions. Indeed, the nature of the problems confronting the faculty at many institutions raises the initial question of whether collective bargaining is a viable and sensible solution.

Managements are often said to have the labor relations systems they deserve. Thus, the elementary and secondary educational systems with characteristically authoritarian managerial styles have been fertile ground for collective bargaining. In many institutions of higher education however, a different style of organization obtains, and collective bargaining is not readily adaptable or useful for resolving problems of the professional staff. This situation was recognized in the 1967 report of a Task Force on Faculty Representation

and Academic Negotiations of the American Association for Higher
Education, which reads in part as follows:

> The case studies indicate that the greatest discontent
> and most visible tendencies toward unionization are found at
> the junior college level. . . . There was considerable faculty
> dissatisfaction over the complete control by the administration
> of curricula and promotions and the rigid application of rules
> governing the conduct of professional duties, such as the re-
> quirement that each faculty member spend a fixed number of
> hours on campus. The new status and prospective growth of
> these institutions make it unlikely that junior college faculties
> will long continue to accept such limitations on their role. . . .
> Similar developments have taken place in the new or
> emerging four-year colleges and universities. In many cases,
> these institutions have grown out of former teachers colleges
> which had a limited enrollment and a specific educational
> objective. In this context, the conventional forms of faculty rep-
> resentation often are shallowly rooted or nonexistent. Conse-
> quently, when the institution is elevated suddenly to a full-
> fledged college or university, many strains are likely to develop.
> . . . Another development underlying faculty restiveness and
> demands for improving procedures for representation is the
> establishment of rationalized, statewide systems of higher edu-
> cation. . . . The movement toward the coordinated-system
> approach has had a sharp impact on the role of the faculty
> on the individual campuses, even on those that have well-func-
> tioning procedures for faculty representation. . . . Issues . . .
> are displaced upward, [and] faculty influence exerted at the
> level of the individual institution is bound to be diluted when
> it is transmitted to the higher reaches of the bureaucracy or to
> the legislature. . . . Although there is an obvious bias in our
> sample, the greatest faculty unrest appears to exist in the
> junior colleges and in the new or emerging public colleges and
> universities. But problems concerning the proper faculty role in
> the administration of colleges and universities also were ob-
> served in the few private institutions examined [American As-
> sociation for Higher Education, 1967, pp. 10–13].

In sum, because collective bargaining, even in those states where it is provided for by statute, is predicated upon freedom of choice (often, although not always, expressed through a secret ballot election), some faculties will turn away from it while others will turn toward it. All that brief analysis can realistically do is to describe collective bargaining United States style, identify its principal characteristics, analyze its functions, weigh its pros and cons, suggest the critical considerations which may tip the choice one way or the other, and identify and discuss some issues which may arise when faculties in higher education opt for collective bargaining.

Characteristics

Collective bargaining is a system of representative government in which members of a body politic (in labor relations parlance, the grouping of jobs constituting the bargaining unit) participate, through a designated organizational representative, in decision-making which affects their working environment—salaries, terms and conditions of employment, and other matters related to their interests as an occupational group. To put this another way, the members of the bargaining unit are the persons who are represented in the collective bargaining process.

Since collective bargaining involves employee participation in decision-making, it assumes the existence of another party—a management with the authority to make decisions in respect to the matters being bargained about. In the private sector it is easy to identify the employer, but for reasons I examine below, such identification is frequently difficult in publicly funded institutions.

Two other characteristics of collective bargaining in the United States should be noted at this point. First, the organizational representative which represents the constituency (that is, the bargaining unit) is the exclusive representative of all members of the unit including those who do not support the organization. Second, decisions in respect to bargaining demands and the acceptance of bargained-out decisions are controlled by the principle of majority rule. In short, the system is one of majoritarianism.

Assuming that management can be identified and that its representatives can be brought to the bargaining table, the process itself is essentially the one which characterizes the marketplace—proposal and counterproposal, action and reaction, give and take—resulting ultimately in deal or no deal, in agreement or stalemate. If collective bargaining is to work, both parties must be, as they are in the marketplace, motivated to reach agreement by fear of the consequences if agreement is not reached. This anxiety is the catalyst which makes the process function.

In collective bargaining in the business and industrial sector the alternative to agreement is usually a strike—an event which works economic injury to employer and employee. The fear of this consequence provides a major motive power for agreement and ordinarily causes each side to compromise. A strike does not have such operative significance in higher education. In privately funded institutions a successful strike—one which substantially curtails or shuts down educational services—may cause the institution to lose tuition and perhaps incidental income. However, these losses are probably more than offset by the savings realized from not paying faculty members for the days they are on strike; personnel outlays constitute a very major portion of the budget, while student tuition fails to cover the cost of operation. In publicly funded institutions this effect is even more pronounced. The enterprise saves money and is subjected to little or no economic injury (except, perhaps, the overhead take from research grants). However, these savings may be diminished if the strike settlement includes an agreement to make up classes.

Many strikes in elementary and secondary educational institutions have been successful, usually because they interrupt the day child care function and thereby generate outside political pressure on institutional decision-makers. A strike in the public sector is said to be not an economic weapon, but rather a weapon of political embarrassment. This is a valid differentiation and characterization if the service interrupted is important enough to activate a cohesive and influential segment of the body politic which in turn generates pressure on managerial decision-makers. Little evidence exists thus far to suggest that such a sanction will work in higher education, whether the institution involved is publicly or privately funded, except where a critical secondary service is interrupted (such as the operation of a medical school teaching hospital).

If a strike went on long enough so that the academic careers of a substantial segment of students were threatened with serious delay, political pressures might generate. However, they would likely be diffused because parents may not be the constituents of the decision-makers who have the power to settle the dispute. This situation may change as eighteen-year-old students assume the franchise, provided they are sympathetic to the faculty's objectives. Moreover, long strikes are anathema to employee organizations whose members cannot tolerate protracted loss of income. Faculty organizations do not ordinarily pay strike benefits, but limit their assistance to interest-free loans and other minimal financial help.

Other sanctions are possible, such as forms of academic sabotage; for example, refusal of faculty to serve on committees or to seek research grants, censure, blacklisting of institutions such as that by the American Association of University Professors (AAUP), and persuasion of professional associations such as the American Association of Law Schools (AALS) and the American Chemical Society (ACS) to threaten withdrawal of accreditation if specified work standards are not met.

The product of collective bargaining in higher education is typically a group agreement which memorializes the deal in respect to the subjects bargained about. The agreement is enforceable either by judicial proceedings or, more typically, if a settlement cannot be reached, by a grievance procedure which contemplates the ultimate decision of an arbitrator selected by administrative and union representatives through agreed-upon machinery.

The group contract or collective bargaining agreement typically contains promises from management in respect to the subjects covered—salaries, incremental increases, fringe benefits, work load. Usually, unless there is a no-strike clause, little or nothing in the agreement obligates performance by the organizational representative or the employees it represents or both vis-a-vis management. Thus, as a practical matter, the grievants are ordinarily employees whose complaint is that management has failed to live up to the terms of the agreement; in this sense, the grievance machinery is a mechanism whereby the employees and their organization police the agreement, that is, make sure that institutional management does what it has promised to do.

In many states (Michigan, New Jersey, New York, Pennsylvania, and most states that have opted for collective bargaining in public education) the awards of arbitrators are enforceable by court action if one of the parties refuses to carry out the award, assuming that the group contract states that arbitral awards are binding. Furthermore, in private colleges and universities to which the National Labor Relations Act is applicable, where the parties have so agreed, arbitrators' awards are binding and judicially enforceable against the recalcitrant party. The courts give presumptive validity to the soundness of the arbitrator's decision on the merits. They usually limit themselves to questions of jurisdiction (so-called arbitrability) and procedural aberrations. Consequently, there is little litigation because the chances of success are limited.

Having looked at the principal characteristics of collective bargaining as a system of decision-making, I now examine the question of how (or whether) it can be adapted to fit the needs of higher education faculty.

Structure and Function

The central problems in respect to the structure and functioning of collective bargaining in higher education can be compressed into one question: For whom and with whom does the collective bargaining representative bargain about what, and who should the representative be? As I pointed out earlier, the answer varies depending upon the institution involved.

The complexity of the problem is suggested, for example, by delineating the potential levels of decision-making (with whom?) in a multiversity such as SUNY: "(1) The level of first-line supervision—the department chairman, or, in smaller institutions, the dean; (2) the second-line level—either the dean in schools which are departmentalized or the president of nondepartmentalized institutions; (3) the third-line level in departmentalized institutions— the president and his staff; (4) the local campus board; (5) the systemwide chancellor; (6) the systemwide board (e.g., the board of trustees); (7) the superboard which caps the entire state system or systems (the board of regents); (8) the executive branch of state government, including the state budgetary agency and the governor; (9) the state legislature" (Wollett, 1971, pp. 23–24).

Traditionally the primary function of the collective bargaining representative has been to protect and advance the occupational interests of those whom it represents in their capacity as employees. If one of their problems generates from inadequate aggregate funding, then the bargaining, if it is to be effective, must be conducted with the person or the group which controls funding decisions. Bargaining over this matter in the case of a private institution must be conducted with the governing board or its representatives. Even then, they may have limits on their authority since their funds derive from other sources, for example, government contracts, private gifts, investments, and student fees. However the problem of who is to be bargained with in respect to aggregate funding is much easier in the case of a private institution than it is in the case of a public institution. With whom does one bargain over this matter in the latter case—the governor, the legislature, or some ad hoc committee consisting of representatives of the governor's office, the legislature, and (in the interests of protecting institutional autonomy) a representative of the governing board? And, who speaks for whom?

Closely related to the question of the money which can be made available by the person or persons with whom one is bargaining is the question of allocation of resources. Indeed, an organization may contend that the question is never one of ability to pay; the question is how resources are to be allocated. Thus, if the union can exert enough pressure to gain its objectives, the problem of funding other commitments lies exclusively with the other side, which, if additional funds are not forthcoming, may have to reduce staff or curtail or terminate programs.

Who has the authority to make these decisions? Again, there is more latitude on the administrative side of the table in the privately funded than in the publicly funded institution. Legal constraints are not frequent in the former situation. Public institutions are more likely to be subject to budgeting practices compelled by law and to legislative action.

Many of these decisions lie in the hands of the governing board, even in public institutions. Many of them, as a practical matter, lie in the hands of the president of the institution or, in multicampus enterprises, may be delegated to the administrative head of a campus. The structure for meaningful collective bargaining has to be tailored to fit the various realities in a particular situation.

In addition to questions of aggregate funding, the allocation of available funds as between operations on the one hand and capital investments on the other and as between professional and non-professional personnel, salaries, fringe benefits, and facilities involves a wide range of considerations and has implications for faculty work load.

How about the distribution of faculty salary increases and the administration of salary schedules? Should increases be distributed across the board? Should they be utilized to correct inequities? Should increments be automatic, geared to mechanical criteria such as length of service, or should they be based upon judgments made to recognize merit? What should be the locus of decision-making authority on these matters? Problems of personnel administration must also be settled—for example, recruiting, promotions, and the decision to nonrenew or to confer tenure; decisions in respect to work schedules, class assignments; and issues relating to environmental matters such as parking facilities, office space, and telephone service; as well as the procedures for meting out (and challenging) discipline.

All these matters, with the possible exception of discipline, have fiscal implications, but once an agreement is reached with respect to aggregate funding and the allocation of money, the problems of determining who has authority to make decisions within budgetary constraints should be resolved by the collective bargaining agreement between the faculty representative and the administration. A bargain struck with a governing board is binding on the president and lesser administrative officers. The board may delegate authority to make local agreements to the chief executive officer or his subordinates.

Another of the vexatious problems in collective bargaining among higher education faculty is the delineation of the bargaining unit or units to be represented (for whom?). The difficulty of the problem is related to the variables among institutions and the complexity of the particular institution involved. If a bargaining unit is

to be a functional entity, its members must have a sufficient community of interest so that they can resolve their conflicts internally
(through intraorganizational systems of bargaining) and ultimately
reach group decisions which permit the organization representing
the unit to operate cohesively in the negotiating process. Community
of interest does not mean identity of interest, but it does require a
broad enough area of common concern to permit the resolution of
internal conflict.

The most common rivalries and tensions among the members of any faculty group are the old versus the young; the tenured
versus the nontenured; and the research-oriented versus the class-
room-oriented. These tensions are likely to be manageable in a small
liberal arts college with essentially homogeneous objectives and more
functional uniformity than diversity. However, rivalries intensify
with the complexity of the institution. In a multicampus situation,
for example, no single community of scholars can readily function
as an effective collectivity. Instead, there are many communities,
and their interests and functions may be so diverse that it is unlikely
that they can resolve their conflicts internally. The problem is accentuated in California, for example, where a nine-campus university system and a nineteen-campus state university and college
system compete with each other.

In dealing with a situation of this complexity, it is useful to
draw a distinction between the voting unit (election district) and
the bargaining unit. The former includes employees who are eligible
to vote on the question of what organization if any will be their
bargaining representative; the latter is the group to whom the agreements reached are applicable. Thus, in a multicampus system, each
campus might be a separate voting unit, the members of which
select their bargaining representative. The representative so selected
bargains on their behalf at all levels of administrative authority. With
respect to negotiations over subjects at the systemwide level or at the
legislative and gubernatorial level, minimal problems occur if each
voting unit chooses the same representative. However, if the faculty
on the several campuses select different bargaining representatives,
there must be either multiple-party bargaining or a coalition to bargain on a coordinated basis.

Special problems are created in respect to faculty who are

also members of a profession external to higher education. For example, doctors, lawyers, and engineers are part of a marketplace larger than the academy. To attract and retain quality faculty within these professional groups, universities often find it necessary to prescribe lighter work loads and larger salaries than those of other faculty groups who are not so fortunately situated. Since collective bargaining is a system of representative government based on majoritarianism, tension is likely between the majority and the minority with professional prestige. The former may want either their salaries and work loads improved to the level of their elite colleagues or the differentials removed and contributed to the collective advantage of the group. The collective bargain may prescribe minimum rates and leave areas open to individual bargaining, thus leaving the present system largely intact. This has been the case in respect to some reporters and columnists because the Newspaper Guild accepts the reality of specially negotiated salaries which preserve the star system.

Other tensions doubtless exist between the teaching members of the academic staff and the nonteaching professionals (NTPs) in student personnel services and various service or managerial offices. The latter were included in the bargaining unit in the SUNY case and have emerged in the Senate Professional Association (SPA), which won the bargaining election, as a group with far greater power than their campus roles and numerical minority would suggest. The result has been some compression of preexisting differentials between teaching professionals and NTPs.

Whether the faculty unit of adjunct professors, lecturers, teaching assistants, and other persons outside the established academic hierarchy who teach part-time should be included in the bargaining unit poses another problem. Since they perform teaching or supportive functions, much is to be said for their inclusion in the unit. However, their primary external commitments and preoccupations militate toward exclusion.

The handling of supervisory personnel is another question. In many institutions, this issue begins at the level of the department head, who is a functional schizoid. He performs supervisory functions but is also a professorial colleague and continues to teach. He may have been selected by the department members and, like the composing room foreman in a unionized job print plant, may identify more with his academic colleagues than with the administration.

Finally, the most complex issue is the place of the teacher who is active in a system of self-governance and spends much of his time performing managerial functions. He may serve on a departmental or divisional recruiting committee, a merit increase committee, or a promotional or tenure committee. He even may be a part of a senate structure with responsibilities so great that he is given released time from the classroom.

How do those who serve in faculty government and as department chairmen fit in a system of collective bargaining long associated with the dichotomy between management and employees? The system of self-governance treasured by many faculty members does not adapt easily to collective bargaining. Indeed, it can probably not survive in this new environment. Managerial decisions, regardless of who makes them, are likely to be the source of complaints and the prime generator of grievances. Thus, for example, a department head's action on course assignments may be a source of complaint, or the decision of a senate personnel committee in respect to promotional or tenure question may generate an appeal. To illustrate further, in 1970 the Budget Committee of the Academic Senate of the Davis campus of the University of California passed judgment on over 550 personnel matters involving appointments, merit increases, tenure decisions, promotions, and changes in academic title. These decisions all involved personnel administration. Many faculty members were aggrieved by denials of merit increases or tenure or promotions which were made authoritatively by the Budget Committee. Many of the grievances in fact did not originate with the Budget Committee but came from departmental action which the Budget Committee approved. Thus, as appeals from some of these decisions moved from the Budget Committee to the Privilege and Tenure Committee of the Senate, it developed that the real source of the complaint was action by the grievant's colleagues. How are these matters to be handled in a collective bargaining system?

The subject matter of collective bargaining was necessarily dealt with above in considering the importance of identifying an authoritative management with whom to do business in respect to a particular matter. The question for examination now is one of legitimacy; that is, what matters should be the subject of negotiations? Or, to put it differently, what subjects should be reserved to unilateral decision-making by institutional managers on the ground that their obligations to the consumers and funders of the enterprise require them to accept responsibility for certain decisions and to retain commensurate authority?

The scope of bargaining is perhaps the most emotion-charged issue which arises in collective bargaining in education, particularly in public institutions. Several state statutes include restrictions. Oregon, for example, limits the scope of mandatory negotiations to salaries, grievance procedures, extra compensation, and related economic policies. Hawaiian statutes make it illegal for public employers to make agreements which interfere with their responsibilities in a number of important aspects. They must retain the authority to direct employees; to determine qualifications, standards for work, and the nature and content of examinations; to hire, promote, transfer, assign, and retain employees in positions; to suspend, demote, discharge, or take other disciplinary action against employees for proper cause; to relieve an employee from duty because of lack of work or other legitimate reasons; to maintain the efficiency of operations; and to determine the methods, means, and personnel by which operations are to be conducted.

The National Labor Relations Act, which applies to private colleges and universities with a gross annual income of one million dollars or more, limits the mandatory subjects of bargaining to rates of pay, wages, hours of employment, and the conditions of employment. These terms have been given an expansive interpretation. However, as a practical matter the scope of bargaining is influenced very little by statutory constraints. The dimensions of the process are in fact a function of the relative power of the two parties and the extent to which the members of the bargaining unit are ambitious to assert authority over and assume responsibility for decisions which bear on the management of the enterprise.

I have already discussed the relative weakness of the bargaining power of faculty organizations; most are unable to force bargaining (or, more to the point, force agreement) over matters relating to educational policy, issues involving the so-called mission of the institution, and matters which may fall into the domain of management and only tangentially affect terms and conditions of employment. Thus, in institutions where the procedures and traditions of self-governance are shallowly rooted or nonexistent, the scope of bargaining is likely to be circumscribed.

But questions of negotiability are not unimportant in such institutions. Professors have traditionally aspired to the same degree of self-government that obtains in the entrepreneurial professions. Like lawyers and doctors, they have sought to establish their criteria for admission into the profession and to fashion and enforce their standards of good practice. Within many colleges and universities, they have pressed for effective influence in policy decisions on admission standards; curricular content; degree requirements; grading standards; academic freedom; standards for student conduct and discipline; and procedures for the appointment of department chairmen, deans, and presidents. Furthermore, they have aspired to determine the conditions which affect standards and quality of work performance—recruitment, promotion, tenure, merit increases, course assignments, work schedules, work loads, allocation of space, and secretarial help.

Professors in institutions where authoritarian administration is the tradition are likely to attempt to use the collective bargaining process to achieve bilateral decision-making in some of these matters. However, their lack of bargaining power is a major disability in attaining such objectives, and the probable result is (at the most) trade-offs for improvements in salaries, hours, and working conditions.

Here again, however, differences in institutional arrangements, structures, size, traditions, and the political milieu have profound influence. Where the traditions of self-governance are deeply rooted and the faculty has historically exercised a meaningful voice in such matters as admissions policy and curriculum, the scope of bargaining is likely to be broad. Indeed, the faculty may use collective bargaining to make its system of self-governance (such as a faculty senate) authoritative by writing it into an enforceable contract rather than relying on the largesse of a governing board which is willing to share authority.

A faculty may, however, trade away a meaningful system of

self-governance for occupational bread-and-butter gains. This choice seems unlikely, although academic administrations attempt to utilize collective bargaining to narrow the scope of faculty authority and meaningful participation in decision-making. In any event, authority which a governing board has been willing to share by choice does not find its way easily into an enforceable agreement which limits the exercise of broad authority by law.

In sum, the two extreme situations in collective bargaining in higher education are the faculty using the bargaining process to achieve professional aspirations and the faculty whose professional aspirations have been recognized struggling to retain their power (and perhaps strengthen it) against a governing board or an administration or both ambitious to reassert authority.

If collective bargaining comes to a college or university, institutional management and the organized faculty have many hard decisions to make in respect to what they should bargain about and what accommodations of interest are desirable. I discuss some of these issues here.

Should work load be quantified? It is not unusual to find in the collective bargaining agreements to date provisions which describe teaching load in terms of student contact hours per week, classroom size, number of courses, and other quantitative measures, especially for two-year colleges. Quantitative controls over faculty members appeal to persons who are ill-informed about how colleges and universities operate, who are interested in economy and efficiency in planning and operating academic programs, and whose psyche finds comfort and security in numbers. However, such controls are likely to be counterproductive in several ways. First, where the rules are expressed as maxima, they protect the faculty against excessive loading by an arbitrary and cost-conscious administration. Second, controls expressed as minima are easy to comply with because they are temporal and spatial, leaving performance unmeasured. Third, the quantification of work load affords a legitimate (if not a compelling) basis for ceasing to work without compensation during vacations, holidays, weekends, and after daily hours. (Although the suggestion may seem whimsical, an accommodation might be found in an agreed-upon provision establishing a professorial time bank into which faculty members make deposits during summers, weekends, and vacations and upon which they may draw when they wish to work a short day or a short week.) Fourth, the concept of a quantified work load is stultifying and, to sensitive members of the faculty, degrading since it is antithetical to the notion that teaching is a profession whose members are client-oriented and not clock-oriented. Fifth, the effectiveness of the most imaginative, innovative, and productive members of the faculty is likely to be adversely affected because their life style is not readily adaptable to standard measures. Finally, rigidity in working rules has serious implications for management. "Collective bargaining is a method of introducing civil rights into the working environment; that is, of requiring that management be conducted by rule rather than by arbitrary decision" (Slichter, 1961, pp. 214–215). The introduction of this principle creates two areas of concern: the importance of preserving a proper balance between the freedom of the administration to manage and the protection of employees from arbitrary administration; and the avoidance of rules which become obsolete. If the administration is given too much freedom, it may take advantage of its situation and destroy the organization. If the administration is too restricted, collective bargaining may become a method of protecting the old against the new, of retarding change, and of protecting vested interests and obsolete methodology.

Should salary schedules and other personnel policies be administered by applying objective criteria rather than by judging merit? Judging by objective criteria may eliminate abuses of managerial discrimination; however, removing rewards for superior perfomance may deprive administrations of ways of stimulating effort. Morale problems may result because the faculty lacks a self-satisfying work environment. Three illustrations, drawn from the studies of the Harvard group headed by Slichter, make the point:

> (1)ʹ In many cases there are almost no exceptions to the application of seniority in promotion—. . . the simple principle appeals to union leaders; and the path of least resistance for management is to avoid making exceptions. . . .
> (2)ʹ The merit principle has tended to disappear and to lose meaning. Where rate ranges exist, advancement to the maximum is more or less automatic. (3) The selective retirement

principle is not used under bargained pension plans. In one
case the possibility of selective retirement was raised with the
management group. With less than two minutes discussion,
management decided that it was impossible because it would
cause grievances [Slichter, Healy, and Livernash, 1960, pp.
950–951].

Should the faculty become involved in decisions relating to
recruiting, promoting, granting tenure, and awarding merit increases? If yes, then must not the faculty also assume the responsibility of meting out discipline? These questions go directly to the
matter of peer evaluation which is grounded on the premise that
the members of a profession should, as part of their obligation of
self-regulation, evaluate each other. In some colleges and universities
the peer judgment, as a practical matter, is almost always dispositive. In others it serves merely as a guide to administration. In still
others it does not exist. The question here is how this procedure
should be adapted to a collective bargaining system. The pros and
cons of peer evaluation are not pertinent to this question. The point
is that the decisions reached are managerial in the sense that they
direct and control (and sometimes terminate) the on-the-job life
of other persons. As we have seen above, collective bargaining is a
system of representative government, predicated upon the principle
of majoritarianism, which operates as a check on the performance
of managerial functions, regardless of who makes the decisions. It
can be argued that self-governance should be guaranteed in the
collective bargaining process and that decisions by faculty should be
definitive, whereas decisions by administrators should be subject to
review by an impartial arbitrator. The argument is not persuasive
unless one assumes that faculty decisions are inherently more equitable and more likely to upgrade the institution than administrative
decisions. Furthermore, a system of faculty authority without responsibility, where the faculty establishment is accountable only to
itself, while administrators must answer to aggrieved faculty members, students, and alumni or taxpayers is not realistic. Therefore,
the members of the bargaining unit are likely to push for provisions
in the agreement which make all managerial decisions related to

working conditions, regardless of who makes them, subject to grievance machinery and ultimately to binding review by a third party.

   Other decisions, too numerous to discuss in detail here, arise;
for example, should the faculty press for a role in the selection of
department heads and deans and the fixing of curricular offerings,
admission standards, and student fees, or should it leave the former
to administrators and be satisfied with a consultative role in the
latter? Basically, should the faculty remove itself from time-consuming, economically unrewarding managerial functions and leave
the propriety of decisions in this area to be challenged by their
organizational representative in the collective bargaining system?

   Now we come to the problem of who should do the bargaining. Three major national organizations compete for the position
as bargaining agent in higher education—the AAUP, the National
Education Association (NEA), the American Federation of Teachers
(AFT). They are aptly characterized in Chapter One and by a report of the Academic Senate of the Berkeley Division, University
of California (*Report of Special Subcommittee*, 1972, pp. 5–6).
There are also civil service organizations such as the California State
Employees Association. "Although they participate in election con-
tests, no such civil service group has won an election in any university faculty unit as yet [including the New York Civil Service
Employees Association, which ran in the SUNY election]. The usual
approach is to offer affiliation with a high degree of autonomy for
local units. [Such an organization is] strong as a lobbyist but with
limited experience with bargaining and local representation" (*Report of Special Subcommittee*, 1972, p. 6).

   In addition to the four organizations listed above, faculty
or academic senates, which are internal organizations (financed
from institutional funds), are common. A senate is typically a representative form of government. The elected senators constitute a
deliberative body empowered to act directly or through committees
or officers. "While the will, determination, and commitment of a
senate to faculty interests may not be weakened or diluted by the
fact it is financially dependent upon the college or university for
operational funds, the lack of an independent source of financing
may disable it from functioning effectively as a bargaining agent. It

is not a matter of 'company domination,' but a matter of resources and ability to perform adequately" (Wollett, 1971, p. 26).

A senate may overcome this financial disability by allying itself with a state or national organization. The statewide SUNY Faculty Senate made this choice in 1968, when it was involved in a representation proceeding under the Taylor Law:

> A joint venture, involving the senate and the American Association of University Professors, seemed to promise mutual benefits, but the AAUP chose to stand alone. Discussions between the senate and the Civil Service Employees Association [CSEA] culminated finally in agreement on . . . terms . . . , but at the last moment CSEA reneged and withdrew from the association. . . . During the winter of 1969–1970, . . . the Senate Executive Committee began discussions with an organization [which] so far had played no part. The State University Professional Association (SUPA), formed in 1967, was designed to draw into a single organization the university's 4000 nonteaching professionals. As the university's stepchildren, the NTPs had long felt aggrieved at their second-class status, particularly as compared with the faculty. . . . The discussions which began between the senate and SUPA were arranged through . . . [the NEA and its New York affiliate, the New York State Teachers Association (NYSTA)]. They led to agreement by both the senate and SUPA late in the spring of 1970 to form the Senate Professional Association (SPA). SPA was the child of this marriage of convenience between the senate and SUPA, a marriage which had been solemnized and financed by NEA-NYSTA [Sherwig, 1971, pp. 5–8].

(After SPA won the representation election with financial and professional help from NEA-NYSTA, it formally affiliated with NEA-NYSTA).

A senate might also choose to establish a separate membership organization to operate as its negotiating arm. The Special Subcommittee on Faculty Organization for Collective Action of the Academic Senate, Berkeley Division, University of California, made this choice, recommending "that a Faculty Senate Association be formed, that it be composed, at least initially, only of faculty members presently eligible for membership in the Academic Senate [with an initiation fee of ten dollars and monthly dues] . . . .The purpose of the Faculty Senate Association is to serve as the collective representative agency of the faculty of the university to the administration and to the regents of the university and to all appropriate state agencies and that it report regularly to the faculty and to appropriate senate committees on matters of concern. It shall also serve to encourage the establishment of similar organizations on the other campuses" (*Report of Special Subcommittee,* 1972, p. 9).

The subcommittee left the door open for ultimate affiliation with an outside organization, stating that "the formation of an independent organization at this time would improve the terms of any future relationship which the faculty might wish to form with other organized groups for the purpose of furthering more effectively both distinctive and mutual interests. The experience of other universities suggests that negotiating with an external organization as a going concern is a useful strategy if alliances with outside groups appear to be indicated" (*Report of Special Subcommittee,* 1972, p. 10)'.

The problem of financing the operation of the collective bargaining representative is a critical one which deserves special comment. For example, the SPA which represents approximately fifteen thousand employees of SUNY, reportedly has a membership of about 3500. The costs of periodically negotiating or renegotiating a group agreement, with all the prebargaining work which must go into the formulation of positions, policies, and demands; the bargaining itself; plus the obligation of policing the agreement—complicated by the fact that members of the unit are scattered over twenty-eight campuses—are formidable. Competent people (who require monetary compensation) must deal with economic analysis, collect and package data, present grievances, handle litigation, plan and execute a public relations strategy, and so forth.

An organization with 3500 members cannot do this job for fifteen thousand persons unless it is subsidized by the state and national organizations with which it is affiliated. While the latter may be willing to do so until the local affiliate gains the loyalties of the members of the bargaining unit and demonstrates its ability to function, the local ultimately has to sustain itself. This must be an objective of any bargaining representative; it can be accomplished by either selling memberships or requiring those who are represented to contribute as a condition of their employment, a situation known as an agency shop. Faculty members can expect to pay approximately $150 annually or contribute an equivalent amount. Agency shop agreements are of doubtful legality in many states, but the trend is toward legalization, and the imperatives of the system indicate that the trend will develop into the norm.

What Choice?

Aaron states, "I think that some system of collective bargaining will eventually become established in many of our colleges and universities, including those supported primarily by public funds. . . . The present drive toward organization and some form of collective participation in decision-making in most of our government institutions seems to have a kind of ineluctable quality that one associates with great social movements. If this is true, it will inevitably include both private and public institutions of higher learning. Whether or not this would be a good thing is something each of us must consider and decide for himself" (1971, p. 13). Assuming that Aaron is right, the issues identified and discussed in this chapter must be faced and resolved. And there are others.

What will be the bargaining unit? In the case of a multiversity, will it be systemwide in respect to certain issues and campuswide in respect to others, depending upon the locus of decision-making authority? Is it possible to have a systemwide unit for bargaining over some issues and campuswide units for bargaining over others? Is it possible to have different organizations do the bargaining in different units? Referring to the comments above, which distinguish between voting and bargaining units, this is the obvious situation in which the two might not coincide, with each voting unit being a component of the bargaining unit with respect to systemwide subjects, with either a multiplicity of organizations or a coalition representing the bargaining unit faculty.

Should the professional schools be separately represented or go unrepresented in campuswide or systemwide units?

If NTPs, part-time teachers who are not on the tenure ladder, and supervisory personnel are excluded from regular full-time faculty units, should they be permitted to participate in the collective bargaining system through units of their own?

Insofar as the scope of bargaining is concerned, should some issues be excluded from the formal bargaining process? For instance, admissions standards and their administration go to the heart of educational policy. But they have a direct impact on faculty work load. Moreover, they engage the attention and interest of other groups—students and parents. If these matters are the subject of formal bargaining, will the process take the form of bilateral bargaining between management and the faculty or trilateral bargaining between management, the faculty, and the consumers of educational services?

The same question arises in respect to demands by faculty which require additional funds or the curtailment or suspension of programs. If additional funds are to be generated by raising student fees or if faculty demands are to be met by allocating moneys to salaries rather than to course offerings, can affected consumer groups be excluded from the process? Is it fanciful to forecast that student unions may be established to protect and advance student interests?

Collective bargaining is essentially an egalitarian activity, at least as we have seen it in operation in the business and industrial sector. Accordingly, it emphasizes utilitarianism, standardization, and uniformity. If these values achieve primacy in higher education, what will be the effect on the quality of service?

Can institutions of faculty self-governance survive a collective bargaining system? Will they not falter and ultimately fail? Will this loss be offset by a gain in managerial efficiency, accountability, and responsiveness to the needs of the community being served? A collective bargaining system is likely to be intolerant of poor administration. In other words, if collective bargaining is functioning effectively, the enterprise cannot afford the luxury of incompetent administration. Costly administrative practices, indecision, dilatory behavior, caprice, and similar inadequacies in the managerial hierarchy are likely to be exposed and eliminated. This is one of the reasons many administrators in educational institutions find collective bargaining threatening.

If collective bargaining is to function, organized faculties must devise and utilize methods for effective political activity. Are faculty members prepared to commit themselves to much greater involvement in political activity than has heretofore been the case?

Collective bargaining in higher education may be necessitated by the fact that administrations, governing boards, legislatures, and governors seem indifferent, if not hostile, to faculties that lack political muscle. Thus, Aaron's prediction (1971, pp. 14–15) may prove out:

> What is missing from this vision of the future, or at least only dimly perceived, is a quality of life in our colleges and universities in which eccentricity and nonconformity can still flourish; in which distinguished scholarship is honored despite its lack of "relevance"—that mean little word; in which the main ties between colleagues are their intellectual interests; in which cost-benefit analysis is not the sole basis on which the value of every course or degree program is judged; and in which these institutions, in addition to administering to the contemporary needs of their students and helping to solve some of the problems faced by the broader community, remain the guardians and transmitters of the world's cultural heritage.

Whether or not this prognosis is correct, one may understand his poignance.

3

Bargaining
Process

David L. Graham, Donald E. Walters

In planning this chapter the editors felt it imperative to seek author-
ship from among persons who were experienced in bargaining
within higher education and who could discuss the topic analyti-
cally. We found it difficult to meet these criteria through a single
author, since those with experience tended to assume highly partisan
attitudes. We believe we have found a workable compromise in
what follows.

The major portion of the chapter has been written by David
L. Graham, a person schooled in bargaining within the industrial
sector as well as in community college and complex university set-
tings. Graham was the chief negotiator for the major portion of the

first negotiations of the Senate Professional Association of the State University of New York. He thus played a critical role in much that is described in Chapter Seven of this volume. His presentation is a systematic development of the approach which a faculty might take, drawing heavily upon his own experience and his perception of the nature of an institution of higher education. It outlines an approach which will provoke much reaction, both favorable and unfavorable, but one which has met the pragmatic test in a variety of situations.

We felt, however, that to obtain balance in this chapter we should include a statement from one whose experience had been on the administration side of the table.

Donald E. Walters represents the board of trustees of the Massachusetts State College System as their chief negotiator in all professional collective bargaining. He suggests in the last section of this chapter, "Administrative Viewpoint," that the ultimate relationships which emerge between faculty and administration will be major in their impact upon higher education and that these relations are functions of the content or substance of what is to be formally negotiated. The treatment is brief but should be provocative and stimulating for those struggling to find a model other than one deriving primarily from an industrial or noncollegiate setting.

E. D. D. and R. S. F.

The essence of collective bargaining is the negotiations process, its substance and its method. The process is dramatized in the meeting of two teams across a table in a frankly adversarial relationship. Selected individuals of the faculty union constitute a disciplined group prepared to propose and counterpropose to a similar group chosen to represent the administration or (in the instance of some state systems) a state executive office. Each group must enhance the interests of its constituency.

In the broader sense, however, the negotiations process involves much more than the sessions at the table. In this chapter the process is segmented into preparation of the proposal, constitution of the bargaining team, formal negotiations at the table, and away from the table communications and arrangements—all of which lead to a formal contract which binds the two constituencies for a definite period of time.

Preparation of Proposal

Preparation of the proposal is customarily the responsibility of the employee representative. Most administrators come to the bargaining table with the current established policies, working conditions, and salaries as their proposal. Their posture is to maintain the status quo. This is not unexpected since the administration is unlikely to propose an item which would increase costs, and presumably is prepared to defend most noncost administrative procedures and policies as they stand. When the parties have negotiated prior contracts, the administration may propose changes in administrative procedures which have proven cumbersome.

Many higher education faculties feel apprehensive about preparing the proposal. Few have participated in collective bargaining, and the questions of where to start and how much change the proposals should encompass cause considerable confusion.

All faculty problems, concerns, and desires must be identified and translated into written proposed solutions. A committee representing every interest group in the bargaining unit should prepare the proposal. The committee must include members who will ultimately form the negotiating team which is charged with presenting and arguing the proposal. This will ensure that the negotiating team member is well-schooled in the proposal and that he will negotiate the faculty's interests effectively.

To identify the faculty interests, the committee must develop a communications system among the faculty. Most faculty members, especially in newly recognized bargaining units, need answers to basic questions about the bargaining process before they can express their own concerns. They may not realize that a specific concern is a negotiable item, that is, that a question regarding due process in denial of tenure relates to internal departmental evaluation. Informal discussions between committee members and members of a department can give the faculty the opportunity to relay its interests to the committee, and many of the issues will emerge and crystallize.

Information garnered from informal meetings can be supplemented by faculty questionnaires which list every possible issue; this can help to determine priorities.

Once the committee has identified the concerns, desires, and priorities of the faculty, it is ready to write the proposal. The first step is to cull the faculty handbook, trustee policy manual, and written and unwritten administrative procedures to identify those which are adequate and should be preserved as written guarantees in the new contract. Some of these will need amendment and others will be eliminated through negotiations.

The second step is to examine carefully other contracts which have been negotiated not only in higher education but in the public school sector and in the private sector as well. Contract language covering insurance protection, grievance procedures, binding arbitration procedures, salary schedules, and other working conditions has often been developed to provide a solution to problems similar to those faced by a higher education faculty. Thorough examination of other agreements will prevent the committee from repeating the mistakes of other faculties and will aid in converting faculty concerns into concise contract language. The committee, however, must keep in mind that contract language is the language of compromise. Ultimately the contract will include phrases such as "when mutually agreeable," "where practicable," or "within a reasonable period of time," which are not included in the original proposal. Many novice committees, fearing committee or faculty censure, are timid in their proposals. Such committees write "reasonable" and "realistic" proposals which promote only moderate change. During negotiations they are forced into a position of obtaining much less for the faculty than was intended.

The committee should attempt to prepare a proposal which would support ideal conditions necessary for an institution of higher education. Such a proposal, if accepted, would mandate optimum policies and procedures and all working conditions that would be in effect if conditions permitted. The fact that a specific goal is not immediately attainable does not limit its legitimacy as a bargaining proposal. The typical arguments that the legislature will not fund it, the public will not accept it, it appears utopian should not be heavily considered in the deliberations of the committee. While the legislature may not fund it this year or the public accept it immediately, it will surely never be attained unless it is proposed.

Once the contract proposals have been completed, they should be examined by an attorney to ensure that they are all legally permissible. If there is some question as to whether a certain one may be permissible, the negotiating team should propose the item and be prepared to document its arguments with an attorney's opinion supporting the proposal.

Bargaining Team

Even if the negotiations proposal committee has succeeded in transferring the needs of the faculty into well-written, concise proposals, its efforts can be rendered useless if equal attention is not given to the choice of the bargaining team. Experienced negotiators find that the minimal requirements for team members are a vigorous advocacy of faculty rights and a strong commitment to the collective bargaining process.

Each member of the team should be willing to employ the full range of bargaining tactics to assure that the proposals become contract guarantees. Should negotiations reach impasse, each team member must be ready to use such weapons as political action, news releases, faculty censure of the administration, community censure, impasse proceedings, fact-finding, and perhaps even the strike. But he must understand the judicial use of these techniques. Perhaps the most inffective member of the team is the one whose first reaction to the frustrations of negotiating is to ask for a strike. That person is unwilling or unable to understand that negotiations is a sophisticated process which may require the use of all the weapons in the arsenal. At the same time, the team member who approaches negotiations convinced that logic, facts, persuasiveness, and good manners will leave no alternative to the administration but to accept, had best stay far from the negotiating table. These reasonable tools, without the support of the other bargaining weapons, will win few concessions.

The negotiator also must be willing to spend long hours at the table maintaining discipline by saying nothing while others speak. He needs patience when the administration calls a caucus for hours and then returns with no progress to report. But perhaps most important, he must maintain an optimistic attitude in the face of constant frustrations and slow progress.

An experienced negotiator looks for that total idealistic and personal commitment in any prospective team member. Nothing can be more disastrous to the negotiating team than to discover at some critical point in negotiations that a member of the team is disagreeing not with the timing of a tactic but with the very issue of whether that tactic is legitimate under any circumstances.

Tough decisions with far-ranging effects have to be made quickly in negotiations, and if an excessive amount of time is necessary to reach agreement among the team members, an error can be made at a critical point. Equally important is that the team member always be present to offer his insights to the committee. The decisions are never made by the chief negotiator alone. His role is to assess the faculty's position and offer advice on the most effective response to the administration. To do so, he must have the thoughts and suggestions of all team members. Thus they must be present at all sessions and should be prepared to be away from their families for long periods of time when negotiations reach crisis stages.

For any bargaining team to be successful, it must represent all the faculty. Procedures used in the selection of the negotiating team are usually more political than functional. Probably the worst method is through the election process. An elected team will need much training and luck to become the functional and dynamic group that bargaining requires. A better process would be to have the team selected by the stronger proponents of collective bargaining in conjunction with an experienced negotiator. This may appear undemocratic, but a bargaining team should not be a discussion group which represents all the pros and cons of collective bargaining. It should be a group committed to the advocacy aspects of collective bargaining.

Many faculty members initially disagree on the need for an outside professional negotiator. The need for his expertise becomes evident in any negotiations and even more apparent when the team meets hostility and distrust from the administration. The individual faculty member may be in a vulnerable position, but the profes-

sional negotiator can face the administration with firmness and reso-
lute force. The talents of an experienced negotiator are especially
valuable during negotiations for the initial contract following an
election or certification of the faculty organization as the bargaining
agent. In the campaign prior to the first negotiations, the competing
faculty organizations are likely to have made statements about the
administration, and in an effort to gain votes may have promised to
remedy all those wrongs in bargaining. The administration then
may come to the bargaining table in a defensive position at best and
a hostile, distrustful position at worst. The novice administration
and the novice faculty may, in such an atmosphere, overreact to
each other's proposals and adopt unnecessarily hard-line positions
from which neither can retreat comfortably. Experienced negotiators on both sides who do not have the political and emotional
commitments of the other members of their teams can often create
a more productive bargaining atmosphere. Eventually during negotiations, the administration will recognize that bargaining is an
orderly and sophisticated process calling for gradual change, and the
faculty organization will discover that bargaining is not the immediate panacea to cure years of administration neglect and faculty in-
difference.

Table Negotiations

The most typical attitude of the novice faculty member is
one of excitement and impatience to get to the bargaining table. He
may feel that once the negotiating team meets the administration
under the aegis of collective bargaining, presents the faculty position
to the administration, buttresses that position by multitudinous arguments, and proposes the obviously logical solution, the administration will have no choice but to accept. Actually, he will find that the
administration may agree totally with the faculty position, but it
will not accept the proposal for any of at least seven reasons: there
is no money in the budget; the trustees will not allow it; one group of
faculty members will benefit at the expense of another; the legislature will be up in arms; the public will be hostile; the governor will
not like it; and it is contrary to the tradition of the university.

Though veteran negotiators realize that well-reasoned arguments standing alone win little at the bargaining table, they further realize that the arguments must be made to determine what problems the administration faces in implementing the faculty proposals. The arguments also have to be made and answered to obtain faculty support when that becomes necessary.

Arguments and supporting data should be compiled for each substantive area of the proposal prior to the first bargaining session—data should not be prepared for the salary alone! The bargaining team, armed with facts, figures, and logical conclusions, is presumably prepared to go to the table.

The team often reacts negatively when the chief negotiator instructs it in the rigors of bargaining discipline. Only the chief negotiator is to make the argument, presentation, and counter arguments. The team member is not to answer questions directed to him, and he is never to correct any member of his team or to disagree with him openly. Understandably, the team member feels affronted by these rules, but successful negotiators demand strict team discipline for two reasons. First, the nature of the negotiating process is very akin to a chess game. The inexperienced player seldom thinks far beyond his next move; the seasoned player is often several moves ahead in his overall strategy. A move that may seem inane to one not privy to the overall strategy may well be the key move in a long-range strategy. Thus the negotiator cannot have the entire team trying to guess his next move. For example, the administrative team may make a statement which every member of the faculty team knows to be erroneous. The novice negotiator would refute the argument immediately. The veteran negotiator, however, may want the statement to stand for the moment, to be used on another issue at a later time.

The second reason for discipline relates to the strategy and style of the opposing negotiator. When an entire team can speak freely, the opposing negotiator knows within a few bargaining sessions how strongly each member on the opposing team feels about each issue. He may use that knowledge to divide and conquer the opposition team. If he can ascertain, for example, that one member of the faculty team does not feel strongly on the need for higher salaries, he will direct all questions on salary to that member. Once a weak statement is made, it cannot be retracted by anyone at the table, and management knows that the team is not solid on the salary issue. For all practical purposes, the weakest position voiced by any member of either team becomes the position of that team. Both chief negotiators and all the members of the team are constantly assessing the responses, facial expressions, and involuntary slips of each member of the opposing team. This is one of the most important functions of the negotiating committee. The assessments are critically evaluated in caucuses called by the teams during negotiations.

The complete proposal should be presented at the first bargaining session. It should not be mailed to the administration prior to that first session, because an early reading may create a number of misunderstandings as to the meaning of the proposal. The faculty bargaining team should hand the proposal to the administration in the first session and then proceed to explain the proposal fully. The first session is not the time to argue for its implementation. Procedures for future negotiation involving frequency, time, and place of future meetings; faculty released time; and other guidelines should be agreed to at the first meeting. At subsequent meetings, the faculty team should begin a more detailed explanation of the proposal and the documentation of the arguments which support the proposal. The position of the faculty must be aired on each issue before the administration can be expected to counterpropose.

Once the faculty's position on each clause of the proposal has been explained and fully understood by the administration, the administration must state its position. The faculty should never offer to move from its stated position until the administration has moved. This does not mean that the administration should be expected to counterpropose to every part of the proposal. In fact, such a procedure would undoubtedly lead to unwieldy sessions.

Most negotiators prefer that the negotiating process be orderly. Both parties should attempt to reach agreement article-by-article, or by groups of related articles. If agreement can be reached on noncontroversial items first, the issues can be brought into better focus and an atmosphere of give and take is set which allows each party to become familiar with the negotiating style of the other. Serious trading on economic items and aspects of other priority items such as tenure, binding arbitration, and dismissal procedures should be held until the less crucial items are off the table.

As agreement is reached on each item, the language should be agreed to as well, especially in initial negotiations. Although parties that have negotiated together for years can often agree in principle to settlement terms and plan to write the language at a later date, this practice is fraught with potential conflict. A host of problems will arise naturally from the changes necessitated by initial negotiations and confusion over intent invariably occurs. It is far more preferable to agree to language as agreement is reached on each article or group of articles.

As negotiations progress and proposals are exchanged, the parties will caucus frequently to assess positions and proposals. Veteran negotiators seldom accept a major proposal at the table. The normal procedure is to ask questions about the intent of the proposal and how it relates to the overall package and then discuss the proposal in caucus. The caucus is the forum for deciding the team's position on the other party's proposal and the response that will be made to the proposal. The response may be made immediately or at some later session, but regardless of what it will be or when it will be transmitted, it must be or appear to be unanimous. A caucus should be called as the need arises.

Good-faith negotiations require that the administration consider each proposal with the knowledge that it must either accept it, offer valid justification for refusing to accept it, or offer a counterproposal. Refusal to offer any of the three options would constitute a breach of good-faith bargaining. A constant refusal to meet at reasonable times and places would be a breach of good faith. Beyond that, the question of good faith depends on such variables as the validity of the reasons for refusal to accept a proposal, the amount of movement that is offered, the number of issues at hand, and their interrelationship. It is a subjective judgment based on weighing these variables.

As negotiations progress, the more difficult items are put aside time and again while agreement is reached in other areas. They are reconsidered occasionally, and differences are lessened or more clearly defined. Ideally, this process of narrowing differences through repeated exchanges of proposals would lead to a settlement without the need for either party to pull other weapons from their collective bargaining arsenal. This may occur, but only in a situation where the administration has the financial resources and authority to effect sweeping changes, or where the faculty is willing to settle for little more than the status quo. An amicable settlement is also unlikely in some institutions because in effect, traditions of many years' standing will be challenged by any proposal that is founded on the assumption that faculties have power equal to the administration. The changes proposed through negotiations will almost invariably be met by resistance on the part of the administration—resistance which has to be overcome by weapons other than persuasion and logic.

Away from Table

The use of tactics other than direct persuasion and logic as an integral part of negotiations marks the most significant difference between public-sector and private-sector bargaining. In private-sector bargaining, the strike or threat of a strike is used eventually to produce a settlement. The underlying philosophy of the National Labor Relations Board (NLRB) is that the greatest labor stability develops when the parties have equal bargaining power at the table. That equality has been achieved in the private sector by balancing the power of employees to strike with the power of management to lock out employees. Because the right to strike is prohibited or severely limited in the public sector, bargainers have developed other ways to increase bargaining strength. These tactics, many of which are incorporated into the law, include public relations, political action on the local and state level, lobbying, mediation, and fact-finding.

Since the threat of a strike is not an immediate tactic for public universities, how do faculties go about bargaining with administrations? They must first exhaust all other tactics short of the threat of a strike. Even in Pennsylvania and Hawaii, which allow strikes by higher education faculty, the other tactics must be exhausted according to state law and because a novice faculty will demand it before they are willing to carry picket signs around the administration building. How does the bargaining team develop those tactics effectively to minimize the necessity of a strike?

The faculty bargaining team members must realize that any of these tactics may be used before negotiations are successfully concluded. The extent to which any tactic will be used depends upon the progress at the bargaining table. A bargaining team that meets recalcitrance at the table and has reached impasse on a number of issues may wish to call on the faculty, community, city, or country or state legislature for support. Many negotiators, both administration and faculty association, eschew the idea of taking the issues to the public, even though by doing so they may avoid a disgruntled faculty and even a strike. Neither party is willing to make a proposal or counterproposal during fruitful negotiations if it is open to public scrutiny, because the negotiations would take on an aura of public debate where each party would play to the public rather than bargain seriously toward a settlement. Each party would lose its authority to negotiate and would in effect be turning the negotiations over to the entire faculty, community, board of trustees, and legislature. However, when the parties have reached impasse, the faculty bargaining team must look for outside support.

To go before any group with the expectation of support necessitates early establishment of lines of communication. Faculty support should be automatic if the faculty has been involved in the preparation of the proposals and has been kept informed on the progress of negotiations. This does not mean that each proposal and counterproposal should be published, but reports should be made after each bargaining session.

Communication with the faculty can produce another important and long-range effect. Most faculties, especially those at large institutions, range from skeptically accepting to frankly opposing collective bargaining. The fact that a majority of the faculty members cast their votes for one organization to represent them in bargaining does not imply that collective bargaining has been fully accepted. To be fully accepted it must be fully understood, and the best time for the bargaining agent to educate the faculty is during negotiations. Reports to the members about the discussions go far toward making the bargaining process an acceptable vehicle of change.

The type of support requested from the faculty members will depend upon the reasons for the impasse. If negotiations have stalled because the administration suspects that their proposals are adequate to reach a settlement, then a simple resolution by the faculty, reaffirming its support of the bargaining team and the proposals, may be sufficient to start the negotiations rolling again. If the reason for the impasse is that the administration lacks the authority for making any further proposals, stronger tactics are necessary. Where the faculty must bring pressure to bear depends upon the oganizational structure of the institution as well as the issues at impasse. The authority to sanction change in a public institution resides in varying degrees in the president or chancellor, the board of trustees, and the legislative body. The degree to which each of these persons or groups exercises control depends upon factors ranging from the size of the institution to state law. Generally, the top administrative office and the board of trustees share authority in noneconomic areas, which include governance, grievance processing, faculty evaluation, and curriculum matters. A board of trustees with a positive attitude toward collective bargaining will delegate its authority in these areas to the administration bargaining team. This action in itself will lessen the conflict at the bargaining table since the noneconomic areas lead to the greatest conflict.

The methods by which the faculty can bring pressure on the president and the board of trustees will vary depending on the seriousness of the issues and the willingness of the top officers of the institution to continue negotiations. The board of trustees may be unaware of strong faculty support for certain proposals, and it may oppose others in order to reserve power for itself or the administration. Effective tactics for promoting change may vary from a resolution from the faculty, to letters and telegrams, to a press conference called to make the public aware of the controversy.

An impasse in negotiations on the economic areas is not only more difficult to resolve but is also more easily reached. Bargaining on economic items is perplexing to both parties. The administration team members may admit that they agree with the faculty team's proposal on wages, insurance benefits, and other money issues. They may also admit that they will offer no counterproposal because appropriations come from the legislature. The best that the administration can offer is that faculty and administration jointly recommend an economic package to the legislature. Though state legislatures have given the responsibility to negotiate to the administrations, they have not given them the full authority to do so. Even in New York State where the legislature has invested much power in the Office of Employee Relations (OER), which is responsible to the governor, this agency can only reach agreement on what it recommends to be funded.

When the novice faculty bargaining team reaches impasse on economic issues, its members become painfully aware of the need for an effective political action arm for their organization and for a lobbying effort at the city, county, or state legislature. Prior to the passage of statutes mandating the right of public employees to bargain, public employee organizations relied largely on lobbying with legislative bodies to obtain benefits for its members. Now with the advent of collective bargaining, the need to lobby has become even more acute. The boom in local, state, and federal appropriations has slowed, and legislators, especially on the state and local levels, may gain favor with their constituents by voting against economic benefits for higher education faculties.

No less important is the fact that college faculties are among the last to bargain and they have the least power in the legislature. Government white-collar workers, blue-collar workers, nurses, and teachers all go to the same public trough for money. It stands to reason that the strongest will drink the deepest, and at present, college faculties have yet to find the trough.

In addition to political pressure, other avenues are available to resolve impasse short of a strike. Two common methods are mediation and fact-finding. These require that both parties agree that progress cannot be made, and they therefore enlist independent third parties to settle the dispute. In many states the procedures are provided for by law. The New York State mediation procedure is typical. When the parties declare impasse, the Public Employment Relations Board (PERB) appoints a mediator selected from a list of private attorneys, retired judges, and other arbitrators familiar with labor relations. Both parties are then contacted by the mediator, who attempts to convince each to compromise on its position in the interest of a settlement. An experienced mediator seldom cares about the merits of the issues. He is interested only in a settlement. The mediator will be of little value if both parties have reached their rock bottom level of compromise. However, he can be effective when impasse was reached because of an inability of the parties to communicate.

Few faculty members realize the extent of bargaining that occurs away from the table to prevent impasse and the need for a mediator. During negotiations at the table, both parties have a number of representatives present. In negotiations at a large university, as many as thirty people may be present during the sessions. The chief negotiators in such a situation are reluctant to make proposals which are in essence feelers or conditional proposals, because with thirty witnesses they become public knowledge and in effect are not retractable. Thus, experienced negotiators often meet without their entire teams in an effort to sound each other out. They may discover after a few hours of discussion the real reasons why movement cannot be made on an issue. Frank discussion may lead to a resolution or a better understanding of the problems. Both parties, through such meetings, in effect call for a truce and attempt to find resolutions in a relaxed atmosphere. If they cannot reach agreement, they return to the bargaining table as if no meeting had occurred. If such meetings do not occur because the negotiators are too inexperienced to realize they are an integral part of bargaining or because the team members are hesitant to trust their chief negotiator, then the chances for reaching impasse and requiring the services of a mediator are considerably heightened.

When impasse is reached because such off-the-record discussions have not been held or have been ineffective, the mediator can often provide the necessary communication. A professional mediator opens the lines of communications and offers compromises which may never have occurred to either party.

Should the mediator fail in his efforts to affect reconciliation, the parties prepare for fact-finding. This involves the casting in concrete form of all the arguments and facts which were used at the bargaining table. The fact-finder listens to the arguments of both sides and issues a recommendation at the conclusion of the hearings. Although the fact-finder's report is not binding, it forces both parties toward acquiescence, since the report is an independent third party's opinion of what constitutes a fair settlement and consequently lessens the validity of both parties' arguments for previous positions.

If the faculty is unwilling to accept the fact-finder's report, it must decide whether to back the bargaining team through the ultimate use of power—the strike. The question arises as to whether the faculty will repeat the history of public school teachers and resort to the strike as a collective bargaining tactic. A comparison of the public school teachers' working conditions and professional participation in the decision-making process with that of the faculty of higher education suggests that, though there will undoubtedly be strikes, there will be fewer, and at four-year institutions and large universities they will not take place for several years. (Sporadic strikes at the community college level have already begun to occur.) The causes for strikes in the public school sector have centered on the lack of input by the teacher into the professional aspects of the education process. In higher education, faculties have long had a great deal to say about such matters; their role has been advisory in almost every institution, but the precedent is there. The question is whether administrations will understand faculty demands that the advisory function become a guaranteed right to share equally in determining curriculum, work load, tenure, class size, salaries, and fringe benefits. If administrations cannot adapt to this fundamental change, faculty frustrations will mount. If legislatures continue to cut back on appropriations and legislate class size and work load, there will be further faculty discontent.

That strikes will occur at four-year institutions is inevitable. The change in the role of the faculty advisory participation to power-sharing under collective bargaining is profound. Administrations and legislatures that are comfortable with the faculty advisory capacity may find it difficult to adjust to the faculty that refuses to take no for an answer. Collective bargaining dictates that administrations meet the demands of faculties with counter proposals which necessitate altering practices and procedures developed by the administration. The natural impulse to resist such change is great, and administrations which find difficulty in adjusting will face the possibility of strikes.

Although it is difficult to assess the impact of collective bargaining on higher education, it is not impossible to predict general trends. Collective bargaining is a process which opens new lines of communication with the administration. To bargain and to discuss issues at the table requires both parties to become experts on administration. During negotiations the practices of the university are examined in great detail. When faculty, who are closest to the daily problems of teaching in a university, are allowed to participate equally in the governance of that institution, the quality of higher education must be improved.

Administration Viewpoint

Collective bargaining is a catalyst capable of altering the basic direction of higher education, and effective control over the processes of collective bargaining lies in the hands of the bargainers. The attitudes which faculty, union representatives, and administrators bring to the bargaining table influence the quality of the contract and the future character of the institution. Two fundamental perceptions of those at the negotiating table determine the outcome of bargaining: the perception they have of the nature of the bargaining process, and the perception they have of the traditions of higher education and the professoriate.

The earliest influences on collective bargaining were industrial. Thus the bargaining process was developed in a milieu which accepted the basic division between management and labor, and which built its foundations on three principles: first, that the relationship and the status of the bargaining parties was that of employer-employee; second, that there was an essential and irrevocable conflict between the interests of the employer and the employee and that their bargaining relationship was basically adversary; and third, that management owns the tools of production and the worker, his skills, so that the worker had no substantive role in deciding what work would be done, by what methods or by whom, or what should be the policies or goals of the organization.

As collective bargaining spread from the private to the public sector, these three principles became such an integral part of the bargaining process that no challenge to their validity was raised. Even when collective bargaining became an accepted process for teachers in elementary and secondary education, a reexamination of these principles did not take place. Thus the nature of the bargaining process at the beginning of the 1970s is still rooted in the seminal notions that the interests of employees and employers are adverse, that the objectives of management and worker are irreconcilably split, and that their prerogatives and concerns are absolutely separate.

In higher education the nature of the bargaining process remains deeply influenced by its industrial origins. Indeed, the most common approach to collegiate collective bargaining builds an entire negotiating strategy on the central presumption that the parties at the bargaining table are adversaries. The tools, weapons, and rhetoric are chosen accordingly. Whether the tool is binding arbitration or the weapon is the strike, no question is raised as to its appropriateness or usefulness in solving the problems of higher education.

However, another approach to the bargaining process deserves analysis. This approach accepts the validity—or at least the reality—of collective bargaining in higher education, but refuses to accept without serious reevaluation a process designed more for the factory than for the university. It begins, therefore, with an assessment of the collegiate milieu in the early 1970s, of the traditions of the academy, and of the relationships and roles of those who comprise the campus community. It requires that collective bargaining take into account, as it once did in industry, the existing conditions of the institution where it is to be applied and the real roles of the parties. It is an approach which challenges collective bargaining to change.

The original principles upon which the industrial bargaining model rested do not so much need to be destroyed as amended. At least four fundamental areas can be modified. First, the original concept of the sharply defined status of the parties as employer-employee fails to take account of the supplementary status of faculty as professionals. Since the status of faculty is different and is more than employee, the expectation about faculty roles in and contribution to the institution should also be viewed from a different perspective. If, as professionals, faculty are to be self-initiating and self-sustaining with respect to their work, goal- and not clock-oriented in measuring their commitment to teaching and scholarship, and intellectually free to set the outer limits of their contribution, then the bargaining process must reflect these objectives.

Second, the notion that there is an essential and irrevocable conflict between the interests of the employer and the employee attaches insufficient importance to the real mutuality of interests between faculty and administration. Conflicts obviously exist between faculty and administration, but the basic relationship does not grow out of conflict. Indeed, that relationship emphasizes the community of interests between faculty and administration in the broader institutional commitments to teaching, scholarship, and service, as well as in the determination of institutional goals and educational policy.

Third, the presupposition that employers and employees are adversaries, or that their interests are, ignores the importance and usefulness in higher education of the concept of collegiality as a set of processes for conflict resolution; the bargaining process may be adversary, but the parties need not be. Too great an emphasis on the sense of conflict between faculty and administration will be devisive at the negotiating table and alter the tone of the relationship between the parties away from it.

Fourth, the rigid distinction between management as owner of the tools of production on the one hand and the worker on the other does not fit higher education. Applied with its original intent, this distinction makes the faculty-administration relationship more artificial. It ignores the tradition of faculty participation in making decisions and tends thereby to isolate the faculty from such decisions as those affecting educational policy, which range from student admissions to academic requirements and programs to faculty personnel policies, and to shut off the voice of the faculty in matters affecting their professional interests.

The challenge for those who engage in collective bargaining in higher education is that of effecting a fundamental change in the character and tone of the negotiations process. More than any other single factor the thrust and substance of the proposal and counter-proposal of the parties at the table will decide whether such change is possible. The nature of higher education calls for unique expectations as to the matters to be dealt with at the table, an approach which may contrast sharply with early precedents. What the parties offer and counteroffer will determine whether the bargaining process as well as the agreement will become a major new medium for integrating traditional academic and collegial values with the needs of unionized faculties.

Thus, the following working hypothesis deserves both attention and analysis, for it suggests a guide for such fundamental change: "The protection of faculty professionalism and the preservation of collegiality can be dramatically enhanced if union and campus representatives can find creative ways to construe 'faculty governance' as a condition of employment to be negotiated into contract."

Doubtless there are risks for the institution as well as for the parties in any attempt to negotiate an entire system of campus governance into a collective bargaining agreement; but any such dangers can be minimized if the parties agree that the process and machinery for governance will exist independent of the union local on campus, outside its exclusive dominion or control, and will not be considered a creature of either the institution or the union local; that every member of the unit represented by the union is entitled to participate in the negotiated system of campus governance (that is, to vote in elections and to sit on committees) regardless of his dues-paying status; and that the system of campus governance negotiated in the contract, although advisory in form and in effect, will at all times be recognized for its integrity by the administration. If the parties bring these ideas to the bargaining table and thereby think in terms of institutional benefits rather than management or labor benefits, then a negotiated system of campus governance can become a compelling force for stabilizing the campus, preserving collegiality, ensuring institutional autonomy, and affirming the rights and responsibilities of faculty members as professionals.

A negotiated system of campus governance offers several benefits: First, it stabilizes the campus by expressly consolidating the common interests of the union and faculty senate in representing the faculty. Contractual governance establishes a single set of integrating processes through which the interests of all faculty may be satisfied. The potential conflict between senate and union can thus be dissolved, and with it the potential for open warfare. A contractual commitment to tripartite involvement of faculty, students, and administrators in campus governance also secures a measure of stability if the contract refuses to isolate the governance machinery from any of these constituencies. Governance thus drives the campus community toward unity by removing the divisive issues that lead to a polarization of the institution.

Second, a negotiated system of governance preserves collegiality by refusing to recognize the adversary relationship which has been an essential of collective bargaining historically. Rather, the contractural emphasis on shared authority through campus governance acts as an affirmation that the goals of faculty and administration are common, not disparate, and that the accomplishment of the goals is enhanced if faculty and administrators work toward them together.

Third, a negotiated system of governance ensures institutional autonomy by allowing decisions affecting the future of the college to be made on merit and at the time such decisions may be required. The parties must agree that no advance contractural commitment should be made that would prevent faculty, students, and administrators from dealing effectively with an unanticipated institutional need or opportunity.

Fourth, a negotiated system of governance affirms the professional status of faculty by its refusal to strip their relationship to the institution back to that of employee. Faculty are employees, but their role and contribution to their institution, students, and scholarship carry them far beyond the limiting concept of that term. All governance provisions of the contract dealing with faculty roles—their rights and responsibilities—must assume that no limits have been placed on the commitment or the contribution of the faculty to the college. Thus, provisions of the contract should not quantify the work of the faculty, but should reinforce the expectations that faculty are self-initiating and self-sustaining.

Obviously, where terms and conditions of employment are at stake, either party is free to propose matters which qualify the governance, substance, and process. Matters such as promotion and tenure may strain relationships such that the ultimate resolution becomes contractual. But would it not be wiser to make the processes for decision-making part of the contract and thus grievable, and to leave the criteria and judgment aspects within the purview of the campus governance process where peer judgment more readily obtains?

What is suggested, therefore, is a restraint upon both parties to examine what is proposed for bargaining so as to minimize the scope of adversarial relationships to matters for which there appear to be no alternatives and to enlarge the role and responsibility of faculty governance such that alternatives are less necessary or sought after. What is at stake for higher education in the collective bargaining endeavor is much more than even the contract. When everything else is stripped away, the relationship of the parties remains. Depending on how they view the negotiations process, the parties will get the relationship they deserve.

4

Grievance
Procedures

Matthew W. Finkin

*Once one has moved beyond the basic economic issues related to
salaries, fringe benefits, and promotion and tenure, the most important questions which have arisen are those related to grievances. In
many respects this facet of unionism more than any other reflects
the break with the traditional organizational relationships. Traditionally, the rights of the faculty member or other professional have
rested legally with the pleasure of the governing board, although
those associated with faculties are typically bolstered by well-established institutional traditions and the practices of the academic profession related to academic freedom. However, the bargained contract may supersede this mode and certainly sets up a grievance*

process based upon its own authority as a legal instrument. More-
over, it usually provides for final review by an arbitrator who is
independent of the board and external from the institution or state
system.

The nature and implications of the grievance procedures
therefore illustrate the most significant change which unionism may
carry into the academic enterprise. More than any other aspect, it
accentuates the possibility that a bargaining contract can become
the primary law of the institution, a fundamental condition which
would carry over into other relationships and policies as they are in-
cluded in the bargaining process.

The author of this chapter, Matthew W. Finkin, recognizes
this difference between the nature of the traditional mold and the
contractual relationship. Finkin has been in an excellent position
in the American Association of University Professors to place the
grievance process in this significant perspective. His chapter deals
first with a noncontractual pattern and then reviews the contrac-
tual procedures. His concluding remark points up difficulties which
have accompanied the imposition of contractually based procedures
upon traditionally established arrangements.

E. D. D. and R. S. F.

A sharp disparity in attitude toward the grievance procedures of
a collective agreement even among management representatives is
illustrated by the following two quotes: "The swift and equitable
handling of grievances is perhaps the most important factor in securing harmonious and cooperative relationships between employer
and professional employees in educational institutions. . . . Properly conceived, grievance procedures can be a boon to both administrators and faculty whose common concern is progress based on
justice and harmony" (Angell, 1972, p. 505). And: "Almost all
collective bargaining agreements contain a grievance procedure, yet
most public employers have no appreciation of the havoc such a
clause can produce. It is a sleeping monster, which can be aroused
by your employees snapping their collective fingers" (Hogan, 1972,
p. 67). These divergences pose vividly the interrelated questions of
what a grievance procedure is for, how it should be designed to ac-

complish its ends, and how it should articulate with an existing system of internal institutional decision-making independent of collective bargaining.

Apropos of these questions, the United States Supreme Court has described the grievance process, culminating in the arbitration of the disputed issue by a neutral third party, as "the very heart of the system of industrial self-government." It is, said the court, "a vehicle by which meaning and content is given to the collective agreement." The implications of the Court's description for unions in academic institutions have particular importance. The professional status of academic personnel gives them a role in the making of decisions which may be challenged through the grievance process. Perhaps no other single aspect of collective bargaining places the tension between the professor's legal status as an employee and his status as a professional so sharply as the terms of the contractual grievance procedure and the manner of its administration. The implications of this issue are a recurrent theme in this chapter.

From the above perspective, the discussion here focuses first on general notions of faculty government as reflected in a noncontractual model for the disposition of faculty grievances. It then reviews the various procedures in a sampling of collective agreements in four-year colleges and universities. Finally, it will center on some of the most critical aspects of resort to arbitration, the most commonly used final stage in the procedure, and some problem areas which require careful attention by parties drafting agreements.

Noncontractual Paradigm

In most universities and colleges the faculty has secured an influential role, and in some a dispositive one, in decisions on faculty status. Through peer judgment the faculty, particularly of a mature university, may influence decisions affecting teaching responsibilities, salary, promotion, tenure criteria, and other working conditions. In the area of dismissals of faculty and allegations of violation of academic freedom, faculties have generally maintained that they possess primary responsibility and expect concurrence by the institution's administration and governing board. Many faculty decisions are potentially subject to complaint by an adversely affected faculty member.

The degree of faculty influence varies widely. In autocratically administered institutions faculty grievances are disposed of by appeal, usually on a purely informal basis, to the chief administrative officer. In other institutions, however, some internal faculty procedures have been used to resolve faculty complaints. These vary greatly in design and degree of detail. For example, the Board of Control of Northern Michigan University, formerly a college for teacher training, has adopted an elaborate internal procedure (now published in a seventeen-page booklet) which is administered by a standing Faculty Hearing Panel. In the most common case the review is less structured. The procedure applicable in New York University (NYU) is a good example. Each school or college within the university has a grievance committee which is available to faculty members after informal channels are exhausted. The committee is advisory to the dean. Further formal appeal to a universitywide committee composed of tenured members of the Faculty Council (the elected faculty members within the overall universitywide senate) may be made only on matters of reappointment, promotion, and tenure, although informal review may be made by the central administration on other issues. In addition, formal appeal is limited to allegations of the procedural irregularities, inadequate attention, or violation of academic freedom. Within specified time limits the committee is to advise the president and chancellor, who must state their reasons to the committee if they fail to concur with its recommendations.

Several aspects of the NYU system reflect a conventional pattern, at least for mature institutions, whereby a faculty disposes of internal complaints: any faculty member has a right to pursue his complaint through all stages of the process; the definition of the grievance allows review of academic freedom questions or of allegations of arbitrary or capricious treatment, but precludes interference with the substantive judgment of the disciplinary peer group concerning the individual's qualifications; the procedure is relatively loose with respect to functional precision and time limitations (the Faculty Council has subsequently adopted internal regulations tightening the procedure on the universitywide level); the review is purely internal to the institution and is conducted by representatives of the faculty peer group; and the judgment of the final grievance review is purely recommendatory to the administration. Similarly the Northern Michigan plan, while more open-ended in the issues allowed for final faculty review and far more detailed in the actual design, typically allows unfettered resort by the individual complainant to the procedure which results ultimately in a recommendation to the administration.

Contractual Procedures

Negotiated contracts invariably provide for formal grievance procedures. For this analysis the provisions of ten agreements are reviewed to highlight their similarities and differences and to provide a contrast with the non-negotiated model just described.

At Oakland University (in Michigan), after an informal attempt to resolve a grievance, the matter may be submitted by the individual or individuals or the bargaining agent to a designee of the administration. If the matter remains unresolved, it is presented to a six-member University Appeals Committee consisting of three appointees of the university and three of the bargaining agent. The committee has the right to hold formal hearings. If the matter remains unresolved, either the agent or the administration may submit the matter for the decision of an arbitrator selected through the American Arbitration Association. A grievance is broadly defined to include any problem relating to employment in addition to the application or interpretation of the agreement, but the arbitrator is prohibited from substituting his judgment for that based upon academic considerations in the classification of a faculty member.

At Central Michigan University, after an informal attempt to resolve a grievance, the complainant must present the matter to a grievance committee of the bargaining agent which has the authority to determine whether the grievance arises out of a violation of the agreement, whether the grievance procedure is the proper method for resolving the grievance, and whether as a matter of policy the agent wishes to pursue the grievance. If it decides the foregoing affirmatively, the matter is presented formally to the provost. If the matter remains unresolved and the agent wishes to pursue a remedy, it is submitted to a four-member committee of two appointees of the administration and two of the agent. If the committee is unable to agree, it may choose a fifth voting member from the academic community-at-large. A grievance is defined as a violation of the agreement.

At Boston State College, after informal attempts to secure resolution, the grievant officially submits the matter to the academic dean, and if he is then dissatisfied, to the president. If the matter is still unresolved, the grievant may present it to the board of trustees if it involves departures from enumerated board policies expressly incorporated by reference in the agreement; procedural irregularities on matters of appointment, promotion, and tenure (except grievances which are concerned with matters of academic judgment); or the failure of the president to recommend tenure for a faculty member who has been recommended by appropriate faculty bodies pursuant to criteria established in the contract. A grievance is defined as a breach of either the contract or board policies incorporated by reference in it.

At Southeastern Massachusetts University, a grievance is presented for the successive review of the dean of the school, the dean of faculty and the president. If the grievant is dissatisfied, the union local may appeal to the board of trustees, and if the matter is still unresolved, the local may submit it to arbitration. A grievance is defined as breach, misapplication, or misinterpretation of the agreement.

At the City University of New York (CUNY), two bargaining agents have agreements which contain identical grievance procedures. They encourage the internal resolution of all complaints and grievances and designate the local campus president or his designee as the first formal stage, with subsequent appeal to the chancellor or his designee. If the matter then remains unresolved, either the grievant or the agent may proceed to arbitration. Each agreement provides for a standing three-member arbitration panel jointly selected by the agent and the administration and composed of persons "familiar with the customs, practices, nature and spirit of the academic community." They serve on a rotating basis. The contract defines a grievance as breach or misapplication of the agreement or arbitrary application of or a failure to act pursuant to the bylaws and policies of the board related to terms and conditions of employment. It is subject, however, to a clause providing that grievances relating to appointment, reappointment, promotion, or tenure "which are concerned with matters of academic judgment" may not be arbitrated. According to the contract, an allegation of arbitrary or discriminatory use of procedure in such decisions may be arbitrated subject to the following contract provision: "In such case the power of the arbitrator shall be limited to remanding the matter for compliance with established procedures. It shall be the arbitrator's first responsibility to rule as to whether or not the grievance relates to procedure rather than academic judgment. In no event, however, shall the arbitrator substitute his judgment for the academic judgment. In the event that the grievant finally prevails, he shall be made whole."

At St. John's University, after exhaustion of informal avenues for redress, the matter is presented officially to the dean of the school. Review by the president may be sought directly on matters affecting more than one school. It may be sought also in determinations by the dean that are unfavorable to the grievant. Finally, the agent may submit any unresolved grievance to arbitration under the auspices of the American Arbitration Association. A grievance is defined in the same fashion as in the CUNY agreements. Exceptions include dismissal of a faculty member (governed by the procedural due process provisions of university statutes); complaints by department chairmen concerning their administrative duties; complaints concerned with the nondiscrimination clause; and complaints "relating to the merits of appointment, reappointment, promotion, academic freedom and tenure which matters are governed by the statutes and practices" of the university.

At the New York Institute of Technology, after informal avenues have been availed of, the matter is presented to a committee established by the Faculty Senate which in turn makes a recommendation to the president. If the agent is dissatisfied with the result, it may proceed to arbitration through the American Arbitration Association. A grievance is defined as a dispute involving the application and interpretation of the agreement and includes the American Association of University Professors (AAUP) standards on academic freedom and tenure and university government.

At the State University of New York (SUNY), after resort to informal channels, a grievance is initiated formally by appeal to the local campus president (or his designee), with further appeal to the chancellor and then to the state Office of Employee Relations (OER). Finally, the agent may insist upon arbitration by one of a standing seven-member panel selected jointly by the agent and the OER. A grievance is defined as a dispute over terms and conditions of employment (except dismissals for cause dealt with in a separate procedural section) or an allegation of failure to follow procedures established by board policies relating to appointment or promotion. The arbitrator is expressly prohibited from substituting his judgment for that of the administrative official exercising judgment on substantive matters and is limited to directing a reconsideration of the case in the event he finds procedural noncompliance.

At the New Jersey State Colleges, after informal channels have been availed of, the matter is presented first to the college dean or academic vice-president and if it is unresolved, to the president. If the matter is still not settled, it is appealed to the chancellor of higher education (or his designee), who may convene a formal hearing. A grievance is defined as either breach of the agreement or, in an explicit second category, as improper application of or failure to follow policies of either the State Board of Higher Education or the local board of trustees related to terms and conditions of employment. Decisions involving the nonreappointment of nontenured faculty are deemed not to be grievable. Further review after the chancellor's decision is afforded to the governor's Employee Relations Policy Council, which, in the first class of grievance, can conduct a form of advisory arbitration and, in the second, can provide a review by a hearing officer whose decision must be in writing, but whose advisory or binding status is not specified.

At Rutgers University, after the exhaustion of informal methods, the grievance is initiated by submission to the appropriate dean or director. If the matter is unresolved, it is submitted to a faculty committee of review established in each college or division subject to certain procedural guarantees such as the right of access to documentation, cross-examination of witnesses, and the like. If the matter is still unresolved, appeal may be made to the provost of the university and then to a six-member universitywide appeals

committee consisting of three appointees of the agent and three of
the administration. The decision of the committee is advisory to the
university president and the board of governors. A grievance is defined as a violation of the agreement or of established university
regulations governing promotion or tenure, except that the agreement is not to diminish "the responsibility of faculty, department
chairmen, and . . . deans, directors and other appropriate administrative officials for the exercise of academic judgment."

Comparison of Approaches

All the foregoing bear some similarities and dissimilarities.
First, almost all the agreements encourage the informal settlement
of problems. Most permit the individual adversely affected to pursue
his own grievance at least in the early stages. In the CUNY agreements it is explicit that the individual also may proceed to arbitration on his own, although it is unclear what the financial arrangement for the arbitrator's fee and expenses in such cases would be.
The grievant may proceed on his own in Rutgers University as well,
but that procedure differs very little from the noncontractual form.
In the majority of agreements, however, the collective agent has
control of whether the final stage of the process is utilized and, in
fact, the Central Michigan University agreement explicitly states
that the agent exercises its discretion to control access to further review as a matter of policy. I discuss the significance of the individual's ability to proceed to the final stage independent of the agent
later in this chapter.

Second, some of the contracts have limited the grievance
procedure to breach of the agreement while others include violation
or neglect of institutional procedures established through other
means. However, a closer look at the former category is required to
ascertain whether the contract formally incorporates such existing
institutional policies or in effect substantially reenacts them. Moreover, the care devoted to the standard for review in the CUNY, St.
John's University, Oakland University, Boston State College, SUNY,
and Rutgers University agreements are not dissimilar to the non-
bargaining approach of NYU. They make clear that in matters of
faculty status the exercise of an "academic judgment" or a decision

on merit by appropriate faculty bodies and administrative officers is not to be reviewed as opposed to the procedural aspects of the decision-making process. This is in keeping with precontract assumptions concerning the desirability of review of substantive peer judgments. I discuss the utility of the language of the standard adopted, however, later when I treat the implications of the use of arbitration.

Third, unlike the NYU procedure all the foregoing are relatively explicit with respect to the timing of appeals, and provide some detailed guide to procedures to be followed. Most of the arbitration provisions accept the rules of the American Arbitration Association.

Fourth, a wide disparity is presented in the composition of the review machinery. At Rutgers University the procedure is almost indistinguishable from a noncontract form and utilizes local faculty grievance committees, administrative appeal, and a universitywide committee composed of both faculty and administration representatives. At the New York Institute of Technology the faculty's internal governing body (with modified composition and expanded functions as a result of negotiations) is given initial review authority. Under the CUNY, St. John's University, Boston State College, Southeastern Massachusetts University, the New Jersey State Colleges, and SUNY agreements, however, only levels of administrative appeal are provided for prior to resort to the final stage of the procedure. At Oakland University a level of joint administration-faculty review is interposed between a purely administrative appeal and the final stage, and at Central Michigan University a similar bipartite body itself provides the final review.

In addition, varying approaches are reflected in the final stage. At CUNY, St. John's University, SUNY, Southeastern Massachusetts University, New York Institute of Technology, and Oakland University, the matter is presented finally to a neutral third party from outside the institution (an arbitrator, or, in the New Jersey State Colleges, a hearing officer). At Boston State College, appeal ends with the board of trustees and at Rutgers University with the president and board of governors. At Central Michigan University a neutral third party may be made a member of the standing bipartite committee to break an impasse on the disposition of any grievance. Thus varying attitudes are reflected with respect to the degree of collegial judgment which should bear in the grievance process and the extent to which the final determination should be made internal to the institution.

Fifth, unlike the noncontractual model, the ultimate review provided in the CUNY, St. John's University, New York Institute of Technology, SUNY, Southeastern Massachusetts University, Central Michigan University, and Oakland University agreements is binding on the institution without requiring further review by the trustees. On the other hand, in Rutgers University and Boston State College the trustees themselves constitute the final level of appeal. In the New Jersey State colleges the outside review is clearly a recommendatory one for one category of grievance and it is unclear whether it is binding in the other. The absence of binding review may indicate a lack of bargaining power, a purely legal question of whether a governing board may commit itself in advance to abide by such decisions, or a degree of satisfaction with internal processes coupled, perhaps, with uncertainty of the wisdom of submitting institutional decisions, which may be faculty-generated, for review by persons outside the institution.

Arbitration

As noted earlier, in the industrial sector it is assumed generally that the grievance process will culminate in arbitration. In fact this has held also for most of the agreements in higher education. The submission of an institutional decision for review and possibly nullification by an individual outside the institution is novel indeed for colleges and universities. It is possible that unilateral administrative decisions may lend themselves rather easily to arbitral review. Thus the advent of arbitration for a faculty of an autocratically administered institution may be viewed in a fashion similar to the industrial experience. Indeed Lieberman (1971, pp. 68–69) suggests that a consequence of collective bargaining will be that the faculty will obtain the arbitration of administrative or managerial decisions in place of its traditional role in the making of those decisions initially. On the other hand, most of the agreements reviewed have not eroded the faculty's influence, and several have strengthened or guaranteed it.

Unlike the industrial experience, then, a cluster of issues critical to academic values grow out of the resort to arbitration by a faculty which participates in institutional decisions. These include the definition of the arbitral standard; the degree of remedial power delegated to the arbitrator; and the selection of the arbitrator in terms of the degree to which he is educated by the parties to the issue or issues before him and his sensitization to the subtle fabric of custom and practice in higher education. A threshold issue on the question of arbitral standard is whether the parties wish an arbitrator to review the merits of personnel actions; that is, whether an arbitrator should have the authority to make a qualitative judgment on matters of faculty status apart from applying those provisions susceptible of decision by resort to more objective criteria.

Perhaps the best introduction to these critical areas is a brief review of arbitral awards touching them. In one case an arbitrator was asked to decide whether the transfer of a faculty member from one department to another violated the guarantee in the agreement of academic freedom (*SMU Faculty Federation,* March 10, 1971). The arbitrator noted that if the evidence showed the transfer was made "for the purpose of denying [the faculty member] the freedom to discuss controversial . . . issues" in the department from which he was being transferred, it would sustain a violation of the agreement. After a full analysis of the reason for the transfer provided by the president of the institution as well as the circumstances surrounding it, the arbitrator concluded that no violation had been shown. The arbitrator, in this case a university professor of long experience, demonstrated an awareness of the issue in the context of a university setting.

In an award in a junior college, however, the arbitrator did not distinguish the concerns unique to higher education from the industrial attitudes about the employment relationship (*Board of Trustees of Schoolcraft College,* 1969). A faculty member had been reprimanded by the administration for writing an article in the student press which the arbitrator characterized as "critical of colleges in general and Schoolcraft College in particular." It called on students to examine whether the college was serving its purpose and whether it encourages or actually hinders learning and free inquiry. The grievant suggested that if the latter were the case, the institution should be closed. The arbitrator characterized the criticism as severe and found the article lacking in mature judgment which "cannot but be understood from a reading of the article that he, the author, considers the school to be of little or no value to its students." Accordingly, he upheld the formal reprimand. The grievant had contended that he enjoyed the freedom to state his views. The arbitrator responded to this point by noting that the faculty member was asked to write the article "because of his interest in the school and its pedagogical programs, not as a disinterested citizen." Thus, although the grievant's rights as a citizen must be respected, his conduct as a teacher was "subject to managerial control."

This attitude toward the relationship of the faculty member to the institution is well-illustrated in another arbitrator's comments concerning the wisdom of a governing board of an institution serving as a hearing body in a dismissal situation:

> The truth is that the board hires and fires. To cast this body, at any stage of an individual's employment stint, in the role of an *"impartial tribunal"* is clearly wishful thinking and at odds with the primary responsibility which the board serves: to protect and advance the interests of the institution. Only secondarily can the board be concerned about the interests of its employees. It is not an arbitral body, standing neutrally between the institution and the work force. It is, in fact, the employer, exerting controls and direction over the employees to the ends of promoting the school's interests. The fruits of due process before a body which is necessarily so management-oriented can be expected to be so bitter that, oftentimes, it would be better not tasted [*St. Clair County,* September 1971].

It is unnecessary to point to the body of law, custom, and comment which gainsays the propriety of a blanket application of industrial attitudes in an institution of higher learning. The awards cited above underline the need to select arbitrators carefully and "to make certain that they are aware of and sensitive to the values of academic freedom, and are knowledgeable and understanding of the ways of the academic world" (Sands, 1971, p. 172).

Turning next to the matter of arbitral standard, I noted earlier that in several of the agreements, most notably at CUNY, care is exercised to distinguish academic judgment from procedural departure. The standard for defining an academic judgment was placed in issue in two cases concerning the nonrenewal of full-time lecturers. The agreement provides that full-time annual lecturers achieve a form of tenure after a requisite number of years of service and defines the position as applicable to "faculty who are hired to teach and perform related faculty functions but do not have a research commitment." In the first case a department personnel and budget committee in Hunter College notified a faculty member of the nonrenewal of appointment due to the unavailability of classes and the individual's failure to pursue a doctorate. The arbitrator held that the first was a matter of academic judgment and that the provision defining the position could be understood to include continued progress toward securing a doctorate: "While my personal evaluation of the necessity for receipt of (or study for) the PhD degree might well vary from that adopted by the grievant's department," he stated, "it is impossible for me to find and conclude other than that this is, in rather pristine form, a matter of 'academic judgment' " (*United Federation,* June 23, 1970).

Several months later, however, another arbitrator held that the nonrenewal of appointment of a full-time lecturer in Queens College because he happened to be lacking a doctorate's degree ran counter to the job definition provision of the agreement. He reasoned that as the PhD is a research degree and as the full-time lectureship carries with it no research commitment, the reliance on the absence of the degree as the sole basis for the decision was impermissable:

> The reading into Article 13.1 [defining a full-time lecturer] a requirement for a PhD as a matter of "academic judgment" appears to the undersigned as a very substantial deviation from the language of the contract, and imposes a condition which was not negotiated by the parties.

This arbitrator recognizes that scholarly research could be helpful to teaching effectiveness. He also recognizes that many academicians equate the possession of a PhD with scholarly research. However, the contract bars the university from using the criteria of scholarly research and the lack of a PhD as the *sole* grounds for denying reappointment [*City University*, May 26, 1971].

The foregoing cases indicate a need to develop as matter of contractual draftsmanship a more detailed and workable standard than "academic judgment."

Another illustration of the institutional implications of the arbitral standard and the manner of its application emerges from a somewhat different perspective. The appointment of a lecturer in CUNY was not renewed in a decision which was later rescinded with a caution that his status would be reviewed carefully. After intense evaluation the department recommended that his appointment not be continued. Due to procedural irregularities a reevaluation was ordered which resulted in the reaffirmation of this position. The faculty member pursued the matter to arbitration alleging the decision to be based on his active efforts in the union and thus in breach of the nondiscrimination provisions covering such activity in the contract (*Board of Higher Education*, June 24, 1971). The grievant had been a graduate and undergraduate student in the department. He was well-known to many of the faculty but not to the new chairman, who testified in the arbitration proceeding to the meagerness of the grievant's academic output. In addition, unfavorable memoranda from faculty members who had observed the grievant's classes were introduced although the authors did not testify.

The arbitrator noted that the grievant's department had been undergoing change and that the selection of a new chairman coincided with a shift in the teaching emphasis and in the curriculum which affected the employment of lecturers. Concurrently, the grievant had served as chairman of the union grievance committee on his campus and was at the center of charges of contract violation against his own department. Thus the arbitrator concluded that the grievant "himself became the focus of the turmoil of the department's changes, as the officer of the union, as a lecturer vulnerable to curriculum changes, and as a faculty member evidently opposed to the teaching changes." These factors then culminated in a consensus in the department that the grievant as "the active unionist and gadfly" was no longed wanted. The arbitrator supported this observation by citing examples of antiunion bias on the part of faculty members evaluating the grievant. One member had admonished the grievant by saying that his union service "actively interfered with his development" in the discipline. Another expressed the conviction that lecturers should not be allowed to secure tenure (one of the union goals). The department chairman criticized the roles of the union in obstructing his plans for the department and of the grievant as a union spokesman.

The arbitrator pointed out the notorious difficulty of proving discrimination for union activity and commented that his determination "must by necessity be derived from the balancing of the substantial evidence consisting of instances of both proper and improper actions." There was, the arbitrator found, an "interlacing of displeasure with the grievant as an official of the union and with him as a teacher." The consideration of the grievant was, he concluded, "tainted by the department's bias stemming from disapproval of the union and his activities."

It is important to note that academic freedom has been understood by the profession to include speech critical of institutional policies. If, as Stevens (1971) points out, collective bargaining is a form of institutional government, it follows that academic freedom extends to activities by faculty members critical of union goals and tactics. This would include the freedom to utter statements critical of the union position affecting a faculty member's own department. In the foregoing the arbitrator failed to distinguish statements reflective of antiunion bias from expressions on institutional policy now subject to negotiation with the union.

Further, in view of the manner in which the nondiscrimination standard was applied it is not unlikely that faculty committees and administrators will become more circumspect in dealing with union activists. A natural caution may mitigate the making of firm judgments on the academic merits in borderline cases in order to avoid the turmoil and expense of arbitration. The consequence may be a chilling effect on the exercise of the right to criticize the goals or methods of the union, particularly by senior faculty. As in the academic judgment cases, more detailed attention in the agreement to the character of evidence may be required.

Finally, a critical area needing review is that of the remedy in the event of contractual breach. The CUNY contracts give evidence of the most careful attention to this issue in a special clause. This provision, however, does not extend to allegations of a breach which does not involve the misuse of procedure or academic judgment. As in the above nondiscrimination case, an arbitral award ordering reinstatement has been afforded where breach of some other contractual guarantee was found. One case, currently the source of much controversy, illustrates the difficulties of contractual draftsmanship. An instructor in Brooklyn College was denied reappointment which would have resulted in the acquisition of tenure. The decision was made without substantial compliance by the department with the contractual evaluation procedure requiring an explicit number of classroom observations and evaluations. The personnel committee of the grievant's department reversed its original negative recommendation in view of the error in procedure but retained its opinion that a better qualified candidate could be found. The college personnel and budget committee also reconsidered the matter but confirmed the prior negative judgment.

The arbitrator observed that the university was under an obligation to ensure proper evaluation so that the department and college committees could render an academic judgment on the basis of a whole record (*Board of Higher Education,* December 1, 1970). Accordingly, he found a gross failure to follow established procedure without reason and thus faced the issue of whether he had the authority to order the grievant reappointed in order to effectuate "compliance with established procedure."

The administration argued that, as a reappointment would confer tenure, such an order would have the effect of substituting the arbitrator's judgment for the academic judgment of the appropriate faculty and administrative bodies, an action prohibited in the contract. The arbitrator reasoned, however, that remand without reappointment would be meaningless in that it would not provide redress "for the arbitrary denial of her procedural rights that clearly are substantive." The arbitrator observed that "this conclusion was reached after much agonizing over the consequences of this award and its impact on the university's committee system that jealously guards its standard of excellence in the grant of tenure." To accede to the position of the university would result, he felt, in providing "no antidote to the wronged and to liberate the wrongdoer." At the time of writing, the Appellate Division of the Supreme Court of New York was divided 3–2 in striking out the order of reappointment from the arbitrator's award (*Legislative Conference,* April 12, 1972). The administration of CUNY has been most critical of the approach taken by the arbitrator (Healey, 1972, p. 3), and the arguments for and against are reflected in the disagreement on the bench. The majority found the award of tenure to be the exclusive prerogative of the Board of Higher Education, to be made on the basis of academic excellence. They found that the contract, requiring remand for procedural compliance in the event of procedural breach, to be consistent with the exercise by the board of its statutory power. Thus they held that public policy, recognizing the importance of tenure in the maintenance of excellence, far outstrips the *"ad hoc* fate" of the grievant. "Tenure," said the majority, "should not be conferred by a 'back-door' maneuver."

The minority, on the other hand, noted that the arbitrator is given explicit authority in the agreement to make the grievant "whole" in the event the grievant prevails. "It seems incongruous that an arbitration should be had," say the dissenters, "simply to come to the conceded conclusion that the Board of Higher Education did not enforce its rules in the first place, and that it could only be told now that there must be 'compliance with established procedures.'" The majority's approach, according to the dissent, would be to "adopt the default of the Board of Higher Education in following its own rules as a natural concomitant of its existence."

Whatever the legal aspects of this case, which at the time of writing is under appeal, it does underline a major difficulty: How much authority should the outside neutral arbitrator be given to remedy procedural errors in matters of faculty status? It also raises a question of the workability of the substance-procedure distinction. In passing, one may question whether the difficulties encountered in CUNY are not compounded by the provision of an elaborate evaluation system which itself increases the likelihood of technical error without perhaps adding significantly to the information before the peer group.

Resulting Problem Areas

One of the most difficult problems for a mature institution lies in the jointure of the grievance procedure with the internal system of faculty government and generally accepted academic customs and practices. The agreements surveyed in the foregoing illustrate a broad spectrum in approach from the almost noncontract style of internal faculty grievance processing of Rutgers University to the pure administrative appeal-arbitration route with some variations including intermediate peer review. It would be expected that a variety of factors, most notably the degree of mutual respect between administration and faculty, the degree to which professional attitudes are shared, and the character of the institution, will strongly influence the style of the resultant procedure.

In fashioning the procedure the parties must focus on a number of problem areas. First, access to the grievance procedure including the final stage: With some variation, in the majority of instances the faculty representative controls access to the final stage. It is not unreasonable to assume that an administration would not wish to be subjected to defending its actions in every conceivable case, including the most frivolous, if it entailed resort to arbitration with its attendant costs. Accordingly, it might demand in the negotiations that the agent have authority to control access to the final stage, presumably so that it would pursue only those cases which appear to have some merit. Balanced against that interest is the possibility that the agent would choose not to pursue the grievance of an unpopular faculty member or an outspoken critic of the organization. This potential is made more ominous if the contract and the grievance procedure for policing it are used as the exclusive internal devices for the protection of academic freedom. Moreover, it is not inconceivable that a compliant union could be persuaded not to pursue an alleged violation of academic freedom (academic freedom complainants are not always the most popular members of the faculty) in return for the promise of some future benefit or as a trade-off for the settlement of some other unrelated case. One way out of this difficulty would be to allow the individual grievant access on his own initiative to all stages of the procedure. Costs in such cases could be borne equally by institution and individual or apportioned by the arbitrator according to the gravity of the case.

Second, formality of the process prior to the final stage: The procedure should doubtless be designed to explore fully all relevant facts and issues. Too rigid an approach in the early stages, however, may inhibit the free exchange of views and information which may be helpful in securing a satisfactory informal settlement. Principal administrators and faculty members may be reluctant to deal informally if the next immediate stage is a triallike atmosphere. Further, too elaborate a review process may protract disposition of the grievance without affording any greater likelihood of a just result. For example, the contractual provisions of the New Jersey State Colleges provide for no fewer than four formal layers of appeal, the last of which involves a hearing officer giving an advisory opinion subsequent to a formal hearing by the chancellor.

Third, critical problems in the use of arbitration: If resort to a neutral is agreed to as the final step, experience suggests that careful attention should be given to the definition of the arbitral standard; the arbitrator's remedial authority; selection of the arbitrator; and the education of the arbitrator by the parties to the issues in the case in the context of the customs and traditions of higher education.

Great care must be taken in the drafting of contracts. The language agreed to should balance the need to correct recognized abuses with an equally important need for academics to exercise professional discretion. Interestingly, the noncontractual grievance procedure of Northern Michigan University makes explicit that the standards for the redress of grievances include not only the policies and regulations of the university but "the developing 'common law' in higher education" as well.

The CUNY agreements spell out most explicitly the attributes of the arbitrators to be selected and, as in the SUNY agreement, provide for a standing panel rather than selection for any particular case. While these provisions are salutory in themselves, some of the awards indicate that greater attention is needed in the selection of the individual arbitrators. The Central Michigan pattern of appeal to an internal administration-faculty committee, supplemented if necessary in impasse situations by an outside neutral from the academic community, may ameliorate some of these difficulties. The committee would be conversant with the "common law of the shop" and particularly sensitive to nuances of fact or personality. The neutral party would be expected to understand the issues and nuances by the arguments of the parties in the proceeding and by the debate within the committee itself.

Fourth, atttiude toward the procedure: The grievance procedure, no matter how it is designed, will only be as effective as those who administer it desire it to be. The vice-chancellor of CUNY has suggested that "a union is a union is a union, even when it is made up of professors" and has charged the faculty's bargaining agents with seriously undermining academic processes by "dragging as many cases as possible" to arbitration (Healey, 1972, p. 5). According to his figures, since the effective date of the agreements in September 1969, approximately 115 grievances on faculty status have been filed, over 60 percent of which have gone to arbitration. This represents an inordinate use of a process which should be resorted to only sparingly. Perusal of many of the resulting awards indicates instances where no serious case was presented. On the other hand, some of the awards have involved clearly demonstrated arbitrary actions. The novelty of a collective agreement for a large university and its ambiguities concerning the grievance procedure may in part explain this excessive use of arbitration. It may be that eventually more cases will be settled at earlier stages. Much depends on what the parties conceive the purpose of the procedure to be. As Angell (1972) somewhat idealistically suggests, the parties should view the procedure as a means of swiftly and equitably resolving honest disputes over difficult problems. On the other hand, as Hogan (1972) implies, the procedure can be conceived of as a mechanism to be used as a bludgeon by the bargaining agent. It may also be used by the administration to delay settling problems or to pass the buck on poor administrative decisions when it is more convenient to blame an arbitrator than to overrule a dean. Aggravated use of the procedure in either instance will not settle disputes so much as it will serve further to exacerbate an existing unhealthy state of administration-faculty relations.

5

Two-Year College Experience

George W. Angell

One dilemma in an assessment of the nature and impact of collective negotiations on the four-year colleges and universities is the novelty of this phenomenon. Professional unionism has sprung unexpectedly upon the academic scene. Thus, in our efforts to present background material preparatory to the accounts of the three typical negotiations cases given in Chapters Seven, Eight, and Nine, we might have looked to the experienced in business and industry, the public schools, public employees, and professional groups such as engineers and airline pilots. However, it became evident that the most pertinent prior experiences lay with the two-year colleges.

As the author of this chapter notes at the outset, the bulk

*of faculty unions have appeared in the public two-year colleges.
They proffer the most complete experience with associations formed,
negotiations conducted, and contracts signed. Their experience provides an overview of the problems, potentialities, and nature of this
activity as it can evolve in other institutions of higher educaiton.*

*The author, George W. Angell, conducted in 1970–1971 a
comprehensive study of faculty collective bargaining in the public
two-year colleges of New York state, a group of institutions typical
of those which have had union organization. His career includes
experience as dean and president in public colleges and as a student
and professor of higher education.*

E. D. D. and R. S. F.

Collective bargaining in higher education found its earliest acceptance in the public two-year colleges. In June 1972, 119 of the
158 separate institutions with recognized bargaining units served
this sector of higher education. Any review of the phenomenon of
academic unionism, therefore, must benefit from a look at this prior
experience which provides the early precedents.

In such a review it is important to recognize that the two-
year colleges have a somewhat different background which is much
closer to secondary education than that of the bulk of the four-year
colleges and universities. It is also important to remember that they
serve far more exclusively for the teaching of students, with less
emphasis on scholarship and research, than do many of the four-
year colleges. Similarly, traditions of faculty participation in institutional affairs and of faculty professional status are far more tenuous,
frequently even nonexistent, in these institutions. In many respects,
including the administrators and faculty members employed, they
look more to secondary than to higher education. Yet, they constitute increasingly a part of higher education. The affiliation of the
community colleges with the State University of New York (SUNY)
represents a major development in this regard.

More significantly, however, they exhibit an academic milieu
related to faculty service, student freedom, departmentalization,
degree requirements, curriculum, and similar facets of their operation that resembles higher education more than the public schools.

In total, they provide an experience which can convey insights of value to those in four-year colleges and universities who are about to launch upon the somewhat tortuous waters of unionism and collective bargaining.

Michigan and New York have had the most extensive experience with bargaining in two-year colleges. These each possess colleges which typify most of the campuses, urban and rural and precollegiate and technical, found elsewhere. The material in this chapter is based upon a study of unionism in twenty-three of the thirty-seven community colleges in New York State. A comprehensive study of the Michigan junior colleges has been made also and is reported in Shoup (1969).

Causes of Unionism

A primary causative factor for unionism in the two-year institutions was the existence of state statutes which facilitated this organization (see Chapter One). Only two of the Michigan and none of the New York faculties were formally recruited by unions prior to the passage of the state public employment relations laws which authorized public employees, including teachers in public institutions at all levels, to organize and bargain with their government employers. Faculties have been organized informally since many of them have voluntary arrangements whereby they consult rather effectively with administrations and boards on questions related to salaries and working conditions. Enabling legislation both spurred additional efforts to organize and turned this effort toward formal associations or unions.

Faculty members interviewed in Michigan and New York gave as their primary reasons for organizing low salaries, unilateral decisions by trustees and administrators, lack of communication between administration and faculty, and a general feeling of being treated as high school teachers rather than as members of a college faculty. As an example, three New York colleges in operation over twenty years did not accord faculty the right of sabbatical leave with pay. In addition, more than half of the faculties were paid substantially the same salaries as some neighboring high school teachers. Few community college faculties had an effective senate or other self-governing device to share the responsibility for determining class schedules, enrollments, calendars, teaching loads, reappointments, promotions, etc., and as a result they had heavy teaching loads, long hours, and few fringe benefits.

Perhaps the most telling factor leading to unionism, however, was the lack of academic freedom on some campuses. During the 1960s many campuses became centers of political activities directed against the war in Vietnam, racism, and autocratic institutions of all types. Faculty members participating in political activities sometimes lost their jobs without a hearing. Angry faculties turned to collective tactics even before they organized unions to protect their constitutional rights.

In both Michigan and New York, community college teachers, many of whom had experience teaching in high schools, sought organizational help from those whom they knew best: primarily the state teachers associations and the National Education Association (NEA). The NEA and its state associations have become more and more oriented toward professional unionism as an effective means to protect teachers' rights. In 1972 seventy-two two-year colleges had recognized NEA affiliations. The American Association of University Professors (AAUP), strong on senior campuses, has apparently exerted little effort to win support of two-year college faculties—only one had an AAUP affiliation in 1972. On the other extreme was the American Federation of Teachers (AFT), perceived as a far more militant organization experienced in bargaining tactics and the use of strikes. While four-year college faculties generally consider industrial-type unionism inappropriate to their ends, two-year faculties were not so certain (thirty-eight had AFT affiliations in 1972). They had seen successful strikes by teachers in New York City and in other large cities even in the face of severe penalties required by law.

Many felt that salaries and working conditions in two-year colleges were equally as oppressive as those in the lower schools and that these conditions would not change without the application of effective mass pressures. It is not surprising, therefore, that in the early stages the AAUP was selected as the bargaining agent for only one of the two-year college faculties and that the AFT was selected by colleges located in or near large cities such as New York, Syracuse, and Buffalo, where this union had long been active. As of the spring of 1971, community college contracts in New York State were negotiated by twenty-four faculty organizations, of which five were members of the AFT, eight were members of the New York State Teachers Association (NYSTA), which is affiliated with the NEA, five were loosely affiliated with the NYSTA, four had no official affiliations but received advice from the NYSTA, and two were independent confederations which permitted members to continue paying their individual dues to the NYSTA or the AFT as they wished. As expected, the campus competition and rivalry among the union organizations increased steadily until 1972 when a merger was finalized between NYSTA and the New York association of the AFT.

Early Problems of Negotiations

Early public employment relation laws were generally initiated and supported by state and municipal employees with little or no help from college teachers, since both two- and four-year faculties were still arguing the merits of unionization versus professionalism. When the first state laws were passed, trustees, administrators, and faculties were caught unprepared both psychologically and technically. This led to a number of early difficulties, the first being a general lack of planning. Trustees and administrators hoped that faculties would not feel the need to organize. Yet within five years after legislation in New York State, more than 90 percent of the faculties in well-established community colleges were actively organized. In many instances, both parties prepared carelessly for bargaining almost as though they were getting ready to attend another committee meeting. Trustees generally expected faculty to approach the bargaining table as friends with mutual interests. Instead they were often met by open militancy and a demand for immediate sweeping reforms in campus governance. Some faculty demands were critical of trustee attitudes and performance. Offended trustees either retreated individually by resigning from the bargaining team or developed an equally tough approach to the issues at hand. Rumors of unprofessional insults being hurled across the bargaining table spread rapidly. In other cases, naive faculty teams faced professionally trained and experienced labor negotiators employed by trustees and felt overwhelmed and embarrassed. Unpreparedness led to a wide divergence in the substance of contracts ranging from those that included almost nothing but salary agreements to those that practically gave away the store to faculty bargainers.

Too many negotiating teams, both management and faculty, were selected on a personal or popularity basis rather than on the basis of training and experience. College presidents, trustees, and elected government officials sat together as the employer team at the bargaining table—and often they were ineffective for a variety of reasons. Concurrently, faculties permitted their most alienated, aggressive members to be self-selected as members of and spokesmen for their bargaining teams—and very few such people were effective bargainers—they often embarrassed everyone at the table including their own associates. When critical impasses required public interviews, the overemotional partisan was at a disadvantage in attracting the public support essential for success. Some negotiation teams were too large to present a well-disciplined, solid front at the table, thus exposing easy targets for opposing teams. Not infrequently large teams engaged in endless and pointless debates, sometimes among themselves.

As experience was accumulated fewer college presidents and executives of government or trustees remained on the negotiating teams. A trustee or government official who participated in bargaining often became well-known to members of the faculty team, and such familiarity sometimes led faculty members to bypass college administrators relative to daily operational problems, severely straining internal campus relationships. For these and other reasons, college administrators turned almost inevitably toward a team that included a well-prepared lawyer to be the team spokesman; a campus business officer who knew how to compute costs quickly; a high-level academic officer, not the president, who understood the implications of each demand for sharing authority; and an official of the sponsoring government (usually from the county) who knew the fiscal and political implications. Backup teams usually included the president, a trustee or two, and one or two government officials.

A number of faculty bargainers were reluctant to argue forcefully with their deans or presidents, and suggested that others do the bargaining. Some faculty unions learned the value of selecting representatives of intellectual stature with diplomatic and ac-

counting skills including a professionally trained spokesman to prepare the demands and lead the strategy.

On both sides well-trained, experienced neutrals often reduced bargaining time, emotions, and costs. They also prepared
contractual agreements with fewer loopholes for misinterpretation
at a later date.

The most serious errors made by both parties in the initial
stages of negotiation were the very ones now being experienced
anew by some four-year college negotiators. Primarily they relate
to a tendency to underestimate the seriousness, resiliency, and objectives of the other party. Initially, presidents and trustees seldom
expect faculty to challenge basic administrative prerogatives. They
think that faculty will limit their serious demands primarily to salary
and fringe benefits and use conventional deliberative campus approaches to the resolution of issues. Few of these expectations are
fulfilled. Faculty are willing to use "boiler plate" tactics from industry when opportune, to denigrate administrators and trustees
whenever it is effective, and to insist that only they are capable of
making intelligent decisions relative to academic matters. On the
other hand, faculty expect most of their demands to appear reasonable to administrators and therefore acceptable to management with
little debate. Such is seldom the case. As a result both parties often
feel offended and react negatively, slowing negotiations to the point
of serious impasse requiring conciliation by outside neutrals.

Conciliation of impasses in the two-year colleges led to further problems. Few mediators, fact-finders, or arbitrators had much
experience in settling public-sector disputes, and even fewer knew
very much about college governance. Rather than being helpful as
conciliators they often needed understanding and consultation from
the negotiating parties. Many mediators tried to use aggressive tactics common in industrial bargaining, but often these were rejected
by one or both parties, and the impasse continued to higher levels of
conciliation. Only the sincerity, naivete, and/or patience of both
parties made it possible to bring into being the first college contracts between faculties and their employers.

Another serious problem facing early two-year college negotiators was the writing of contracts. One tendency was to write
agreements in precise detail that left little or no flexibility in the

administration of contracts. The result was considered by presidents and trustees as a serious intrusion of their responsibilities. Insistence on minutiae also was a cause of impasse, and when included in the contract, often led to a plethora of grievances. Instead of writing contracts which are statesmanlike proclamations of faith in higher education spelling out common goals, joint responsibilities, and the unique roles of each party, contracts being written suggest adversary roles, no mutual bonds of shared experience, and an overwhelming desire for self-protection rather than service. Such contracts become instruments of frustration consuming energy and resources to the neglect of other legitimate needs. Experienced negotiators emphasize inclusion in the contract of regular consultation procedures to settle differences in interpretation of more broadly stated agreements about principle. This helps both parties agree to the omission of detail in the contract.

Perhaps the most inflammatory of all issues faced at the bargaining table was the nature of the last step in a grievance procedure. Everyone agreed that the contract should include an official grievance procedure and that the first step should be informal while the next should be a more formal administrative review. The teacher unions were associated with state and/or national groups indoctrinated at least partially by industrial unions which used binding arbitration of impasses and grievances in private sector bargaining. But in the public sector a serious question of sovereignty arose. Could a government yield its final authority to an outside arbitrator? Since college trustees are ordinarily vested by law with final authority in matters of campus governance, could they legally agree to a contract that assigns a sharing of their powers to arbitrators in the final steps of grievance?

After several years of debate, experience, and court decisions the question of binding arbitration still defies a clear response. The weight of court decisions and legal opinions tends toward the acceptance of arbitration as a means to determine the presence or absence of campus due process and the rejection of arbitration on matters of substantive judgment. For example, where an arbitrator in a case of nonreappointment determines that there was a lack of due process, he should require the administration to use procedures identified in the contract to reprocess the decision on campus; he would not, however, be allowed to substitute his judgment for that of the trustees relative to a candidate's qualifications for reappointment. This matter of limitation and delegation of powers must be decided by the highest tribunal of each state or the legislature must include in its legislation a precise description of management rights and the scope of bargaining.

Contract Provisions

Faculties in community colleges of New York and Michigan enjoy approximately the same relative levels of working conditions, and collective bargaining has, without doubt, speeded the process of improving those conditions. Conditions in twenty-three New York institutions are described in the following analysis. Wide variations exist within the state, with faculties of urban institutions generally enjoying more liberal working conditions than those accorded to their rural colleagues. Most of the benefits described are either stated directly in the negotiated contracts or preserved by clauses which refer to benefits already enacted by trustees or by administrators outside the formal contract.

All twenty-three college contracts included negotiated salary agreements, with those in the region of New York City having the highest salaries. Some community colleges now have higher salary scales than the majority of four-year colleges. This may have a serious impact on the ability of private four-year colleges to compete successfully for quality in new faculty. The sharp rise in salaries might have occurred without the contracts as a result of increased cost of living and the natural competition for professional services. However, an analysis of the rise in community college salaries in comparison to increases in civil service salaries, four-year college salaries, and cost of living indices from 1968 to 1971 indicates almost spectacular relative gains for community college faculties, and these have been caused at least in part by bargaining. Such increases were sometimes made by sacrificing other benefits such as long-range salary schedules with mandated annual increments. This indicates a shift in relationships whereby faculty have come to depend on dynamic processes of bargaining for improving their salaries and working conditions rather than on the more static structures of salary schedules and traditional advisory bodies.

In addition to salary increases, faculty unions made unusual progress in obtaining fringe benefits formerly exclusive to faculties of older, more liberally oriented senior colleges. Nineteen of the twenty-three community colleges now have sick leave, cumulative sick leave, extended illness benefits, maternity leave, military leave, medical expense insurance, and personal leave with pay. All but one have sabbatical leave with pay. More than half have disability insurance, job liability insurance, holidays for nonteaching professionals (NTPs), and jury duty leave. Just beginning to appear in contracts are dental insurance and personal property insurance. Four-year colleges which do not offer such benefits may be forced to provide them.

Until the advent of bargaining few community colleges offered much job protection. Bargaining has led to dramatic changes. All twenty-three New York college faculties have negotiated specific grievance procedures by which any faculty member, tenured or not, may have his grievances heard and resolved first by informal hearings and later, if warranted, by formal administrative reviews during which charges may be heard, witnesses called, and due process followed. Eighteen contracts provide the option of settling a grievance by an outside arbitrator specifically employed by both parties to settle that particular grievance in accordance with contractual policy. At other institutions the trustees or an all-campus review committee is the final arbiter. In any case, the chief administrator can no longer be the final authority. Also, twenty-one of the twenty-three contracts provide for peer evaluation as the first step in preparing recommendations relative to faculty reappointment, tenure, promotion, and discretionary salary increases. In addition a number of special protections are being negotiated: seventeen of the campuses have negotiated specific time limits and advance notices of job termination together with severance pay regardless of the cause for early termination; more than half the faculties have negotiated protective clauses relative to teaching summer, extension, and evening classes, which in effect, give faculty the first options on opportunities for extra pay; about 15 percent of the faculty unions protect their members against arbitrary position, building, or campus transfers. Management rights relative to employment and assignment of faculty are being diminished, possibly at some cost in administrative efficiency. Furthermore, the roles of department chairmen and deans are being complicated by new policy restrictions which require considerable consultation with affected parties before almost any academic decisions can be made. In effect, the new contracts require management to spend much time in prior consultation or to face the loss of more time to handle consequent grievances. Because colleges now face severe budget cutbacks, collective bargaining may have arrived just in time to help prevent possible inequities and unilateral decisions which historically have followed financial crises. Regardless of current public demand for strict fiscal accountability, taxpayer support for strengthening justice and resolving inequities is widespread. Only this broad support has prevented some legislatures from emasculating public employment relations laws by placing severe limits on the scope of bargaining and by reasserting dictatorial powers of boards of trustees.

Collective bargaining has also brought about contractual controls of the assignment of work loads. These controls are aimed at protecting faculties from unduly heavy work loads and upgrading the quality of educational services. Twenty of the twenty-three New York contracts specify work-load limitations such as the maximum teaching hours per week (usually 12–15) and the maximum size of classes (usually 28–30); thirteen specify a formula for equating laboratory teaching with lecture hours and the maximum number of class preparations per week; and the majority of contracts require reduced teaching loads for department chairmen. A few contracts limit the number of consecutive classes to be taught and the length of any single work day (the latter prevents administrators from assigning an 8:00 A.M. and an evening class on the same day). The work loads of NTPs are also controlled by some collective contracts. As a matter of equity, many faculty members felt that reform work loads for NTPs was long overdue.

As mentioned above, additional faculty income is provided for in contracts which give faculty members first options on summer and evening teaching for extra pay. Some contracts allow faculty special privileges of notification about new positions and administrative vacancies to be filled. A few campuses contractually guarantee funding for faculty research. Additional fringe benefits which have begun to appear include tuition for faculty and family to continue their education, the cost of medical examinations and academic attire, reimbursement for joining at least one professional organization, and reimbursement for job-related expenses.

Almost all New York contracts contain a general statement guaranteeing academic freedom on campus. Other specific guarantees have been added to some agreements. For example, most contracts permit a faculty member access to his personnel file, which is the basis for decisions concerning his reappointment and promotion, and include the right of the faculty member to respond to negative statements and to submit new materials. Less frequently contracts include statements which give faculty increased freedom in determining their own teaching methods, textbooks, and source materials.

A great variety of special privileges also may be found in contracts. Where parking is a problem, the institution is often required to furnish special parking space for faculty members within a reasonable distance of their offices. Consultation with faculty is called for before canceling classes in about a fourth of the contracts and before changes are made in the academic calendar in most. A few give faculty copyright privileges for material they develop on or off the job. Clauses are beginning to appear which establish seniority rights relative to such matters as class schedules and job retrenchment. About half the contracts establish tax-sheltered annuity programs. A third state the minimal size for a faculty office.

As would be expected, unions have negotiated special benefits for themselves such as automatic renewal of an agreement if a new one is not yet negotiated; contract reopeners when warranted by conditions such as increased cost of living; use of campus facilities, information sources, and office space; reduction in teaching load for chief union representatives; and released time for union delegates to attend union meetings. About half the contracts require the president or his representatives to meet with union officers on a regular basis to discuss interpretation of the contract, pending complaints, and potential grievances. At many campuses, union officials have special privileges such as receiving advance notice of and attending trustee meetings. Contracts usually require trustees to share at least the expenses involved in employing private conciliators for arbitration, fact-finding, or mediation. In general the institution is required to absorb the cost of printing and distributing contracts.

As faculties have insisted upon having more and more of their rights and working conditions spelled out in clear and unequivocal terms, trustees and administrators have felt obliged to counter with corresponding statements of faculty responsibility that give some assurance to students and taxpayers that reasonable services will be rendered for salaries paid. As a result, most contracts specify the length of the employment year; minimal office hours; attendance at meetings, ceremonies, registration activities, etc.; return to campus following sabbatical leaves; a procedure for canceling tenure; restriction of outside employment; and administrative evaluation of teaching. Few faculties have objected to this last item as long as the evaluations were based at least in part on peer judgments. Most of them insisted that only peer judgment of teaching effectiveness was valid, yet none argued successfully against the right of administration to make the final judgment relative to reappointment, tenure, and promotion. Interestingly, in at least one instance faculty are bound by contract to submit to evaluation by students.

Following the early contracts, faculty challenged as never before almost every traditional prerogative of administrators and trustees. This resulted in many arguments, much loss of time, undesirable adversary relationships, and excessive numbers of complaints and grievances. To clarify the situation, trustees decided to negotiate more and more contracts clearly stating their rights as established in law. Almost all contracts now include a general statement entitled "management rights." In addition, the majority of contracts establish either the trustees' or the administration's responsibility and duty to control such matters as assigning teacher work loads; reducing size of faculty; setting time limits for faculty to accept reappointments; assigning space and financial resources; mandating retirement age; and limiting sabbatical leaves. Sometimes management rights clauses include the creation of new positions outside the bargaining unit; control of copyrights and patents; and the selection of textbooks.

Outcomes

Faculty unionism and collective negotiations have produced a mixed bag of consequences—some real and some imaginary, some progressive and some apparently retrogressive. More than a hundred faculty members on twenty-three New York campuses were asked whether they felt collective bargaining had been successful. They were practically unanimous in thinking it had been sufficiently successful to increase union membership and assure the continuance of collective negotiations. Among other achievements, those cited as being most noteworthy were higher salaries (in rural areas an estimated $500—1000 higher, in the New York City area an estimated $3000—5000 higher); a more important role for faculty in college governance (on many campuses, the new relationship was described as governance by mutual consent); a broad extension of fringe benefits comparable to those offered in senior colleges and progressive industries; increased communication between faculty and administration through regularly scheduled meetings and grievance procedures; more businesslike and standardized treatment of faculty, accompanied by a decrease in paternalism and favoritism; prevention of overloads in times of financial crises or unexpected increases in enrollments; shared responsibility for selection of administrators and supervisors; and speedier and more accessible grievance machinery which is more likely to produce judicious decisions based on written policy and legal agreements.

Fifty-four trustees and administrators from the twenty-three institutions were asked to evaluate the effect of bargaining on campus governance and educational programs. The majority were inclined to believe that the overall effects were more negative than positive. Most, however, felt that some favorable outcomes were the following: management rights, although shared with faculty, students, alumni, and government agencies, are more clearly stated in contracts and in law, more readily accepted by all parties concerned, and more easily sustained through formal, businesslike grievance proceedings; faculty responsibilities and duties, as well as rights, are more clearly delineated and limited, facilitating certain types of administrative decisions including those relative to promotion and reappointment of faculty; automatic salary increases and salary schedules are being abolished in favor of periodic negotiation of salaries which are consistent with current economic and market conditions; offices of employee relations are being established to handle routine aspects of collective negotiations, grievances, and contract administration, leaving trustees and administrators more time for higher-level responsibilities; and more responsibility is placed on the faculty for determining specific levels of professional conduct, subduing colleagues who are chronic complainers, and disciplining members who fail to meet minimal standards of professional service (more responsibility is also accepted for screening invalid claims of grievance at each stage of review).

Impact on Institutional Effectiveness

Both faculty and administration on the twenty-three New York campuses studied recognize certain areas of incipient danger that are at least partially caused or accentuated by the bargaining process. Perhaps it is more accurate to note that the greatest concerns to both parties have arisen from a lack of experience in predicting and responding diplomatically to the moves of the other party. Often one party, in trying to take advantage of its political position, creates a situation that is disadvantageous to both parties. Often a team, when frustrated, turns to emotional threats, name-calling, filibustering, and withdrawal techniques that lead to intransigence and costly impasses. Often one or both parties are careless about making public statements that advertise internal campus problems. In other words, the misuse of the bargaining process by neophytes creates unnecessary obstacles to the accomplishment of institutional priorities. Regardless of the causes, the resulting concerns are real and must be met with diplomacy, wisdom, and cooperation.

No campus has complete autonomy, being subject to a higher authority usually vested in legislatures, courts, donors, and public opinion. Yet, historically the college and university perhaps more than any institution other than the church has been free of sustained public attack and control. Some trustees and presidents of community colleges, however, were less than forceful in asserting their responsibilities for employee relations. New York State educational law vests a board of trustees with powers as the executive body of a public college, whether it be a community college or SUNY. The New York State Employee Relations Act (Taylor Law) makes it clear that bargaining is an executive function. Yet, in more than half the institutions, trustees deferred completely or partially to county officials who decided to bargain directly with faculty representatives. (At SUNY the faculty representatives negotiated directly with the governor's representatives and only secondarily with the trustees' representatives, as described in Chapter Seven.)

When a faculty union bargains directly with county government, it loses some respect for the board of trustees and president and for their authority. Thus, faculty-presidential-trustee relationships become weakened by the intrusion of a fourth, powerful body of government officials who no longer look supinely at the campus from a distance. In some cases government officials discounted the role of the president and trustees, and they were willing to bargain away campus internal governance power in return for a few dollars saved. Now county executives often give orders directly to the community college president relative to certain political and economic concerns. Some presidents must seek approval for budgetary fund transfers or expenditures directly from county government, practically bypassing trustees. In several cases county governments have interfered with campus academic and cultural affairs by threatening retaliatory action in future negotiations and budgets.

To minimize such interference two important steps must be taken: prepare the trustees to act as executive employers by accepting full responsibility for negotiating with faculty; and help shape new or amend old employment relations laws in a manner consistent with existing education law. This is a common concern and responsibility of administration and faculty. In shaping laws and contracts, both sides have an interest in protecting the autonomy of the institution from intrusion by overzealous elected officials, courts, and arbitrators. Although both parties support binding arbitration as the final step in grievance procedures, their common belief in the principles of self-governance almost requires that binding arbitration be limited to procedural rather than substantive decisions.

Another common concern of faculty and administration is the apparent loss in effectiveness of campus leadership in the early years of collective bargaining. Some boards of trustees now hesitate to act on policy matters without lengthy consultation with county legislators or executives who may disapprove their actions as preempting possible issues at the next round of bargaining. Some college presidents now hesitate to act without consulting the trustees, the county attorney, a faculty senate, and faculty union officers because each decision may be grounds for reprimand, legal action, or grievance. Again, some presidents are expected to obtain approval not only of trustees, but county executives and legislatures, before taking certain actions.

Deans more than anyone else have felt a loss in decision-making power. Faculty members often launch petty complaints as a first stage of grievance and vice-presidents or other officers designated to review grievances are compelled to ask the deans to change their original decisions. Such pressures usually decrease a dean's effectiveness and job satisfaction. In turn, considerable confusion arises on some campuses as to the authority of deans and their responsibility for leadership. Some deans and directors have tried new techniques of leadership by persuasion, but few have indicated that such techniques were effective or satisfying. In some cases trustees and presidents have attempted to reestablish effective leadership of deans and directors by promulgating new job descriptions, but this has not proven successful in general.

Some trustees and presidents have also tried to increase their own effectiveness by reducing political intervention—few claim success. The general feeling is that elected officials, once involved in campus affairs, find it too politically alluring to resist future temptations.

Effective faculty leadership is lost wherever confusion arises as to the locus of faculty authority and responsibility—a faculty senate and a faculty union on the same campus are not always compatible. The resulting competition for support and power doubles the administrative burden for consultation required in making even simple decisions. Faculty on some campuses were also confused as to whether the negotiated contract superseded old trustee policies, the body of education law and tradition, and procedures established by earlier faculty bylaws or senate actions.

Another factor in diminishing both faculty and administrative leadership was the time consumed by the machinery of bargaining, grievances, and contract administration. Political activities of competing unions related to election of the bargaining unit, watchdog activities of the losing union, preparing and conducting negotiations, preparing the contract, rewriting handbooks and policies to conform with the new contract, union meetings and rallies, publishing a union newspaper, preparing and conducting grievance reviews, regular meetings between top management and union officials —all these activities undeniably devour time with unabated appetite. In the early years, neither faculty nor administration employed extra professional help. The net result was many overworked people too tired to push ahead with needed academic reform.

Another concern, difficult to describe but vital to the academic community, is the element of humane relationships among students, faculty, administration, and trustees. Collective bargaining requires businesslike procedures seldom characteristic of campus life in prebargaining days. Some faculties and administrations condemn the new relationships as being adversary in nature and unbecoming to the intellectual life. Yet, some faculty welcome the new standardized procedures as being more equitable and less paternalistic than the old style of administration. One concern of faculty, however, is that the new relationships may not attract to administrative vacancies the genial scholar-dean of yore, and in some cases the new campus milieu has certainly helped to speed the demise of the genial and to attract the more toughminded managerial types who enter administrative work at least partly because they like power and want to use it for achieving such goals as increased productivity, efficiency, and accountability among students and faculty. Thus efficiency, an almost unrecognized academic goal only a few years ago, is becoming one of the more compelling bywords on campus today.

Teacher unions are facing new types of negotiation battles with new types of employers. And in the wake, some time-honored academic traditions of town hall decision-making, seniority power in professorial ranks, private personalized bargaining between the individual faculty member and his president, hush-hush collection of secret testimony to determine promotions and reappointments, and above all, Mark Hopkins on one end of the log and his prize student on the other end are apparently being banished to the status of mythology. Many administrators and some faculty members view such changes as a loss in the humane character of the campus; the majority of faculty, however, see it as progress toward justice.

Some academics also see a loss in what they call campus community. Students, through mass action in the 1960s, became a more effective participant in campus decision-making processes. Contracts negotiated in the early 1970s, however, seldom mention students, leaving them to fend for themselves in a new world of labor-management relationships. Many administrators and some faculty believe that students will eventually organize their own unions to bargain on a statewide and even a national basis. If these unions were effective, campuses could become a union versus union battleground of entirely new and unpredictable dimensions.

Another common concern is the loss of campus privacy, prestige, and public support. Bargaining, impasses, contracts, and grievance reviews provide excellent grist for the news mills. Threats of strike and demands for more salary and better working conditions exhibit publicly the human qualities and aspirations of academics. No longer are they generally observed as the intellectuals who put thirst for knowledge above the material life. On some campuses, soon after internal campus politics were made public during bargaining impasses, campus prestige, privacy, and public support came under fire by taxpayers and public officials. Attempts to control campus operations by passing new laws which stipulate statewide parameters for faculty loads, travel funds, sabbatical leaves, salary schedules, and scope of bargaining can be anticipated. Such action would defeat the basic purpose of both the education law and the public employment relations laws.

Implications for Senior Colleges

The junior college experience seems quite similar to the emerging senior college situation. Faculties want the same things, namely more salary, fringe benefits, security, and shared governance. Wherever these needs are unfulfilled, the trend toward unionization and collective bargaining is inexorable. Management in the senior college has problems similar to those in two-year colleges, especially in relation to increasing campus efficiency, faculty responsibility, and quality of the educational product. Public colleges are more closely supervised than private colleges by politically oriented legislators and government executives. However, the private institutions are under the aegis of the National Labor Relations Board (NLRB). Since human motives and the rules of the game are everywhere roughly equivalent, or soon will be, the problems, procedures, and outcomes among junior colleges can be expected to be distributed equally among senior colleges, both public and private.

In summary, community college administrators advise four-year college administrators that they would be wise to prepare themselves well in advance for the entire process of appointing and schooling a bargaining team for the complex problems of negotiating, writing, and administering the contract. Especially, they should employ a lawyer skilled in labor relations; conduct seminars in labor relations for key executives and the board of trustees; mend fences and improve communications with government officials at all levels; designate well in advance those who will constitute the table team of negotiators and train them; develop an understanding as to what roles the trustees and government officials will play in the negotiations; persuade trustees that they are, by law, the executive body in charge of planning and supervising negotiations so that any challenge to the integrity of the university by outside political agencies will be prevented; persuade government officials that they should not interfere with the right of trustees to plan and supervise negotiations lest they reduce the trustees to a powerless appendage; determine well in advance the scope of management rights and the proper limits of bargaining; determine whether statewide bargaining is feasible in order to eliminate whipsawing from campus to campus; and persuade the legislature as to these convictions, preferably before passage of the first public employment relations law covering college faculties.

Experienced faculty negotiators also have advice for the uninitiated. They suggest attempting to strengthen collegial governance in advance of negotiations so that principles of shared governance will already be well-established and not become a barrier to substantive negotiations; plan in advance the most effective type of leadership for the bargaining table (alienated, talkative, or emotional people are often ineffective and sometimes embarrassing to the profession); determine in advance the relationship between the existing governance body (usually a faculty senate) and the yet-to-be-negotiated union; determine in advance the optimum relationship between the local union and state/national unions which will soon be wooing individual faculty members; improve communications with government officials; and help shape any new laws governing public employees.

Man's most serious problems seem to grow out of his ignorance, and educators above all others should know the value of advance training and planning. Yet the community college experience in collective negotiations is an epic feature on the theme of learning by doing. Can the senior colleges learn otherwise?

6

Contracts of Four-Year Institutions

Kenneth P. Mortimer, G. Gregory Lozier

In a review of the process of bargaining it is appropriate to consider the outcomes. What have the faculty representatives and their administrative counterparts negotiated about? Do the signed contracts deal solely or primarily with the bread-and-butter questions of faculty economic welfare? Is there evidence of the broader professional concerns about scholarship and teaching normally associated with the academic enterprise? Have contracts provided for faculty role in institutional governance? What has proved to be the primary orientation of negotiations? What does the future portend?

The authors of this chapter answer these questions on the basis of a comprehensive analysis of the initial fourteen contracts covering four-year colleges and universities. Their report constitutes a picture of the scope of collective bargaining as it has evolved. Their speculations about the future clarify some of the limitations of our knowledge and suggest that a homogenization and bureaucratization of the academic professional will accompany unionism. Professors are likely to find themselves associated with other professional personnel who are involved in the bargaining representation, as they are likely to find traditional academic distinctions muted. Concurrently, they probably will have to learn to cope with new bureaucratic relationships associated with a new organizational dimension imposed by the faculty associations and the procedures necessary to implement the variety of contractual arrangements, especially those related to grievances.

Kenneth P. Mortimer currently is conducting long-range research on collective bargaining, especially as it develops within the Pennsylvania State College and State University systems. His assistant author, G. Gregory Lozier, has been collaborating with him in these studies.

E. D. D. and R. S. F.

The incidence of collective bargaining in four-year colleges and universities has not reached as dramatic proportions as in two-year institutions. Only forty-five four-year colleges have a recognized faculty bargaining agent compared to over 120 two-year colleges, and less than one-half of these had negotiated a contract by June 1972. For some of the remaining four-year colleges negotiations have been proceeding for more than a year without producing a ratified agreement.

Collective bargaining contracts place in written legal form a great deal of the substance and procedure of faculty-administrative relations heretofore either traditional or specifically delegated. In so doing contracts expand this relationship in scope and in the degree of codification. Here we will describe and analyze contracts in four-year colleges and universities pertaining to the following five areas: constituency of the bargaining association; provisions for salaries, fringe benefits, and working conditions; association rights and privileges; personnel policies, including grievance procedures; and provisions for faculty participation in governance.

Fourteen contracts have been used for this analysis. Five of the local agents that signed the contracts have an affiliation or some formal association with the National Education Association (NEA), five with the American Federation of Teachers (AFT), three with the American Association of University Professors (AAUP), and only one has no national affiliation. Eleven of the contracts were signed with public institutions: Massachusetts—Boston State College (AFT), Southeastern Massachusetts University (AFT); Michigan— Central Michigan University (NEA), Oakland University (AAUP); New Jersey—New Jersey State College (NEA), Rutgers, the State University (AAUP); New York—City University of New York (NEA, AFT), State University of New York (NEA), United States Merchant Marine Academy (AFT); Wisconsin—University of Wisconsin at Madison (independent). Three contracts were from private institutions: New Jersey—Monmouth College (NEA); New York—St. John's University (AAUP); Rhode Island—Bryant College of Business Administration (AFT). Of these, twelve are from Massachusetts, Michigan, New Jersey, and New York, where 55 percent of all collective bargaining agents in higher education are active (*Chronicle of Higher Education,* May 15, 1972, p. 2). Twelve of the fourteen contracts are first-time agreements. In the cases of Central Michigan University and Bryant College of Business Administration, a second agreement was available at the time of this writing. The second contract at Central Michigan is discussed in Chapter Eight and is also included in this analysis. The teaching assistants at University of Wisconsin at Madison did renegotiate before their initial contract expired in September 1971. However, at last report the local bargaining organization had faltered and it did not appear that the Wisconsin teaching assistants would have a contract beyond September 1972.

Of the three potential legal bases for collective bargaining in higher education, three of the contracts reviewed here came under the National Labor Relations Board (NLRB) as private institutions; ten came under the authority of state enabling statutes and thus state labor relations board; and the one federal institution was covered by President John F. Kennedy's Executive Order 10988 which gave federal employees the right to bargain collectively. (Interestingly, this has been the only service institution or federal university to take advantage of that order.)

An important factor in formulating the contracts was which administrative or managerial agency or office negotiated them. Legally and formally in higher education, institutional boards have ultimate authority and accountability for all institutional decisions. A significant development in collective bargaining has been the extent of external assumption of the role of negotiator for the institution, especially in multicampus institutions negotiating a single contract. Although each of the six New Jersey State Colleges has its own board of trustees, the agreement for the faculty of these colleges is between the faculty association and the State of New Jersey. A similar situation developed in New York, where the executive branch of the state negotiated with a bargaining team representing the twenty-six campuses of the State University of New York (suny). Local boards were also bypassed at the nineteen-campus City University of New York (cuny), where the contract was negotiated with the Board of Higher Education of the City of New York. Significant implications for college and university governance are brought about by these multicampus contracts: local boards and administration are relegated to the role of implementing the contract; since it is difficult to accommodate individual campus peculiarities, adaptation of the contract depends upon local implementation. This is particularly significant in complex multicampus systems which include community colleges, four-year colleges, and graduate centers.

A different situation exists in Massachusetts, where the individual state colleges held separate elections and will negotiate separate contracts. In each instance the board of trustees of state colleges will be the state's negotiator. Four of the state colleges have elected an aft affiliated agency, three an nea affiliate, and two have yet to elect any agent. As of June 1972, only Boston State College had completed negotiations and ratified an agreement, while Worcester State College finished negotiating in October 1972.

Constituency of Bargaining Unit

For the purposes of collective bargaining a distinction must be made between employees and management, and employees with a viable community of interest must be designated. Although the parties to the unit determination question may informally agree on a definition of the unit, more typically a hearing is held before the appropriate state or national labor relations board, which then renders a decision on the appropriate bargaining unit.

Determination of the department chairman's role as supervisor or nonsupervisor has received the most attention of all the unit determination issues. Of the twelve contracts for full-time faculty reviewed here (the AFT CUNY contract covers only lecturers and teaching assistants and the University of Wisconsin contract covers only teaching assistants), Monmouth College and the United States Merchant Marine Academy are the only units that exclude department heads. The remaining ten either specifically include them or do not specifically exclude them. This trend to include department chairmen is in sharp contrast to that in two-year institutions, where the trend is in the opposite direction (Mortimer and Lozier, 1972).

The assertion of the NLRB's jurisdiction over private higher education has created new developments which may alter the above trends. In five decisions since September 1971 the NLRB ruled twice to include department chairmen in the unit (Fordham University and the University of Detroit) and three times to exclude them (Manhattan College and the Brooklyn and C. W. Post Centers of Long Island University). The full force of the NLRB's role has not yet been realized.

Another significant feature of the unit determination issue has been the inclusion of professional support personnel. Most bargaining units go beyond inclusion of teaching and research personnel and include counselors, librarians, and many of the student personnel staff. At SUNY, approximately 27 percent of the bargaining unit is made up of these professional support staff members. We give further attention to the inclusion of support personnel in our review of tenure in collective bargaining contracts later in this chapter.

The bargaining unit issue has particular significance in CUNY, which has two separate units and contracts. CUNY has an approximately equal number of full-time faculty with academic rank and instructors with the titles of lecturer or teaching assistant. Many of the latter teach on a part-time basis and hold positions which do not ultimately lead to tenure. Accordingly, the New York Public Employment Relations Board (PERB) ruled that two bargaining units be established and separate elections held. The contracts for these two units, one represented by an NEA affiliate and the other by an AFT affiliate, were being renegotiated in 1972. The two local associations merged in the spring of 1972 and are negotiating a single contract.

The contracts analyzed here are unclear as to whether all constituent professional schools in a complex university are included in the same unit. For example, at Fordham University, which eventually voted for no agent, the law school faculty constituted a separate unit. The SUNY contract calls for separate review of salary schedules in the colleges of medicine and dentistry at the health sciences centers, even though personnel of the centers are represented by the Senate Professional Association (SPA), the recognized bargaining unit for SUNY. A proliferation of bargaining units within the same institution appears to be possible and may be an important aspect of the evolution of academic collective bargaining. It is difficult to predict whether units will tend to merge, as at CUNY, or proliferate, or whether the pattern will be eclectic.

A final point should be made regarding the determination of a bargaining unit. Prospective bargaining agents may include or exclude certain groups simply to gain a political advantage in the election. A national association's position may vary with the circumstances. The information available to us does not permit an assessment of the consistency of the positions taken by the three national associations in hearings before various labor relations boards.

Salaries, Fringe Benefits, Working Conditions

Salaries, fringe benefits, and working conditions are the common subjects of collective bargaining. An accurate assessment of gains in each of these areas would require ascertaining their status prior to negotiations, a task beyond the scope of this chapter. Our intent here is to describe the extent of coverage relative to these areas.

Two of the fourteen contracts have no provisions for salaries. Because state legislation stipulates faculty salaries for the state col-

leges of Massachusetts, the Boston State College contract does not
cover salaries. Similarly, the Merchant Marine Act of 1936 au-
thorizes the Secretary of Commerce to establish faculty compensation scales for the Merchant Marines. Since this authority is not
delegated to the administration of the Merchant Marine Academy,
the academy's contract does not include a negotiated article on
salary.

Seven of the contracts provide for salary increases on a percentage basis, ranging from 6 percent at Bryant College, the SUNY,
the New Jersey State Colleges, and Rutgers University, to 12 percent for the first year at St. John's University. While the contracts
at Bryant College and Central Michigan University call for slightly
greater percentages the second year, the percentage at St. John's
University drops back to 9 percent, which is still higher than any of
the other contract provisions. In addition to percentage increments,
increases are made for the minimum salaries in rank at Rutgers
University, Monmouth College, and Bryant College. The SUNY contract has a provision for reopening negotiations on salaries for each
year of the contract.

The most dramatic salary increases probably occurred at
CUNY. Over the three-year period covered by the full-time faculty
contract, full professors at the senior colleges receive increments for
the various steps ranging from $4500 to $5075 to a top salary of
$31,275, associate professors from $3830 to $4500 to a top salary of
$25,500, assistant professors $3830 throughout the rank to a top
salary of $20,830, and instructors from $2650 to $3250 to a top
salary of $17,150. Over the three-year period the salary scales
eliminate the differentials between faculty of similar rank in the
senior colleges and community colleges throughout the system. That
is, the contract calls for an exactly comparable salary range at each
campus for each faculty rank for the year beginning October 1,
1971. The contract also calls for a change in the rank distribution
from 19, 22, 35, and 24 percent for professors, associate professors,
assistant professors, and instructors, respectively, to a distribution of
30, 30, 30, and 10 percent by January 1972.

In the Rutgers University one-year contract, for instructors
increments range from $431 to $636 with a minimum-maximum
salary range of $8613 to $16,543, for assistant professors from $524

to $774 with a salary range of $10,470 to $20,114, for associate professors from $636 to $940 with a salary range of $12,727 to $24,444, and for professors from $812 to $1459 with a salary range of $16,244 to $37,925. The Oakland University salary schedule uses a salary index. After establishing minimum salaries for level in rank, index factors are multiplied to the base salary to determine increments based on discipline (school or department) and merit.

With one or two exceptions, salaries provided for in the contracts analyzed are keeping the faculty even with or slightly ahead of the current rate of national inflation. This could be regarded as a significant achievement given the current financial stringency in higher education. On the other hand, similar raises might have been granted without collective bargaining.

A controversial issue relative to salaries is whether collective bargaining will retain or encourage merit in the allocation of salaries. Garbarino (1971), after visits to CUNY, Southeastern Massachusetts University, Rutgers University, Central Michigan University, and SUNY, reported that, where money was available, the unions had not reached agreements with any of the administrations on a long-range system of distribution. The contracts covered here reveal that SUNY, Rutgers University, the New Jersey State Colleges, Southeastern Massachusetts University, and Oakland University either provide procedures for dispensing merit raises or suggest that merit raises may be applied in addition to the salary benefits provided, but in the light of Garbarino's information, we cannot conclude that merit pay provisions are, in fact, operative or that they will become so.[1]

A second part of the economic package is fringe benefits. Several types of benefits commonly appear in four-year contracts. (The number of contracts studied which cover each is noted in parentheses): insurance—life (7), health (6), plus two more programs yet to be developed or funded, and disability-liability (7); leaves—sabbatical (9), sick (8), advanced study, research, travel (8), maternity (4), jury duty (4), personal, leave of absence (3),

---

[1] The 1972 amendment of the contract at SUNY provides for allocation of merit increases by action of the board of trustees upon recommendation of the chancellor.

and bereavement (2); and tuition, loans, grants—for faculty self-improvement (6), for faculty children (2), for spouses (1).

Seven of the contracts make reference to eight or more different fringe benefits, with Central Michigan University having the most at thirteen while Rutgers has none. The teaching assistants' contract at Wisconsin provides for sick leave and an agreement that the university will request funds for a health plan with coverage equal to that for Wisconsin state employees. The original contract for the Bryant College of Business Administration has a section providing that all benefits currently in existence but not included in the contract are to be continued on the same basis. In its second contract, a long-term disability insurance plan, a program to provide the children of deceased tenured faculty members with higher education benefits, and a plan to provide faculty members with advanced payments for masters or doctoral study are added to the agreement. Five contracts specifically refer to retirement benefits. These plans are, however, continuations of existing retirement programs, most typically the Teachers Insurance and Annuity Association and College Retirement Equities Fund (TIAA-CREF). For a faculty member participating in TIAA-CREF, Oakland University will contribute an amount equal to 10 percent of the faculty member's monetary compensation while the faculty member himself contributes 5 percent. At St. John's University, if a faculty member contributes 5 percent of his contract salary, the university will provide an amount equal to 9 percent of his salary the first year of the contract, and 10 percent commencing with the second year.

Some contracts also provide the following benefits related to working conditions (the number of contracts which cover each is again noted in parentheses): teaching load (10), teaching overload (8), travel reimbursement (5), summer employment (5), office hours (4), scheduling of courses (4), academic or college calendar (4), class size (3), office space (3), off-campus teaching (3), secretarial assistance (3), parking (4), dining facilities (2), lounges (2), secretarial assistance (1). Articles or sections of the contracts dealing with working conditions are not as prevalent as are those for fringe benefits. The NEA-negotiated contracts at Monmouth College, with thirteen provisions, and CUNY with nine, cover the most working conditions of the contracts studied.

Once again, the Rutgers University contract has no sections concerning working conditions, and in this category it is joined by the contract from SUNY. While the Merchant Marine Academy agreement has provisions for limiting teaching loads and reimbursement for professional or institutional-related travel, other working conditions are determined to be matters for consultation and discussion between the faculty and the administration.

Bargaining Agent Rights and Privileges

Sections dealing with bargaining agent rights and privileges follow salaries in frequency of inclusion. Of the fourteen contracts negotiated, all but that for the Wisconsin teaching assistants declares that the respective faculty association is the exclusive bargaining agent. Twelve of the contracts (excluding St. John's University and the Merchant Marine Academy) stipulate a provision for voluntary dues checkoff and payroll deduction by the college or university for the exclusive bargaining association. None of the contracts provide for the adoption of agency shop status for the bargaining association. However, the SUNY and both CUNY contracts stipulate that negotiations can be reopened if a legislative amendment is passed in New York permitting public employees to enter into an agency shop agreement. Evidence from Michigan, where agency shop agreements are legal and several community college contracts have made them, indicates that it is possible that they may become a standard part of four-year college and university contracts.

Eight contracts stipulate a means for establishing ongoing consultation between the faculty and presidents, boards, and state governments. Typically, discussions are to be limited to prearranged agenda. The Boston State College contract requires two meetings with the board director per semester, as well as one each month with the president. The NEA CUNY contract requires two meetings per semester with the chancellor, and two per semester with local campus presidents. The SUNY contract has similar provisions for association-administrative meetings with the chancellor twice each semester and the campus president once each month. The contracts are careful, however, to indicate that these special consultations do not eliminate the possibility of other discussions between the association and the administration or between any individual faculty member and the administration.

Three additional provisions appear in contracts which guarantee communication and information flow between an association and a board of trustees. Four contracts (SUNY, two at CUNY, and the New Jersey State Colleges) afford representatives of the bargaining association the right to appear before the board of trustees during regular trustee meetings. Furthermore, at the same institutions and at Southeastern Massachusetts University, copies of board agenda and minutes are to be sent on a regular basis to the association. The Boston State College contract and the five noted above instruct the board and the administration to provide the associations with all budgetary data and other information pertinent to negotiations for faculty salary, etc. These provisions clearly rest responsibility with the board of the college or university, while the right or privilege is given to the association. The major responsibility of the association is to notify the board in advance of its desire to meet with the board.

The contracts tend to establish the viability of the bargaining association and to make it an integral part of the system of communication within the institution. They also include provisions which (in eleven contracts) permit the use of campus buildings, (in twelve) allow the use of bulletin boards, (in eight) grant the use of mail services and equipment, and (in eight) provide released time for association officers.

Personnel Policies

A wide range of issues included in contracts may be classified as referring to academic personnel policies. In addition to tenure, academic freedom, and grievance procedures, which are discussed below, nine common issues and the number of contracts in which they appear are nondiscriminatory hiring practices (9); appointment (9); reappointment (7); promotion and criteria for promotion (9); causes and procedures for dismissal or contract nonrenewal (9); definition and requirements of academic titles, that is, professor, associate professor, etc. (7); evaluation of faculty (6); time for notice of nonrenewal (5); and personnel files (5).

The contract for the New Jersey State Colleges contains a typical article negotiated for faculty personnel files. It requires that a faculty member's file contain all communications dealing with his competencies, academic achievement, and research. Each faculty member is free to submit any appropriate materials for inclusion in his own file. All documents dealing with his teaching ability, service, character, or conduct must be signed by their originators. Any faculty member may review the contents of his file, and all materials in the file, excluding those secured from sources outside the university, must be made available to him. Permission may be given by the faculty member for a representative of the bargaining association to view the file simultaneously. Finally, the faculty member has the right to respond to his president about any document in his file, and a copy of his response shall also be included in the file. The St. John's University article dealing with this issue avoids withholding confidential materials from sources outside the college by maintaining two categories of files, one a preemployment file, the other a record of employment, professional accomplishment, and evaluation of performance.

Policies dealing with personnel files are only one step in the elimination of secret procedures in the processes leading to reappointment, promotion, and tenure. The argument for secrecy—to protect the integrity of those submitting the materials and the faculty member—is giving way to the faculty member's right to know.

The ability to review their files is also the first step in assuring due process for faculty in personnel matters. The first section of the article in the Southeastern Massachusetts University contract dealing with tenure is entitled "Definition of Tenure and Due Process." This demonstrates the inextricable relationship which is developing between tenure and due process as a result of collective bargaining and the intervention of the courts into higher education. Due process guarantees to the tenured faculty member the right to a hearing of his case, either before the board, the administration, or a committee of his peers. Typically he has the additional right to be faced by his accusers. Of the eight contracts with articles or sections dealing with tenure, however, only four alter the established tenure policy.

Van Alstyne (1971) suggests that collective bargaining may

have two effects upon tenure: first, tenure, along with academic freedom and due process, might be traded-off for more immediate gains such as salary and fringe benefits; and second, faculty probationary periods might be reduced to one or two years. The contracts in four-year institutions to date do not confirm either hypothesis. The chances of the latter occurring is somewhat likely, as it has already happened in two-year colleges. Several of the four-year college contracts which indicate probationary periods maintain times of five to seven years. New Jersey State Colleges and Monmouth College are exceptions to this. At Monmouth, assistant professors are eligible for tenure after four years (or three years for holders of the earned doctorate or its equivalent). Faculty members coming from another teaching position may become eligible after two years. New Jersey state law provides state college faculty with tenure after three years of employment.

That tenure will be bargained away for other types of compensation is less likely, as it is even more sought after as job security. The AFT contract at CUNY contains an article entitled "Job Security," which grants to all lecturers with five or more years of full-time employment an administrative certificate of continuous employment. Termination of these lecturers can be for no less reasons than those for the removal of a tenured faculty member. The contract further stipulates that after the first year of appointment, denial of reappointment on the basis of professional incompetence can be made only if two of three evaluations of the teacher made during the three previous semesters indicate unsatisfactory professional performance. After the first reappointment, this contract guarantees job security for continuing full-time lecturers.

In anticipating the extent to which job security will be granted to nontenured as well as tenured faculty members, it is helpful to review a section from the model contract drawn up and distributed to local associations by the NEA's National Society of Professors. Under the heading "Annual Continuing Contract" it states: "A member of the bargaining unit who has received one continuing contract will receive succeeding annual continuing contracts unless specific charges are placed against him including a request for dismissal from the institution" (National Education Association, 1970b, Section 0205.2). The section also stipulates pro-

cedures for due process. We think that future contracts will realize
a greater incidence in agreements assuring the continuous appointment of nontenured faculty. To terminate employment the institution will have to prove professional or personal incompetence of the
faculty member, or demonstrate the financial situation which renders the institution unable to continue the position.

Collective bargaining may go beyond extending job security
to nontenured faculty, by reaching further to nonteaching academic
personnel. Except for some librarians and personnel under civil
service laws, these staff members have been largely unsuccessful in
obtaining tenure. Their inclusion in the bargaining unit may be the
means to extend to them the job security enjoyed by faculty members. For the moment, however, this is limited to speculation.
Tenure provisions in existing four-year college contracts refer only
to the granting of tenure for faculty members. If support personnel,
or even administrators not in the unit, have joint appointments as
faculty members, they may maintain tenure as faculty members, but
not in their other positions.

The AAUP has held that academic freedom is a nonnegotia-
ble item. However, all three of the four-year college contracts
negotiated by an AAUP agency have included a statement on academic freedom. Two of them (Oakland and St. John's) voice support of the AAUP's 1940 *Statement of Principles of Academic Freedom and Tenture* (American Association of University Professors,
1970)', while the Rutgers contract recognizes the principles of academic freedom previously adopted by the university's board of
governors. We can conclude from this that since a statement on academic freedom is appropriate for a collective bargaining agreement,
it constitutes an appropriate subject for negotiations. Seven of the
remaining contracts reviewed support such a conclusion, four contain an original statement on academic freedom, two support existing institutional policy, and one subscribes to the AAUP's statement.

Historical review of tenure and academic freedom in higher
education reveals that these concerns have been conceptually and
procedurally related. The AAUP's 1940 statement affords evidence of
this association. In contrast the collective bargaining contracts in
existence reveal that academic freedom and tenure exist as important and essential separate entities. Typical of an original statement

on academic freedom is the article in the SUNY contract (Article
I)':

> It is the policy of the university to maintain and en-
> courage full freedom, within the law, of inquiry, teaching and
> research. In the exercise of this freedom the faculty member
> may, without limitation, discuss his own subject in the class-
> room; he may not, however, claim as his right the privilege
> of discussing in his classroom controversial matter which has
> no relation to his subject. In his role as citizen, every employee
> has the same freedoms as other citizens. However, in his extra-
> mural utterances he has an obligation to indicate that he is not
> an institutional spokesman.

This article does not relate tenure to academic freedom, and no
article in the contract provides for tenure. Except for contracts
which adopt the AAUP 1940 statement, the dependence of academic
freedom upon tenure appears to have been rejected. In collective
bargaining, each principle stands separately. As noted above, if anything can be associated with tenure it is the principle of due process
as reflected in grievance procedures.

All contracts reviewed contain a grievance procedure; these
range from three to five steps. Grievance procedures have developed
to settle disputes arising from the administration of the contract,
and they are therefore used in personnel cases as well. The first step
is typically an attempt to arrive at an informal adjustment of the
grievance at the department level under the authority of the chairman of the department. If an appropriate department committee
exists, the grievance may be taken informally to that committee. At
Central Michigan University, an informal grievance may be taken
to the office of the provost. If that proves unsatisfactory, it goes to
the Association Committee on Contract Grievances where it is determined whether to undertake formal proceedings.

The distinguishing characteristic between informal and formal procedures is that with the latter all matters pertaining to the
grievance must be commited to writing. A written record of all letters of appeal, decisions, and hearings must be maintained in the
faculty member's file. The time lapse between the offense and its

submission of the written grievance is usually specified. Time specifications are also placed at each step upon the person or persons charged with resolving the grievance and upon the faculty member and his association in filing appeals. Every effort is made to expedite a solution. The faculty member can typically choose to represent himself or be represented by his bargaining association during the procedure. If he chooses the former, contracts guarantee the association the right to send an observer to all hearings.

The final step in the procedure in nine of the contracts is binding arbitration. Either the association or the institution may file an appeal to the American Arbitration Association for a final and binding decision. However, the arbitrator's decision is limited to the application and interpretation of the provisions of the contract. He is not free to add to, subtract from, or in any way alter or modify the contract. Nothing in the contracts requires that the arbitrator be knowledgeable in the area of higher education, which has made many opponents of collective bargaining in higher education fearful. Among the limitations placed upon the arbitrator, however, are the preservation of academic decisions in the realm of professional judgment. The Oakland University contract stipulates that the arbitrator does not have the authority to interpret any policy, practice, or rule which does not relate to wages, hours, or conditions of employment, or to substitute his judgment for academic judgment in the establishment of the classification or change in classification of any faculty member. Should a grievance relating to faculty reappointment, promotion, or dismissal get to binding arbitration, the arbitrator's judgment can only consider whether procedural due process in matters of appointment and promotions as set forth in the contract have been carried out. He cannot judge the professional competence of the faculty member, but is limited to remanding the matter for compliance with prescribed procedures.

Faculty Participation in Governance

One of the most intriguing issues is the effect of collective bargaining on internal decision-making processes in colleges and universities. In the absence of collective bargaining, many forms of faculty participation in governance, from department committees to university senates, rest on traditional practices or have been specifically delegated by administrations and boards of trustees. Many such practices can be changed with or without faculty consultation. A contract, on the other hand, cannot be changed without concurrence from the bargaining agent. The faculty governance processes which are written into a contract may be mere adaptations of pre-existing policy or they may be major transitions in an institution's policy. The latter is frequently the case in many of the two-year and emerging four-year colleges. But at whatever place along this continuum an institution may lie, collective bargaining gives faculty participation in governance a legal guarantee which it may not have had before.

Limitations to this guarantee must be recognized. Policy which is not written into the contract does not have the same legal guarantee. Eleven of the fourteen contracts reviewed have a management rights clause which is typically short and states clearly that all the authority, rights, functions, and responsibilities vested in the board or the state are retained unless they are expressly abridged or limited by the contract. Hence, the legal entities which govern the institution retain powers and duties provided by law. Only the powers and duties assigned to the faculty by the contract are non-revocable by the board or the state, provided they are consistent with the law. Even the items included in the contract are subject to legal interpretation and may be subsequently ruled in conflict with federal or state statutes. Ultimately, guarantees of management rights are much more general and encompassing than provisions stipulating procedures for faculty participation in governance. The faculty provisions, however, do indicate how collective bargaining makes faculty input part of the decision-making process. We cite some examples below.

The contract for the New Jersey State Colleges is the only one that has provision for faculty input in the selection of college presidents. The contract stipulates that any committee assigned a role in the selection of a college president must include a member of the bargaining association.

Two contracts have provisions for the selection of academic deans. At St. John's University a search committee composed of four tenured faculty members elected by the faculty submits to the university president the names of no fewer than three candidates. The president in turn submits one of the names to the board of trustees for its approval. He cannot recommend any candidate whose name has not been submitted by the committee. (See Chapter Nine for further details of this procedure.) At Southeastern Massachusetts University, a seven-person screening committee must be established to nominate candidates to fill the vacancy of any deanship. Three members of this committee must be tenured faculty appointed by the faculty federation. Three others are appointed by the university president, and a student member is selected by the student senate.

Three contracts have provisions for selecting department chairmen. At Southeastern Massachusetts University the dean of faculty appoints chairmen subject to consultation with the appropriate college dean. Faculty members of the department may make recommendations for the vacant chairmanship. In the New Jersey State Colleges department chairmen are elected by members of their departments and are approved and appointed by the college president. The contract further stipulates that in exceptional circumstances a chairman may be appointed by a college president with the consent of the faculty association. The Boston State contract provides elaborate procedures for both election and recall of department chairmen. Within the first month after endorsement of the contract, every department is required to elect three members of the department for nomination to the chairmanship. The elections must be supervised by the faculty federation. All members of a department are eligible to vote and to be nominated. After each election the president of the federation submits the list of nominees to the president of the college who, within seven working days, must appoint a chairman from the list of nominees or decline to appoint any of the nominees. In the latter instance, the nomination procedures begin again. The normal term of appointment for department chairmen at Boston State is three years. However, the faculty of a department can recall a chairman. Upon receipt of a petition signed by one-third of the faculty members in a department, the college dean sets the time and place for a meeting to consider the petition. The president of the faculty federation appoints an impartial faculty member to conduct the recall meeting. By a two-thirds vote of the department members, a recommendation is forwarded to the college president to request that he declare a vacant chairmanship. After receiving this request and a written record of the meeting, the president calls for a new election according to prescribed procedures. Finally, the contract states that the college president may at his discretion declare a vacant chairmanship at any time.

Some observers of collective bargaining fear that the role of faculty senates will be subverted by bargaining agents and contracts. Despite a potential conflict between the means and objectives of collective bargaining and of faculty senates, in some instances contracts support the senates. The agreement with St. John's University stipulates that the senate as well as other existing and duly constituted organizations shall continue to function as long as they do not interfere with or modify the bargaining contract. The management rights clauses in the CUNY contracts provide for the maintenance of the rights of all entities and bodies within the university which are granted under board bylaws unless they conflict with the terms of the agreement. One of the bodies preserved is the University Senate, with its responsibility for the formulation of educational and instructional policy (Finkin, 1971). In other instances, however, collective bargaining contracts place critical limitations upon the operations of a faculty senate. In a clause entitled "Internal Governance," the New Jersey State Colleges contract specifies that the recommendation of a college senate or other faculty governing body implemented by the administration and trustees shall not violate the terms of the agreement. In general, the language of the contracts does not provide sufficient information to judge the viability of faculty senates under collective bargaining.

More clear than the relationship between collective bargaining and faculty senates is the contractual establishment of faculty participation on committees. In some instances, the faculty association is guaranteed a role in making appointments to these committees. The Southeastern Massachusetts University contract creates a committee for awarding sabbatical leaves composed of two federation and three college presidential appointees. This contract also calls for an Academic Review Committee composed of two trustee representatives, two federation representatives, and the dean of the faculty and the federation president, who serve as alternate chairmen. The purpose of this committee is to review changes in academic programs which directly affect wages, hours, and conditions of employment specifically covered by the contract. This contract also provides for the formation of six academic councils, one for each academic division, to participate in the review and recommendation of faculty for tenure. Members of these councils are elected by the tenured or senior faculty in each division.

The contract for Bryant College of Business Administration establishes committees dealing with appointment and curriculum. The Curriculum Committee and the Rank and Appointment Committee each consist of five voting members to be elected annually from the faculty by the faculty federation.

Not only do collective bargaining contracts establish committees, they also frequently guarantee agency representation on these committees, as noted in some of the circumstances cited above. At Central Michigan University the faculty association has representation on committees which create policy for establishing a distinguished professorship; recommend policy on teaching loads and sabbaticals; and debate policy affecting office space and equipment, salaries, and fringe benefits. Committees established by the Monmouth College contract are related primarily to procedures affecting appointment, promotions, and tenure. These include Department Qualifications Committees, elected by department members and open to suggestions by one or two upper-class students who are majors in that department; the College Tenure and Promotions Committee, one member of which is appointed by the faculty association, one by the college, and five elected by the faculty; and the Faculty Appellate Committee, the membership of which is not specified in the contract.

Except for the involvement of the faculty bargaining association, many of the committee structure provisions discussed above are not radically unlike those in existence at many four-year institutions. Even at Boston State College, where the major thrust of the contract is upon the governance structure of the college, many provisions are not drastically different from policy in other colleges and universities. The contract establishes committees at the department, division, and campuswide levels on a wide variety of issues, including faculty evaluation, curriculum, work load, scheduling of course assignments, promotion and tenure, reappointments, college development, budget consultation, and governance review. Student participation is also provided for on some committees.

Whether the Boston State contract will serve as a model for future agreements can only be a subject for speculation. The negotiations for the other Massachusetts state colleges are leading to similar governance arrangements. The student participation sections of the Boston State contract were negotiated without student input and incorporated into the contract with the provision that they would be effective only if approved by a student referendum. Although the contract was subsequently approved, students objected to being left out of the negotiations process. As a result of this experience, students at other Massachusetts state colleges are being consulted regarding student participation in the governance provisions negotiated in the contracts.

Significance

What impact will all these provisions and stipulations have for four-year colleges and universities? For several reasons this analysis can only speculate about impact. First, an analysis of contracts alone does not provide an adequate base for judging the impact collective bargaining has or may have on higher education. To assess the probable impact, we would have to know more about the conditions at a given institution before bargaining, more about items that were negotiated during the bargaining process but not incorporated into the first contract, and more about how contracts are being administered.

Second, collective bargaining is too new to four-year institutions to permit generalizations. With only two exceptions, the contracts reviewed in this chapter are first agreements. It may be that if the more typical issues (salaries, fringe benefits, etc.) become stabilized, future contracts will consolidate the gains of the first contracts and seek to enlarge the scope of negotiations. This appears to us to be a reasonable prediction, but the courts, legislatures, or arbitrators may be called upon to redefine the scope of negotiable items or to settle bargaining impasses, and we cannot be certain as to the directions that will be taken.

Third, in reviewing contracts we must be aware of the

special circumstances which apply to each institution. For example, the problems of arriving at a single contract for multicampus systems are quite different, and appear to be more complex, than negotiating a single-campus contract.

Fourth, the contracts reviewed here are not a representative sample of all four-year institutions that have adopted collective bargaining for faculty. The paucity of final contracts negotiated to date may not reflect accurately the conditions that will prevail when other institutions complete their contracts.

Two general points can be made about the contracts we have reviewed. We offer these below as hypotheses to be tested in the light of future experience. First, the definitions of bargaining units include a wide range of nonteaching professionals (NTPS). This homogenization of professional personnel includes full-time faculty, librarians, counselors, some administrative but nonsupervisory titles, some part-time teaching titles, and department chairmen. It is likely, in our opinion, that future contracts will apply to the entire unit, faculty and NTPS alike. For example, it is possible that the term "continuous employment" will apply to a wide variety of titles and that little, if any, distinction will be made between it and the term "tenure." It also may be difficult to maintain salary differentials among faculty members in two-year, four-year, and graduate school campuses within a multicampus system. The homogenization of professional personnel into one bargaining unit seems certain to require compromises within the unit, prior to bargaining, on these and other issues, and the results of these compromises will be incorporated into contracts.

Second, contracts codify and specify procedures for faculty-administrative relations in a wide variety of areas, most of which are discussed here. In some cases, contracts merely put in writing some of the normal practices of the institution. In other cases, notably in grievance and appeal procedures, provisions for binding arbitration, and bargaining agent rights and privileges, contracts institutionalize a new set of procedures and rights. Contracts give legal status to what may have been informal practices and extend this status to new areas.

7

Public University System: State University of New York

Robert S. Fisk, William C. Puffer

The State University of New York constitutes one of the two largest university complexes operating under a collective bargaining contract (the other is the City University of New York). Thus, the case which follows should raise a series of major questions which other public, multicampus systems of higher education may face as they approach the negotiations process. To this end the authors have described the process of choosing the bargaining association to represent faculty and other professional personnel, the negotiation of the first contract, and the implementation of this contract during its first year.

The State University of New York experience serves to highlight such considerations as the definition of the bargaining unit and the organizational problems resulting where faculty members and nonteaching professionals from very different types of units over a large geographical area are formed into one bargaining association. It leads to speculation as to whether this kind of comprehensive association or smaller, more homogeneous units would prove more appropriate and whether the grouping of all professional staff members can best serve the interests of each group and the university as a whole.

The analysis of the negotiations process which follows attends to the dynamics of the relationships involved. It emphasizes the question as to whether the discipline exacted upon each member of the bargaining teams constitutes an appropriate approach to relationships in an academic institution. It highlights the question of the role for experienced professional negotiators. Also, since the professional association is viewed by some to have stemmed from a statewide faculty senate, it offers a perspective in the dichotomy between models associated with traditional faculty government and those associated with the public school or industrial setting. Finally, the chapter provides an opportunity to see some of the strains upon colleges and universities that occur when legislatures define procedures which affect a total system of public higher education and create rules which challenge some of the independence and authority of a governing board and its chief administrator.

Robert S. Fisk brings to the case experience both as a university dean and director and as a faculty member. Currently, his special concern is for policy studies in education. During the past two years he participated actively in the professional association as a member of its executive board and of the team that bargained for the first contract. William C. Puffer is currently undertaking an intensive analysis of the development of the Senate Professional Association which represented the faculty and professional staff in New York. The authors assume full responsibility for the chapter, which was prepared independently of the association, without requesting its sanction or approval.   E. D. D. and R. S. F.

The State University of New York (SUNY) was one of the first complex institutions of higher learning to move toward collective bargaining. The State Employee Relations Act (known as the Taylor Law); the organizational efforts of most other public employees throughout the state; the brief history and lack of traditions within SUNY; and the presence of several organizations desirous of representing the faculty and the professional staff all contributed to the momentum toward bargaining. Even the many who would have preferred to avoid unionization were led inevitably to support one organization or another for fear that still another might ultimately win control.

Founded in 1948, for some years it was difficult to conceive of SUNY as a university in anything more than name. Its establishment was not met with universal enthusiasm—the president of one private university stated, in the presence of the governor and the Board of Regents at a major convocation, that New York should never have to endure one of those monstrosities of the midwest, the state universities. It began with a nucleus of eleven state teachers colleges, six agricultural and technical two-year institutes, a maritime academy, and a college of forestry. It soon acquired two medical colleges by absorption from existing institutions. It also assumed developmental and programmatic supervision, but not direct control, over the growing community college movement in the state for which it also shares in the financing.

The governor nominates the trustees of SUNY, making it essentially an arm of the executive branch of state government. As a statutory body it enjoys substantially less autonomy than the long-established board of regents whose members are chosen by the legislature and which has constitutional status and general supervision over education at all levels within the state. During its formative period the presidents and trustees of SUNY engaged in a spasmodic struggle with the regents as they sought autonomy in development.

By the late 1950s, however, SUNY had gained considerable autonomy as a unit of state government and was beginning to grant greater autonomy to its various units. Its central administration appeared to view its role as a master planner, a primary advocate to a sympathetic governor and a compliant legislature, and an interceder with a variety of state offices and agencies. Primary authority for the SUNY system rested with its board of trustees and the chancellor, subject to appropriations from the legislature and budgetary supervision from the executive department of the state.

For the various segments within SUNY the 1960s were years of expansion beyond the dreams of most. Its four university centers acquired prestigious faculty, attracting them with both salary and a vision of greatness to be achieved. While SUNY's overall salary schedule was not uniformly good, salaries for its university centers placed them among the top thirty universities in the country by American Association of University Professors (AAUP) standards. Its undergraduate student body also became increasingly a select academic group. Individual graduate departments became nationally and internationally visible. SUNY engaged in a major building program, spending approximately 2.6 billion dollars on its physical plant during the decade 1962–1972. It grew from approximately 34,000 students in 1960 to 117,000 in 1970, exclusive of the community colleges, and to twenty-eight separate units as follows: twelve university colleges with programs through the MA, four university centers with graduate and professional schools, four health science centers, six agricultural and technical institutes, and two specialized colleges. Nothing seemed impossible.

With the approach of the 1970s the climate changed and trouble converged upon SUNY from all sides. The chancellor departed after a shorter stay than many had anticipated. Increases in financial support were questioned by friends of private institutions who voiced doubts about the need for continued expansion of SUNY and by the governor and legislature who were concerned about the costs generated by SUNY. Student and faculty cultural and political activism aroused public antipathies and eroded support. Moreover, the state remained unsure of its commitment to public higher education and was inclined toward taking greater pride in its many prestigious private institutions.

Setting the Stage

The legal basis for negotiation with the 14,000 or more faculty members and professional staff was established by the 1967 legislature with the enactment of the Taylor Law which is definitive with regard to many aspects of the negotiation process. It gives employees the right to organize and join unions which may enter into negotiations and legally binding contracts with the state over the terms and conditions of employment of their membership, but it continues the former prohibition of the right to strike.

For the administration of the personnel processes evolving from the Taylor Law the Office of Employee Relations (OER) was established within the executive department of the state government. The OER and its director negotiate with the various bargaining units representing the several categories of state employees, a very critical aspect of the bargaining process which places OER opposite the union at the bargaining table. The role of the chancellor of SUNY and his representatives at the table is at times difficult to determine. We discuss this later in the chapter.

The Public Employment Relations Board (PERB) was charged with implementation of the Taylor Law and has the power to respond to the request of an employee organization for certification as the bargaining unit within a given category of employees. Several groups within SUNY asked for certification, and PERB began hearings in July 1968 to define the bargaining unit. In addition to the central administration (the chancellor and his immediate staff, located in Albany) five employee organizations appeared: the Council of Affiliated Chapters of the AAUP in SUNY; a group of five locals of the State University Federation of Teachers (SUFT), an affiliate of the American Federation of Teachers (AFT), American Federation of Labor-Congress of Industrial Organizations (AFL-CIO); the Civil Service Employees Organization (CSEA), a large group of state employees with a long history; the SUNY Faculty Senate, which represented faculty interests to the chancellor and his administrative officers while it exhibited many traits associated with faculty senates (for example, financial support from the central administration and a blending of administrative personnel with faculty representatives); and the Faculty Association of SUNY, a group which emanated from the faculties of the former state teachers colleges, but had difficulty establishing itself and subsequently dropped out of the proceedings.

The PERB hearing amplified the enabling legislation in setting the ground rules for the bargaining process. The issue of unit determination held significant implications. It encompassed a number of issues which had a great impact upon subsequent events related to the representative election and organizational development. These included the geographic scope of the unit, the personnel to be included, and the determination of which organizations qualified as potential bargaining agents.

The question of the geographic scope of the unit centered upon whether there should be one statewide bargaining unit or a separate unit for each campus. There appeared to have been no serious thought given to subgroupings of similar institutions such as university centers, state colleges, and technical institutes.

The SUNY central administration found the question to be a crucial one since it felt that campus-by-campus negotiations would impair its statewide coordination and development functions. For the other agencies of state government involved, primarily PERB and the OER, a campus-by-campus unit raised the question of a potential whipsawing effect, playing one campus against another. And an even more significant question was whether the local campus administrations had the power to make meaningful agreements, since ultimately their budgets required the endorsement of the central administration, the office of the state budget director, and the legislature.

For the petitioning organizations the implications of the geographic unit issue were political and structural. A statewide unit would favor an organization whose strength or appeal was statewide, rather than limited to a type of institution such as the four-year colleges. Thus, an organization would have to appeal to a wide range of constituencies in a statewide unit. In a campus-by-campus unit, organizations could appeal to the particular interests of that unit such as those of the medical centers or the Maritime College.

SUFT was the only petitioner to argue in favor of a campus-by-campus unit. The central administration and the others favored a statewide unit.

The second major issue revolved about the personnel in the bargaining unit and was, primarily, a question of whether the non-teaching professionals (NTPs) should be included with the faculty. The additional question arose of when faculty and NTPs became management and thus should be barred from the unit. The inclusion of the NTPs would mean that the bargaining association would have to accommodate to a greater diversity of interests, both in organization and in the substance of negotiations. For the NTPs it would mean an alliance with the faculty in negotiations which very likely would give them greater strength but entail some risk from unsympathetic academics.

The position of the central administration on the personnel to be included was based on the New York education law which defines professional service as including both faculty members and professional support staff in the libraries, student personnel services, financial and managerial offices, and other nonacademic components of the institutions. In addition, the administration argued that, in contrast with other state employees, the nonteaching and teaching staffs of SUNY had common interests. Common trustee policies and SUNY administrative procedures recognized this community of interests. Further, any separation of the two professional staffs could potentially lead to conflict or competition between them, thereby hindering the educational effectiveness of SUNY.

The AAUP and SUFT argued against this position, stating that a separation of the two categories had always existed. They contended that this was recognized by the policies of the board of trustees on tenure, appointment procedures, and campus faculty senate voting procedures. These two groups also parted company with the others on the matter of who should be considered management—they requested the inclusion of associate and assistant deans and directors in that category.

The third issue to be considered was the question of the qualifications of an organization deemed eligible to become the employee bargaining agent. It centered specifically on the SUNY Faculty Senate. For the senate it was a question of its viability as a potential candidate for the role and, to a degree, its efficacy as a faculty representative to the SUNY administration. For the other organizations it became an issue of principle and politics. The principle involved the right of a possible company union to represent employees. Political considerations evolved from the desire to eliminate an indigenous, well-established, and at least somewhat influential organization from the competition.

Senate adherents argued that criteria concerning company unions drawn from the industrial model of collective bargaining were not applicable to higher education and that it had long represented faculty interests in the SUNY system. If the senate was certified, they indicated that other means would be found to finance its operations.

The hearings extended over eight months and involved almost four thousand pages of testimony. The decision, by PERB's director of representation, stipulated that the geographic unit would be statewide rather than campus-based; the membership of the unit would include NTPS; associate and assistant deans and most directors were not to be excluded from the unit as management personnel; and the Faculty Senate was not eliminated as a potential candidate for bargaining agent.

Following the decision by PERB's director of representation SUFT appealed the judgment to the entire board. In October 1969 the board sustained the director's decision. SUFT took the matter to the courts. In October 1970 a ruling was handed down stating that the Faculty Senate was eligible to act as a bargaining agent under the Taylor Law. It sustained PERB on all the issues.

While the matter was in the courts there was a good deal of organizational activity within the state in preparation for the representation elections. Much centered around the senate's attempt to find a more acceptable means of actively involving itself in the collective negotiation process. One possible solution was a coalition with another organization, preferably one with sufficient financial resources to assist in startup operations. An arrangement was made with the Civil Service Employees Organization (CSEA) during 1968 and 1969, but was dissolved in the fall of 1969. [A lawsuit arising from the breakup and related matters has made it difficult to obtain precise information on these endeavors. For some details see the quote from Sherwig (1971) in Chapter Two.]

Parallel with these developments a number of NTPS began to organize to gain better representation of their approximately four thousand colleagues before the SUNY central administration. They were aware of the imminence of collective bargaining and wanted to ensure that their interests would be adequately represented by the agent ultimately selected. Thus in October 1969 the State University Professional Association (SUPA) was organized to maximize the representation of NTPs in the upcoming contract negotiations.

In early 1970 another development occurred. Some of the leaders in the senate decided to form a new, independent organization in combination with certain of the leaders of SUPA. The new relationship appeared to be a good match. By involving themselves in the development of a new organization the NTPs could ensure that their interests were recognized within the organization and concomitantly, in the contract negotiations. The alliance with elements of the senate provided an academic faculty appearance which SUPA did not have. For the senate the new organization provided an independent association in which it could instill some of its philosophy as faculty in collective bargaining and yet give its leadership the political strength of access to a likely NTP bloc vote. Thus, the Senate Professional Association (SPA) was formed in May 1970 and formally adopted a constitution on October 10, 1970.

The SPA constitution provided for a dual representation system by which membership in each campus chapter and representation to the statewide policy-making body—the Representative Council—is divided into academic and professional (nonteaching) categories. Each category elects its own representatives from each campus. One vice-president is drawn from each category. Thus the constitution established a voice in policy-making for NTPs equal to that of the faculty although the NTPs actually constituted a minority in a ratio of about four to ten. The constitution also provided for a relatively strong voice for the smaller campuses whose collective number in the Representative Council conceivably may be in excess of those from the larger campuses, and, in particular, the university centers. Much of this grew out of the organizational efforts of the NTPs and the momentum they established.

Prior to the adoption of the constitution, however, much had to be accomplished. Although SPA had a potentially sound constituent base, its funds were meager and its membership was minimal. It lacked the resources necessary to carry on an effective campaign or, if it won, to handle the contract negotiations. Following earlier informal contacts the interim executive committee of SPA held a meeting on September 24, 1970 with representatives of the National

Education Association (NEA) and its affiliate, the New York State Teachers Association (NYSTA). The NEA was interested in an affiliation with SPA for two reasons: given the SPA structure, it felt that with help SPA had a chance of winning the election; and the New York State representation election was an important one in terms of collective bargaining in higher education nationally and SUFT appeared to be the most likely group to win it. The NEA leaders felt that they could not ignore the challenge, although they recognized that SUFT was well-established on several of the university college campuses. The NEA took some risks in that SPA was viewed as related to the university administration. In addition, SPA wanted financial support with no strings attached regarding policy should it win. It sought an alliance rather than a merger. The result of the meeting was an informal agreement in which NEA and NYSTA agreed to provide funds and resources—primarily in the form of personnel—in anticipation of a more formal affiliation in the future.

Campaign and Election

The president of the faculty senate requested the substitution of SPA for the senate on the ballot in the upcoming representation election. Accompanying it were the AAUP, CSEA, SUFT, and a "no agent" choice.

During the campaign AAUP stressed long experience as the guardian of academic freedom and faculty tenure and made its appeal almost exclusively to the faculty voters. The controversy among its membership and supporters over whether AAUP should engage in collective bargaining weakened its efforts.

On the other hand, SUFT ran a well-organized campaign which stressed its affiliation with the AFL-CIO. Its major strength was based in some of the four-year colleges. Within the medical centers and the university centers SUFT's militancy and union identification tended to undercut the effectiveness of its campaign.

The SPA campaign emphasized the organization's indigenous aspects. Among the faculty it stressed its ties to the Faculty Senate, and among the NTPs it stressed its ties to SUPA. However, the question of SPA's association with NEA may have been detrimental to its campaign.

The CSEA was rather late in starting its campaign and was never really in the running. While the no agent choice was not without advocacy, apprehension that SUFT might win led to votes for one of the other organizations on the part of many faculty members.

When the mail ballot was finally tabulated on December 29, 1970, none of the organizations had won a majority. SUFT had the largest percentage, followed in order by SPA, AAUP, CSEA, and finally, the no agent category. A run-off election was scheduled between the two top contenders for a week and a half later.

The leaders of SPA deemed the timing propitious, believing they were gaining momentum. The campaign strategists felt that although SUFT was more solidly established, with a more committed membership which would be sure to vote, its militant posture would not attract many new converts in only a week and a half. SPA, however, with its more moderate posture was likely to pick up votes from those who had supported the AAUP and those who were not ready to accept SUFT's aggressive collective bargaining position. SPA's problem, of course, was to get these people to vote. Thus, the SPA campaign tactic was to get out the largest vote possible.

Throughout the first and second campaigns many involved with one or another of the organizations were aware of the seeming lack of interest in the whole endeavor on the part of much of the faculty and professional staff. The scope of collective bargaining under the Taylor Law and its potential for radically affecting working conditions and the university as a whole was little understood. In its effort to get out the vote SPA contended with this apparent lethargy partly by directing its appeal to a large and diverse constituency.

This was reflected in its contract goals which had been developed by the SPA executive board for the first election. They dedicated SPA to "three principles of academic and professional growth: 1. Negotiation of a master contract that will enable the State University of New York to retain and attract the best qualified professional personnel in the nation; 2. Uniformity of rights and benefits within that contract for both teaching faculty and non-teaching professionals; 3. Maintenance within the framework of that contract of a strong element of local autonomy for individual university campuses." The specific goals could hardly have been more comprehensive—they dealt with salary; fringe benefits; professional provisions including leaves and support for other professional activity; workloads; a grievance procedure including binding arbitration and full due process; career service appointments for professional personnel (NTPS); academic freedom and tenure consistent with AAUP standards; equal academic status for librarians; the unique concerns of the health science centers; the principles of the Women's Rights Caucus; maintenance of prior rights and privileges; and local autonomy in governance.

The SPA won the election and was certified by PERB to be the collective bargaining agent for SUNY on January 29, 1971. Although it won, for many months it was unclear who or what SPA was; that is, it had to solidify its organization at both the campus and the state levels. This organizational process caused the SPA leadership, uncertain of its statewide organizational support and wary of elements of the bargaining unit critical of SPA, to function in what often seemed to be a closed manner.

While any commentary on the election is speculative, since the ballots were secret, certain conclusions may be drawn. First, the active support of the NEA and NYSTA was a critical factor in SPA's ultimate success. They evolved the strategy, and provided the financing, staff, facilities, and communications network which made a blitz campaign possible.

Second, SPA's appeals to various constituencies succeeded. Certainly, the NTPS through their organization, SUPA, were a major force in the election. Feeling themselves effectively disenfranchised and largely without job security they saw the most immediate gain from a contract.

Similarly, the health science centers of SUNY and in particular the medical schools sought and obtained assurance from SPA that they would be granted, through an organization known as the Medical Caucus, the right to considerable autonomy in developing their statement of demands and in pushing these to mediation and fact-finding if necessary. The caucus had other requests which were denied by the SPA leadership as challenging the basic authority of the bargaining agent, but it then was satisfied to the extent that it raised a special fund, hired an attorney, and put together a complex proposal for inclusion in the ultimate package placed by SPA on the bargaining table.

Particular attention was given to the concerns of some faculty for economic parity within SUNY and with the City University of New York (CUNY); to the interests of such groups as the librarians and the Women's Rights Caucus; to the desires of those with long-standing loyalty to AAUP and its various standards; and to individual campus commitments to local governance traditions and policies. Each of these factors added to the accumulation of the support needed for ultimate victory. And each later became significant in the bargaining process.

Negotiations

Preparation for the election and the bargaining process had gone forward almost hand-in-hand in SPA. This was believed imperative, since the New York state legislature was to conclude its current session in mid or late Spring, and by provision of the Taylor Law, it would have to approve all contractual provisions requiring the expenditure of funds or statutory change. All parties were aware of the desirability of immediate bargaining so as to complete the process prior to adjournment of the legislature.

With the winning of the election, therefore, the SPA leaders plunged into the final stages of preparing a negotiations package. The executive committee, supplemented by representatives of constituencies not reflected in the executive board, formed a negotiations committee of eighteen persons. In lengthy weekend meetings it tackled each article in the election statement. It was guided in this process by a detailed statement based upon extensive study of an NEA model agreement, the CUNY contract, and other available precedents.

The process was physically exhausting, and apparently contributed to the resignation from office of SPA's first president, an academician from one of the university centers. He was succeeded by the former vice-president for the NTPs who had been closely involved in the earlier organization of SUPA, the establishment of SPA, and the campaign, and was largely responsible for the development of the initial bargaining proposals placed before the committee. His ascendency to the presidency added strength to the NTP point of view in subsequent developments.

At times the development of the negotiation proposals threatened the disaffection of representatives of several segments of SUNY. In the midst of the process the two representatives from the faculties of the university centers (one of them the former president of SPA) resigned from the committee. Questions were at once raised about SPA's potential to represent adequately the interests of committed academicians such as those to be found among senior faculty in the colleges and the university centers. The two representatives who resigned were clearly disenchanted with the philosophy and direction of the bargaining proposal as it was developing, particularly in its economic demands, as well as increasingly critical of the SPA leadership.

This might have led to a separatist movement on the part of some or all of the university centers. However, the chapter presidents of each of the four centers conferred and concluded that representation on the negotiations committee was still desirable. The new representative proposed was accepted by the new SPA president and immediately joined the committee for the final two sessions.

Two weeks later an extensive document emerged which included the material submitted by the Medical Caucus. A bargaining team of four persons was selected by the negotiations committee; it was constituted of two NTPs, including the new SPA president, and two faculty members, one the SPA vice-president for academic personnel and the other the representative of the Medical Caucus. Two others, an NTP technical assistant and the new university center faculty member, were selected as alternates, but were informed that they should consider themselves full participants in the bargaining process.

On March 17, 1971 the two bargaining teams met. The SPA had on its side a professional negotiator from the NEA, a member of their staff in higher education with both business and educational bargaining experience, who although he was present during the formulation of the initial proposal had remained silent. Also present was a research staff member from NYSTA whose assignment was to anticipate and provide data in support of the SPA demands.

On the other side was the director of OER, the assistant
director (who carried the main burden of the negotiations), the
deputy vice-chancellor of SUNY, the vice-chancellor for finance, the
vice-chancellor for personnel, a campus president, and several persons including observers from the office of the director of the budget
and from the office of the legal counsel of SUNY. Following an informal introduction a brief discussion of the ground rules ensued.
The SPA team indicated it desired to function as a committee of the
whole. The OER position was that it might at times prefer committees functioning in parallel. Assuming that all offers were tentative
until final agreement was reached on the package as a whole, the
OER director stressed the confidentiality of the offers and demands
and the need to avoid publicity during negotiations. On the assumption that SPA would present a proposal the OER director suggested
a meeting for clarification and a session following for formal response.

At the meeting the SPA chief negotiator presented a formal
set of proposals, a ninety-page double-spaced catalog of twenty-four
articles, which included a preamble summarizing SPA's commitment to the basic purposes of the university and its desire to develop
a relationship with the state characterized by shared governance.
The proposal's size and detail came as an apparent surprise to the
state team. It can be conjectured that the state team had anticipated
that a number of factors, including the soon-to-be-ending legislative
session and the recency of the bargaining election, would cause SPA
to limit its demands largely to economic matters.[1]

[1] While the authors had access to much of the SPA background
thinking, they did not have similar access to the activities of the OER
and of the SUNY central administration. In response to a request to
discuss procedural and organization endeavors within the SUNY central
administration the chancellor replied that he had been advised "that
it would be inappropriate for us to enter any discussions such as the
type you suggest. We're still at this time too close to the events and
their impact upon future operations of the university to be able to
engage in any kind of public analysis which might seriously affect our
freedom of choice." He concluded with a regret that his position
"stems in part from the posture imposed upon the university by the
collective bargaining process." Thus the material here is largely oriented

The SPA team at this point began to function within certain ground rules. The negotiations committee had agreed earlier that the details of the proposals would not be discussed outside the committee except to reiterate their consistency with the campaign statements. The SPA bargaining team decided to adhere to the same policy. Next, the chief negotiator for SPA insisted upon strict discipline at the table. It was made clear that no member of the team was to volunteer a comment of any kind without prior consent of the negotiator and that the posture at all times was to be a formal one. Should any member of the team wish to advise the negotiator he was to do so in writing. On the other hand, members were to be prepared, at the negotiator's request, to respond to or to take the initiative in the discussion of any given point. Finally, each member of the team was to organize his professional duties so as to give the bargaining process first priority. This was facilitated by holding all sessions away from any campus, in Albany. The desire of the state and SPA to bargain as one unit rather than campus-by-campus was thus fulfilled also.

The rules for the state were of the same order. Primary communication was through the assistant director of OER who served as chief negotiator. (The director came to the table only once or twice after the first session for discussion of economic issues.) Team members for the state varied in number, sometimes with approximately twenty-five persons including visiting campus presidents and SUNY central administration officials. The chancellor never appeared, although it was felt at certain times that he was not far.

Secrecy became a major issue when it was learned that the SPA proposal had been distributed to the campus presidents and then leaked by some of them to subordinates on campus. Thus non-members of the bargaining unit could comment upon certain proposals to members of the bargaining unit and SPA who were themselves almost totally in the dark. At an early session the state agreed to instruct the campus presidents to respect the confidentiality of the proposal document.

During the bargaining process it seemed evident to the SPA

---

to the SPA side of the endeavors and is speculative as concerns the state.

team that maneuvers of the state were directed entirely by the OER. The SPA leadership maintained team discipline. If any informal conversations between members of the two teams occurred, they have not been disclosed.

An early incident established the determination and discipline of the SPA team in the eyes of the state representatives. As the third session began the state's chief negotiator distributed what amounted to a complete reorganization and restatement of the SPA proposals, entitled "SPA Demands." It omitted the preamble and stated the demands in terse, direct language. The state negotiator then stated that his team rejected the language of the SPA proposal, that it had analyzed the demands, and it desired to discuss concepts rather than language. With that introduction (made before an unusually large state team including several SUNY campus presidents), he proceeded with a detailed oral response to each item in the state's analysis of the SPA proposal, objecting to some, rejecting others, inquiring as to the purpose or meaning of many, alleging the illegality of a few, pointing to the great expense involved in the economic package, stating the state's willingness to discuss some at a later point, and holding out the hope that the two sides could come to terms on a few of the items.

Following this statement the SPA chief negotiator requested time for a caucus and the state contingent left the room. The SPA team was stunned by this virtually complete rejection of its proposals, but the chief negotiator quickly analyzed the tactic as a major test of the SPA team and proposed that the response be a complete rejection of the state document and a charge of bad faith bargaining on the basis of failure of the state to respond with proposals of its own in appropriate language. He proposed that the team should be prepared to terminate the discussions unless the state responded positively. The team agreed, and then, after a short interval, invited the state team to return.

The SPA negotiator immediately delivered a hard-line oral statement reminding the state that it had broken the confidentiality of SPA's original demands and charging that in its failure to counterpropose it was guilty of bad faith bargaining. He stated further that the SPA team would waste no more time in unproductive meetings, but that it would meet the following afternoon to hear the state's counterproposals. The mood was one of confrontation and, in a few cases at least, persons who had been friends and colleagues with those across the table now sensed the meaning of an adversary relationship. When the state's response was primarily to remind SPA of the necessity to reach an agreement before the legislature adjourned, the SPA negotiator terminated the discussion and stated that the team would be available the following day. As the last of the SPA team stalked out of the room the state negotiator suggested that it not wait too long the next day.

The following day the sessions were renewed with an obvious effort by the state negotiator to clear the air. He stated that a letter had been sent to all campuses dealing with the confidentiality of the SPA proposals, and he then made a brief, conciliatory explanation of the rewriting of the proposals. Its ostensible purpose was to provide a systematic approach to the various points. After further discussions of procedure the session adjourned amicably, setting a meeting for the next day. At that time the state team began to counterpropose using the SPA proposals in their original form. A note of informality began to characterize the discourse, and fewer university administrators were present. The SPA team members speculated that the confrontation session had been an effort by the OER to demonstrate its command of the process to SUNY administrators, but that the OER now realized that the SPA team was fully prepared to approach the table as peers.

In spite of the procedural progress and many long sessions the state team remained unconvinced during the next two months of the firmness of the SPA commitment to certain basic issues. The principal matters at issue were grievance procedures including arbitration; job security and career development programs for the NTPs; inclusion of many of the written policies of the board of trustees in the contract so they could be grievable; and economic provisions. Despite the imminence of legislative adjournment, the SPA team stood firm, particularly when the state would not compromise on economic proposals. Discussions on these last were clouded by SPA's suspicion that the data provided earlier by the state, in compliance with PERB policies, and used subsequently by SPA to make its analyses of costs had been inaccurate or incomplete or both.

By early May the SPA team concluded that progress was

not being made. Following an extended discussion of term appointments that typified an obdurate position by the state on many points, SPA decided to go to impasse, a procedure under which PERB is requested to provide an impartial mediator. This led to the appointment of a mediator and two weeks of desultory efforts by both sides to find common ground. The director of OER appeared to urge the SPA team to accept an improved economic offer which was approximately twice the original proposal but still less than SPA felt was essential. At that point SPA broke off negotiations and stated its intention to request PERB to appoint a panel of fact-finders. SPA was prepared to claim that the state had provided it with inaccurate data and was showing little inclination to bargain seriously on a number of essential noneconomic proposals.

Under the Taylor Law fact-finding is a process by which, unless the two parties reach agreement through their own efforts, there is ultimate public disclosure of the fact-finders' conclusions. SPA was confident that the OER would not wish events to reach that point and so took a calculated risk. It recognized that the legislature was about to adjourn and thus there could not be implementation of economic provisions in a contract. Yet SPA thought that the OER officials and the SUNY central administration wanted to reach an agreement with SPA rather than risk no agreement and a consequent challenge by SUFT or another organization leading to a new representative election which was almost certain to follow. Thus SPA felt the fact-finding petition to be a sound tactic to get the negotiations back on the track toward an agreement which could be defended.

Nearly three months passed before agreement was reached. Normal bargaining had come to a halt in May. The complicated gathering of data for fact-finding began, and PERB was about to appoint a panel. Parallel with these developments, however, informal discussions between the leadership of the two teams (and without the presence of representatives of the SUNY central administration) led finally to the return to the bargaining table in early August, approximately four weeks before a call for a new representative election could have been initiated. By this time SPA had been provided by NEA with a new chief negotiator, a lawyer of considerable stature in labor relations and the one who had been the negotiator for the faculty at CUNY in its highly successful effort the year before.

The approach to bargaining changed markedly. The state team diminished in size until on occasion only the negotiator and the SUNY vice-chancellor for personnel were present. SPA's team began to function more informally. Individual members were encouraged to take the lead on discussions of matters of particular interest to them or to their individual constituencies. Contract language in written form began to flow freely across the table in both directions. Several long caucus intervals occurred during which one or more members of each team conferred privately in an effort to find agreement. Shortly an economic proposal from the state met SPA's minimum fallback position.

At this point agreement on most matters was reached very quickly. Two major points still at issue were job security and career development for NTPs and a cluster of financial and other concerns of the Medical Caucus. These were temporarily resolved by agreement to appoint study committees. All other primary issues were resolved through specific contract language.

In mid-August the SPA negotiation committee was called to Albany to approve the tentative agreement for submission to the membership of SPA. The date was awkward for most academic calendars, but a signed contract was important if SPA were not to be challenged in a new election and if SUNY were not to be faced with another year of uncertainty in its personnel relationships. The agreement was approved by a vote of 1775 to 106 and was signed in early September by the president of SPA and the director of OER with the chancellor of SUNY as an observer. The contract covered the period of three years until June 30, 1974 with reopeners possible on basic salary matters and for resolution of the concerns of the NTPs and Medical Caucus when their respective committees had reported.

From the point of view of most of the SPA leadership the contract was most significant for having achieved a modest (across-the-board) salary increase; a grievance process leading to binding arbitration on procedural matters; inclusion in the contract of important articles from the policies of the board of trustees; improved job security for NTPs in the form of term appointments during the interval when the study committees were at work; a policy on retrenchment respecting seniority in position; and provision for monthly consultations between local chapters and the campus presidents, periodic consultation with the chancellor, and two health science center study groups.

The SPA leadership felt that the contract, while less than that proposed, was still substantially in excess of what had been anticipated by the OER. The latter seemed insensitive to SPA's willingness to stand on principle on matters of governance, on the grievance process, on prior policies of the trustees, and on job security for the NTPs. On the other hand, SUNY central administration and the OER were surprised at the willingness of the SPA team to accept a provision making it possible "for the university, in its discretion, to grant . . . further upward salary adjustments to individual employees" (from the agreement). The university centers, in particular, had insisted that the prospect of discretionary or merit raises be continued, a matter of less concern to other lower-paid segments of the SPA constituency.

Commencing in November 1971 with the appointment of a new negotiations committee and concluding in late April 1972, this time prior to the adjournment of the legislature, SPA negotiated a new salary agreement for the 1972–1973 fiscal year calling for across-the-board adjustments plus a merit increase of 1.5 percent of the payroll on each campus to be distributed to no more than 30 percent of the academic employees and to no more than 25 percent of the NTPs. The increases were to be made on action by the board of trustees based on recommendation by the chancellor. Informally it was agreed that the increases should emerge from local criteria carrying the confidence of local personnel and within guidelines established by the SUNY central administration and agreed to by the statewide SPA. The contract is still subject to reopening on salaries for the last year of its life. Also, an effort will be made in the future to begin discussions on improving the minimum salary structure throughout the university. Finally, with the help of the OER, SPA gained two agreements with the central administration establishing formal procedures for improving the job security and the career development of the NTPs. A study committee to deal with the problems of another special interest group—the librarians—is also to be established.

Retrospect and Future

The SUNY experience is too recent a phenomenon for us to to examine objectively. Nearly all who are familiar with the situation have served as interested participants committed to one side or the other. Nevertheless this new experience must be chronicled and an effort must be made to analyze it. Hopefully, the case study will serve in the process of refining hypotheses and documenting conclusions which may provide guides to action in other settings.

A number of elements stand out more than others. Clearly the definition of the bargaining unit has been demonstrated to be critically important. It affected the nature of the bargaining organization, the philosophy which undergirded its leadership, the priorities at the bargaining table, and the events which followed. Inclusion of the NTPs dictated the use of much of the SPA resources. The statewide approach to bargaining led to a number of organizational adjustments within SPA.

One result was the wide variation in the numbers of faculty and other professional staff members for whom individual members of the policy-making and executive board spoke. Limiting management personnel to the very top fringe of central and campus administrative staffs left the campus presidents, for example, with very few associates to share administrative confidences and dilemmas. The fact that SPA was the sole bargaining agent for a complex, multi-campus institution was reflected in its representation campaign and the appeal to a wide constituency. Thus, SPA had to accommodate a multiplicity of special and sometimes competing interests from the health science centers, librarians, various minority groups, and faculties of widely differing campuses. All this emphasizes the importance for viability of a kind of organizational eclecticism on the part of the bargaining association. It must be broadly concerned with the interests of its various groups if it is to gain recognition and if it is to survive.

Equally important has been the kind of immediate resources,

both dollar and personnel, made available to the association through affiliate groups. SPA would not have survived and emerged victor without the NEA and NYSTA commitments.

The statutory and regulatory offices and bodies concerned with bargaining make a critical difference. At least annually the negotiations process provides the opportunity for faculty members and NTPS, through their leadership in SPA, to deal directly with representatives of the executive branch of state government. This means that established administrative channels leading to the central administration and board of trustees are bypassed. The latter two groups face serious consequences including responsibility for a university governed in a significant way by a contract for which they were not completely responsible.

In another dimension, SUNY's experience demonstrates the importance of preparation for the negotiation process. SPA made far greater gains than many anticipated because of its considered positions on a wide range of faculty and professional concerns. In contrast many of those at the table felt a lack of preparation, in the form of reliable data at least, on the part of the state team.

Similarly, the availability of skilled negotiators is clearly an imperative. The SPA experience demonstrated the importance of recognizing when a change of pace and of approach is needed. This calls for dispassionate leadership such as is the province of the professional. Experienced, professional negotiators, in the SUNY experience, supported that essential condition at the table in which personal sentiments and educational convictions remained dormant and a careful calculation of possibilities for give and take were accentuated. Yet it did not preclude the intrusion during the latter months of a more informal relationship between the members of the two teams. The mandated conference between administrators and SPA; the check on the accountability of the chancellor through SPA's access to the state's political leadership; the check on the accountability of local presidents through the conferences with the chancellor; and the restraints on everyone brought about by the reality of the bargaining table cannot but have major impact over the years. One immediate possibility is a move within SUNY toward centralization of most personnel-related endeavors and away from much campus autonomy in these matters. Equally likely, however, is an ordering of administrative procedures generally so that no one will be vulnerable on procedural grounds. These in themselves may formalize rapidly administrator-staff relationships and supplant much of the informality which some cherish.

That the entire process is demanding of time, energy, and dollars is readily apparent. Whether the regularization and increased predictability or efficiency to be gained warrants the cost will continue to be debated. Faculty governance has always been demanding where significant. Whether the employee organization will attract the same kind of continuing commitment from strong academicians that some AAUP chapters and many university senates have known remains to be seen. As yet SPA has not gained this commitment from other than the few who have sought or responded to requests to serve leadership roles at the campus or statewide level.

The complexity of the task of collective bargaining in the SUNY experience, a condition which continues to mount within both parties to the negotiation, likewise accentuates the need for skilled professionals who are well-informed as to their legal options and much aware of the importance of precedents. This is most clearly demonstrated in defining and administering the grievance process, which has created significant differences within the SUNY administration and the SPA organization. SPA members and administrative officers in the central headquarters and at each campus have been forced to make major commitments of time, thought, and personnel to the organization of the comprehensive grievance process, something for which most campuses are ill-prepared. At one university center the president, with the support of the local SPA leadership, instituted a grievance procedure which functioned collegially through the faculty senate and a newly formed parallel body for the NTPs. Until now the procedure has functioned in a satisfactory manner, but both the SUNY central administration and the state executive board of SPA have questioned the validity of soliciting peer judgments in what they feel to be a hierarchical process of review and decision.

Whether a permanent and predictable relationship will

emerge between faculty and administration that is significantly different from the often praised collegiality sought in the past remains to be seen.

Equally of interest is the contemplation of the effect of collective bargaining upon other forms of faculty governance. Some within the SUNY senate fear its gradual demise because it no longer will be significant in the grievance process. At the local level, however, there are instances of support by SPA for the established governance systems and efforts at clear delineation of powers and provinces.

For the present one hallowed tradition of most strong universities endures, namely, that of reward for merit. It is premature now to draw any final conclusion until an assessment can be made of local morale and the statewide impact upon SPA of the 1972 effort to reward for merit. As noted before, the last economic package did include provision for such increases and this provision has been implemented.

One major concern to some is the apparent bypassing of the SUNY board of trustees in the negotiations process. If this signals a significant decline in the board's power, it may reduce the attractiveness to persons of influence of board membership and thus reduce the board's capacity to serve as a buffer between university personnel and undue external influence—one of its most important functions. Possibly the bargaining association will provide a more suitable and adequate organization for this purpose.

It is rumored within SUNY that a former administrator stated that in New York the chancellor should be on the same side of the table as the faculty. The statutory nature of SUNY and the stipulations of the Taylor Law provide the executive and the legislative branches of state government with a kind of detailed policy and administrative control over SUNY that severely limits it from functioning with the autonomy major universities usually seek. On the other hand, statesmanship on both sides of the table may lead to the development of a force for autonomy which could exceed that which SUNY has known. Autonomy based upon the sanctions of a contract may ultimately prove superior to that based upon tradition alone. The exacerbation of stress and strain upon all of higher education during the early 1970s is readily apparent. We can at least hope that the mission of the university may now be given strength and new legislative interpretation through intelligent leadership from its employee organization, a task its forerunners were largely incapable of assuming.

8

State College:
Central Michigan

Neil S. Bucklew

For our second case study we turned to another public institution, Central Michigan University, which has the distinction of being the first four-year campus with a collective bargaining contract and which presently is operating under its second contract. In contrast with the State University of New York this is a single campus, but like the latter it has emerged from a period of very rapid growth and significant changes in function.

This case illustrates clearly the differences between a single-campus and multicampus organizational and bargaining endeavor. It also is an illustration of the tactics and procedures within the administration and the faculty association as their adversary rela-

*tionship matured. Both sides entered the second round of negotia-
tions with a substantially different preparation and information
base. The administration attempted a more aggressive stand, and
the faculty stand was drawn more from campus models than from
other educational settings.*

*Finally, in this instance there were primarily positive out-
comes in the sense that faculty participation has become more consistent, traditional faculty decision-making endeavors do continue,
and both faculty and administration are more effective in personnel
procedures. One may also observe that the faculty association has
had to adjust its internal organizational processes, organizational
relationship to the state association, and efforts to communicate
with the faculty as a whole. Thus the chapter should be helpful in
anticipating the normal growing pains and likely outcomes of the
negotiations process. (In this chapter the use of the term* university
*to designate the administration as opposed to the faculty is based on
the formal terminology used during the negotiations at Central
Michigan. In other chapters, faculty and administration are referred to as such. In certain instances the terms* employees *and*
management *are used.)*

*The chapter has been written by Neil S. Bucklew, who
represents the administration of the Central Michigan University
campus on matters related to collective bargaining with the professional staff. He holds a PhD in industrial relations, was active at
the University of Wisconsin in one of the first campus bargaining
endeavors—that of the graduate assistants at that campus—and has
made a career of personnel work in higher education.*

E. D. D. and R. S. F.

Central Michigan University is a multipurpose state institution
offering undergraduate and graduate study in professional, pre-
professional, and arts and science programs. It was founded in 1892
and achieved status as a university in 1959. It includes the following
schools or colleges, most of which offer both graduate and undergraduate degree programs: arts and science; education; business
administration; fine and applied arts; health, physical education,
and recreation; off-campus education; and an institute for per-

sonal and career development. The student body numbers approximately fifteen thousand and the full- and part-time faculty total is about seven hundred. The university is governed by a board of trustees of eight members appointed by the governor with the confirmation of the state senate.

Central Michigan University is located in a state with an extensive history of formalized collective bargaining. Important and significant milestones in the development of private sector labor history have occurred in Michigan. Among the best-known has been the development of industrial unionism in the automobile industry in the late 1930s and early 1940s. In education, Michigan, along with New York, has been the location of the earliest and most extensive experiences in public school negotiations.

Collective bargaining in higher education has its roots in the community college system of the state. By 1972 all but two of the community colleges in the public higher education system were unionized. Central Michigan University, in 1969, became the first single-campus, four-year institution of higher education to enter into a collective bargaining agreement with its faculty. At that time the only existing collective bargaining agreement in an institution of higher education involved the City University of New York (CUNY). The first contract at Central Michigan University covered the academic year 1970–1971, and a second agreement reached upon termination of the first covers 1971–1974. Both of these are reviewed in the analysis which follows.

The reasons for the development of a collective bargaining unit on the Central Michigan University campus are numerous and diverse, but the general milieu of unionization in the state of Michigan was clearly a significant influence. Another factor was the existence of a state statute which provided a mechanism for the determination of this issue. Research has illustrated that the existence of a legal structure for the determination of collective bargaining interest on the part of employees is the single most consistent predictor of the presence of formal collective bargaining relationships (Bucklew, 1971, p. 61). (See the discussion of enabling legislation in Chapter One.)

A recounting of the determinants of unionization by the

faculty at Central Michigan University is descriptive of that particular university, of course, but it also may be indicative of similar developments at other institutions. Some of the causes will be particularly applicable to emerging universities, many of which have an historical development pattern similar to Central Michigan University.

The background for unionization at the university is best understood in the context of its development during the 1960s, when it was undergoing changes in both function and purpose. Central Michigan University was an institution in transition—from an organization primarily concerned with teacher education to a regional university offering a general education at undergraduate and graduate levels. The university concomitantly increased in size and complexity. Its student body expanded from approximately five thousand to more than fourteen thousand. Moreover, the makeup of the student body changed, with an increasing proportion coming from metropolitan suburban areas of the state.

Another significant change was the nature of the faculty, which approximately tripled in size. Its profile showed a higher level of academic preparation; a wider range of disciplines and academic interests; a more youthful pattern when measured by both chronological age and years of service at the university; and a higher proportion of faculty at the instructor and assistant professor ranks.

At the end of the 1960s a totally new administration came into power within the space of two years. It was headed by a president who had been an executive officer at the University of California at Berkeley. By 1970 ten new individuals filled the positions of the executive council of the university. Only one had served in an administrative post at the university prior to the appointment of the new president and only one other had been a member of the faculty prior to this time. Two factors largely accounted for this rapid and significant change: three members of the previous administration, including the president, retired. A number of major or executive administrative positions in the university were expanded. Under the new administration, four new positions were instituted. The remaining vacancies occurred due to a death, in one instance, and normal relocations.

Another factor inherent in this changing environment was a change in style associated with the new administration. Many historical relationships were no longer honored or continued, and new ones were developed. For every faculty member who found support and encouragement in the new administration, another faculty member felt threatened and uneasy by the lack of continuity.

An example of this new administrative posture involved the recruitment of minority group students. A program was implemented just prior to the start of the academic year with the goal of recruiting a specified number of minority group students. For many faculty members this program represented a welcome innovation for a campus largely unrepresentative of minority students. For other faculty members, however, it loomed as a form of double standards. The short timetable used to implement the new program had not permitted a thorough discussion of such concerns. The new administration, in fact, was viewed by a large number of faculty as student-oriented. For some faculty this orientation was interpreted at times as "student interest before faculty interest."

The rapid growth and change in character had an unsettling effect for some faculty members and represented factors accounting for faculty interest in unionization. Also, some faculty members wanted to develop forms for faculty involvement in the governance of the university. The last half of the 1960s had witnessed the development of a University Senate. Pressure from the faculty then eventually led to the formation of an Academic Senate for the university. The new faculty also influenced the decision for collective bargaining. Many of the members were young but fully credentialed and often frustrated with the traditional senior peer review structure of the departments. This frustration was a specific manifestation of a general distrust of authority and established patterns of decision-making. These new individuals were involvement-oriented and demanded immediate recognition for their academic activities. This dynamic and pressing constituency was countered by the existing structure of senior faculty members who were reluctant to change the existing structure. For paradoxical reasons members of each group saw collective bargaining as a way of either changing or maintaining the status quo according to their particular need and philosophy.

Undoubtedly other reasons accounted for the decision to choose collective bargaining, but those noted above were the most important.

Organizational Campaign

The organizational campaign for the unionization of the faculty began in the spring of 1969. Formal petitions were circulated by the campus local of the Michigan Association of Higher Education (MAHE), an affiliate of the Michigan Education Association (MEA) and the National Education Association (NEA), to determine the interest in a collective bargaining relationship between the faculty and the university (the term "university," used in the formal negotiations, is used here to mean the administration). Individuals were urged to sign the petition no matter what their actual position would be if an election were held. The completed petitions with the necessary percentage of signatures were filed that same spring with the Michigan Employment Relations Commission (MERC) which scheduled an election for the following September.

The petition filed by the local chapter of the MAHE included a bargaining unit description that covered all academic positions filled by individuals with faculty rank, as well as counselors, librarians, and coaches. It did not include graduate assistants, administrators, support staff, or other professional or nonteaching staff. Deans and major academic officers were excluded, but department chairmen were included.

A hearing was scheduled by the MERC to determine the position of the parties concerning the petition and the bargaining unit description. The university decided not to challenge the unit described, although it was concerned about the inclusion of department chairmen, because the administrative leaders wanted to proceed with the vote and resolve the question of faculty interest in unionization. Also, the university felt that the inclusion at this time of staff members such as department chairmen would tend to encourage a no vote.

The American Association of University Professors (AAUP) also evidenced an interest in the upcoming election. The local chapter previously had maintained an informal posture of no interest in becoming a collective bargaining agent. This change reflected the shift in the national position of the AAUP at that time.

The local chapter of the MAHE launched an active campaign including provisions for a number of speakers from outside Central Michigan University to give opinions on collective bargaining issues and the collective bargaining process. A series of letters were sent to faculty members describing the goals to be pursued and obtained through collective bargaining. A major thrust of the MAHE campaign was that the union would be interested in economic matters and not academic policies—a vote for the union would not represent a vote against the continued role of the Academic Senate in the area of academic policies.

The basic posture assumed by the administration during the campaign was one of guarded neutrality. This was heightened by faculty reactions to comments by the president at the first faculty meeting which were intended to be neutral, but were perceived by some faculty members as antiunion. The general attitude among many members of the administration and faculty was that the proposition for collective bargaining would not be accepted by the faculty.

More than 80 percent of the eligible faculty voted in the election. The local chapter of the MAHE was chosen in September 1969 as the exclusive bargaining agent for the faculty by a vote of 239 to 221.

Preparation for Bargaining

At this stage the administrators reluctantly recognized and accepted the fact that they must prepare for formal negotiations and a new relationship with the faculty. They began a search for information—information that was simply lacking in the experiences of other institutions of higher education. A series of issues and concerns slowly emerged which ranged from bargaining procedures and techniques to some of the broadest policy considerations yet to be faced by the new leadership.

One general conclusion was that professional assistance must be obtained. An attorney was available who was experienced in general labor relations, negotiations, and public sector bargaining, and he was familiar with the university and its operations, having represented the university as legal counsel and played an active role in the university's labor relations program in the staff employee area.

Prior to the assignment of a spokesman for the negotiations the university had proceeded with the establishment of a bargaining team, which after much deliberation included the five academic deans as the core members. This decision was contrary to predictions that the use of deans would affect adversely their capacity to function in roles other than bargaining. However, the university judged that this assignment would serve as a learning experience for them and would assure a more sensitive and realistic treatment of issues by the university bargaining team. The deans were supplemented by administrative officials who had budget and personnel expertise. The attorney was to coordinate and speak for the administration team. In turn the team was to receive general policy guidance from the executive council of the university and, more specifically, from the provost (vice-president of academic affairs) and the president.

By January 1970 the university team was involved in extensive preparation for negotiations. The program included attendance at a national conference sponsored by a private consulting service which dealt specifically with collective bargaining in higher education. The emphasis in this type of conference historically had been on community college negotiations, but the staff of the conference were anxious and willing to work with representatives from the university. The conference provided an introduction to the process and procedures of collective bargaining and included simulated negotiations as well. In addition, the university sponsored several on-campus meetings where invited participants and advisors from other universities were asked to discuss collective bargaining issues with the university team.

Extensive consideration was also given of the issues anticipated in the upcoming negotiations. Team members gave nearly their full time for two months in an extensive analysis of all the potential issues that could be identified as possible bargaining concerns. The purpose of this preparation was to develop a positive program for accomplishing the goals of the university in collective bargaining. The team determined that a purely defensive or reaction-oriented model would not be productive.

Even more basic was the development of a policy regarding collective bargaining on the campus. The team concluded that the collective bargaining activity and resulting agreement should deal primarily with matters of wages and fringe benefits and directly related conditions of employment. The university intended to maintain, separate from the collective bargaining process and resulting agreement, the traditional system of faculty personnel decisions (appointment, reappointment, tenure, promotion, etc.), curriculum development, and other academic processes.

The local chapter of the MAHE was simultaneously involved in preparations. The district (a designation for the faculty association in the first contract) recognized that it represented only a minority of the faculty members and that it had to organize a structure designed to assure faculty input on bargaining postures and demands. As a result, the faculty bargaining team was composed of members from the actual bargaining unit—none of the members were from outside the faculty.

The district bargaining team devoted a great deal of time and effort to develop their proposal. The state office of the MEA provided consultative services on both the process of contract negotiations and the bargaining issues. In addition, the team set up a structure for identifying the needs and desires of bargaining unit members; the executive board of the district included elected representatives from each of the schools who were responsible for soliciting such information from faculty members in their respective areas. These matters were then analyzed for inclusion in the original bargaining proposals.

In February 1970 the district presented its contract proposal. These original demands were based primarily on a pattern contract provided by the MEA with some specific campus issues added. The use of a model contract (designed for public school and community college situations) resulted in provisions which lacked pertinence to the situation at Central Michigan University. Hepler (1970) describes the original demands in the faculty proposal: "It detailed financial matters, spelled out procedures for academic departments in relationship to department chairmen, listed concepts about promotion, and made statements pertaining to other matters of personnel. It was clear that if the MAHE contract were adopted, the district would control financial policies for the staff as well as many other facets of personnel policy."

With the delivery of the demands of the district it became clear that the parties were to begin bargaining from distinctly different postures as to the basic role of collective bargaining.

Negotiations and First Contract

Formal negotiations began on February 13, 1970. The teams quickly moved to an intensive bargaining schedule which included Saturday and Sunday as well as many night meetings.

The overall bargaining process was fairly simple in pattern. The university took the initiative by asking to explore in some depth the original demands from the district. The exploration was extensive and thorough. The approach of the university was that after a thorough discussion of the issues underlying the specific demands the university would prepare a complete counterproposal to the original contract proposal of the district. The exploration sessions consumed a majority of the time spent at the bargaining table prior to agreement. This approach proved frustrating for the district bargaining team, and charges of stalling were evident. Finally, the university prepared and presented a counterproposal. The give and take of the exploratory sessions had set the stage for acceptance of many of the concepts in the university proposal. A general agreement began to develop. Pressure for a settlement was introduced by an offer from the university to implement the salary aspect of the contract early if it could be ratified immediately. In the early morning on March 18, 1970, a tentative agreement was reached. A ratification vote was scheduled for March 23.

The faculty of Central Michigan University approved the new collective bargaining agreement by a vote of 369 to 82. The ratification vote stood in distinct contrast to the vote for collective bargaining just six months previously.

The basic provisions of this first one-year contract related to wages and fringe benefits. The contract largely reflected the posture previously adopted by the university regarding the description of the appropriate role and parameters of collective bargaining. Hepler (1970) notes that "there is no escaping the fact that in the contract, which the MAHE team kept referring to as a 'professional contract,' cold cash was its most important commodity."

Administration of Contract

Prior to the first negotiating session the university decided to create an office to be responsible for collective bargaining and faculty relations. The new office was established as part of the academic affairs division of the university with responsibilities covering faculty personnel matters and including responsibility for general academic administration. Collective bargaining and contract administration were to represent a major focus of the activities in the new office. The director of the new office was designated the vice-provost for administration. An individual was appointed to this position whose background included a doctorate in industrial relations and previous experience in university administration, including employment relations and labor relations.

Three general mechanisms were developed for contract administration. The first was an extensive committee structure provided for in the contract. Committees to deal with wages and fringe benefits included membership of equal proportion from the university and from the district. Committees to deal with broader subjects included membership from other groups such as the Academic Senate or the Student Senate. Separate committees were established to consider salaries, fringe benefits, teaching loads, sabbatical leaves, tuition refund program, and office space and equipment. Each committee was provided with a specific charge and had the responsibility to make studies and give recommendations to some designated group or groups. The committees did not have decision-making powers. In addition to the general contractual committees, a few with more narrow responsibilities were formed. They included a sick-leave committee, a committee for the distribution of professional awards, and a committee for selection of a distinguished visiting professor.

The parties agreed that the vice-provost for administration

and the president of the district would serve as members on all committees. These appointments encouraged coordination and permitted sharing of information among the committees. The committees, for example, cooperated in a joint survey of other institutions. The parties asked that the committees provide a summary status of their deliberations by January 1, 1971 so that an information base would be available for future negotiations.

The effectiveness of the various committees differed. The Teaching Load Committee, established under the original contract, was continued under the second contract and retained the same basic membership. It developed a sophisticated method of workload analysis and distribution which was implemented on a trial basis during the 1971–1972 academic year. As a result of that experiment the committee revised the system for the 1972–1973 year, and it is once again being used as the basis for analysis of teaching load. The committee has sustained a long-term effort without any subsequent direction from the collective bargaining parties other than a letter of agreement extending its charge.

The Salary Committee adopted a completely different pattern of operation. It carried out an extensive survey within the faculty to determine response to the salary settlement and methodology used under the first contract. It also prepared a report based on external surveys. In addition, the committee identified a series of alternative methods of faculty compensation for the consideration of the parties during upcoming negotiations. It also developed a computer program designed to cost out the various methods of compensation. This program was made available to both bargaining teams so that subsequent negotiations would be assured of a common basis of analysis of salary demands. In essence the Salary Committee's approach was to provide a sound factual basis for subsequent negotiations. The material and system developed were used extensively in bargaining.

These two examples illustrate the range of approaches adopted by the committees. In some cases the committees served as subcommittees in preparation for negotiations. In other cases they assumed a quasiadministrative and continuing role.

The second structured method of contract administration was the Special Conference clause in the contract, which provided for meetings to consider important matters to be arranged at the request of either party. The arrangements were to include a specific agenda to which the meeting would be limited. In operation each party normally selects two to four individuals to attend such meetings; the district has appointed bargaining unit members and the university has appointed administrators. Any agreements reached by the parties concerning a particular issue may be reduced to writing and if so serve as a precedent for future similar issues. It should be noted, however, that "special conferences shall not be used as a substitute for negotiation of agreements between the district and the university" (Central Michigan University, 1971, p. 7).

The intent of the Special Conference provision was to provide the parties with a method of considering important issues as they might appear rather than assuming that such matters could only be considered at the time of formal negotiations. While such discussions are not a substitute for bargaining, they recognize a commitment by the parties to meet and discuss and, if an agreement can be reached on any items, to use that agreement as a precedent where appropriate. Special conferences under the first agreement provided clarification on such matters as the appropriate amount of compensation to be received upon obtaining a doctorate or a promotion. Policies on these matters had been in effect for some time, but it was felt that the parties would be helped if the clarifications were in writing and made available to all faculty members. Special conferences have been called as a formal manner of communicating concern. For example, a conference was held to discuss an administration proposal for revision of the tenure policy to which the district expressed objections. The district also asked for a special conference to communicate its concerns about some aspects of the planning process instituted by the academic affairs division of the university. Some special conferences have resulted in written statements of agreement while others have served only as formal communication devices.

Study committees and special conferences served to relieve the adversarial, crisis nature of negotiations. They created a formal and recognized channel for the consideration of issues of concern at the time they arise. In traditional bargaining relationships many issues take the form of grievances or even frustrated thrashing at a system which is designed to resolve major differences only at the time of negotiations. The Central Michigan University experience indicated that if the parties develop a tradition within which issues can be considered during the life of an agreement, a more healthy climate is produced for the negotiation of a new agreement. Such a tradition means that many issues do not have to be contractualized because mechanisms are available for resolution of difficulties if they should arise.

In addition to the above two formal methods for contract administration an invaluable system developed of regular weekly meetings between the vice-provost for administration and the president of the Faculty Association (the term "Faculty Association" was substituted for "district" prior to negotiations for the second contract). These informal discussions have permitted representatives of both parties to share information on a wide range of matters. The vice-provost for administration reports on appropriate agenda matters considered that week by the Academic Council (Dean's Council) and the Executive Council (President's Council), both of which include him as a member. The president of the Faculty Association presents matters of concern to the association and its individual members. The weekly sessions are expanded to include other individuals when either party believes that would be helpful.

Second Contract

The university appointed a slightly different team for the second negotiations. The coordination and spokesman duties were assumed by the vice-provost for administration. The team was smaller and included two academic deans and the university librarian, controller, and attorney. The attorney was the same person who had served as coordinator and spokesman for the first negotiations and who had since become the university counsel.

The university developed a more sophisticated and formalized pattern of preparation for negotiations than it had previously. The bargaining team developed a series of analyses of university positions. These were discussed and shared with each dean and with others who had administrative concerns. Necessary policy questions were reviewed first by the Dean's Council and when necessary by the President's Council. Selected issues were given the special attention of the board of trustees. The entire process was conducted by the vice-provost for administration.

The university bargaining team accepted as an operating premise that preparations for negotiations would be complete only when all possible subjects that might appear at the bargaining table had been previously analyzed. The goal of the team was to clarify all necessary policy questions and develop parameters prior to actual negotiations. It assumed a positive stance in relation to negotiations, developing a series of proposed revisions and changes in the first contract which it believed to be important for the upcoming negotiations.

The faculty bargaining agent officially changed its name to the Central Michigan University Faculty Association on the basis that this was a more useful and appropriate designation than district. The certified agent was a campus group, and the MAHE was not a direct party; therefore, the new name was consistent with the legal description of the bargaining agent. (The Faculty Association has maintained its affiliation with the MAHE but has no legal obligation to continue to do so.)

The Faculty Association maintained its approach of the previous year. All members of the bargaining team were faculty members from within the unit. The association held a series of meetings to invite input from individual faculty members concerning proposed changes in the contract. It also sponsored a survey of the faculty to determine the response to the various provisions of the first contract.

The association, however, did introduce several new methods of communicating with its constituency concerning the negotiations, including a newsletter, the *Courier*. This newsletter was used to describe and gain support for the association point of view on specific bargaining topics. A second major effort to improve communication was introduced when a draft of the proposed contract was placed on review for bargaining unit members. A room in the University Center was reserved and a schedule for review established. Association bargaining team members were present to discuss the proposals and register responses and comments. The information obtained was used by the bargaining team in preparing its initial proposal.

The Faculty Association team submitted its initial proposal in February 1971 and negotiations began on March 1. The demands were extensive in scope and were not taken from a model contract as were many in the first round of negotiations. On the whole the negotiations followed the same general format as previously. An extended period of analysis and discussion concerning the initial Faculty Association proposal was followed by a major counterproposal by the university team.

Unlike the first negotiations the counterproposal did not form the basis for an agreement. The parties decided to divide the issues into three basic areas and to consider them one at a time: one area included the economic matters; the others were personnel-related and nonpersonnel issues. The latter two areas were discussed first, and a tentative agreement was reached contingent upon an appropriate economic settlement.

Throughout the second negotiations the university maintained that the collective bargaining agreement should be limited basically to wages, fringe benefits, and directly related subject areas. It also sought a contract which would extend over several years.

The Faculty Association maintained its support of a more detailed contract. This position eventually centered on provision for extended grievance procedures and a clause dealing with the decision-making process within academic departments.

Tentative agreement was reached by the parties on April 5, 1971 in the form of a three-year contract proposal. Two major deviations from the first contract emerged. One was the addition of a departmental procedure clause which outlined a system to assure the democratic participation of faculty members within an academic unit in the development of a constitution or procedures for decision-making within that unit. The other was a new clause which gave the Faculty Association a role in the general university appeal procedure. For matters of general faculty concern and not as a review process for questions of contract interpretation, a faculty member was given the option of selecting a Faculty Association or an Academic Senate grievance committee as a first stage. Previously this initial appeal was limited to the senate group. Then, as the second step, with the approval of either committee, according to the new contract a hearing committee could be constituted. Members of this group were to be selected at random by the executive board of the senate. From then on, the traditional procedure serves. This involves the use of a special hearing committee to review the case and report to the president of the university and a final appeal opportunity by either party to the board of trustees.

Questions related to the interpretation of the contract were to be processed through a procedure which follows the traditional model of administrative review steps. The final step is a tripartite committee which, in effect, renders an advisory arbitration opinion.

A ratification election held on April 21, 1971 failed to approve the agreement by a vote of 222 to 173. Several factors accounted for this vote: the faculty bargaining team had not maintained a close relationship to the executive board members of the Faculty Association who were unaware of the substance of the new settlement; the elected leadership of the Faculty Association publicly stated its unwillingness to support the proposed settlement; the bargaining team accepted unenthusiastically the responsibility to obtain a favorable vote; and an agreement to last three years without any reopener clause was strongly opposed by the faculty.

Following the vote the parties returned to the bargaining table to develop an alternative agreement for consideration prior to the close of the academic year. A clause was introduced which provided that a salary reopener was possible if the consumer price index had changed by 15 percent by February 1973. Other minor changes also were included in the revised agreement, which was presented to the faculty on May 12 and passed by a vote of 248 to 88. Thus, the university and the Faculty Association entered into the first multiyear contract at a single-campus, four-year institution of higher education. This also represented the first instance of a second contract in a four-year institution.

Conclusions and Implications

The experience at Central Michigan University has illustrated that the process of collective bargaining represents a viable decision-making system for certain issues. It provides a logical structure for the consideration of wages and fringe benefits, for example. The agreements reached concerning these matters have an acceptance level that is quite high. However, experience does support the concern that bargaining tends to produce a contractualized approach to issues that may benefit from greater flexibility and openness to contingencies. An example of a contract provision that both parties have come to recognize as over-structured or legalistic is a departmental procedures clause covering departmental governance which led to procedures often incomplete and different from those envisioned.

It was noted above that the Teaching Load Committee has provided an ongoing and responsive series of experimental systems for the analysis of faculty teaching loads. The Faculty Association, however, had proposed initially to contractualize an earlier version of one of these systems. If that system had been contractualized, it is quite unlikely that the revised teaching load structure would have been developed.

The presence of a collective bargaining model at Central Michigan University to date has not led to the demise of the traditional academic decision-making systems. The experience has illustrated that the two can coexist. To date, disputes over areas of responsibilities have been adequately resolved, although overlap and pressures do exist. It is quite plausible that, given the Central Michigan University experience, these areas of responsibility may evolve a tradition of their own and the two systems will not require mutually exclusive environments. Some experience suggests that each system functions in an improved manner as a result of the delineation of areas of responsibility. For example, the Academic Senate can direct its energies to the academic program and policies of the university without having to maintain structures and use energy directed at fiscal and salary issues. The evidence is not conclusive but would appear at least to draw into question the supposition by many that the advent of collective bargaining on the campus represents the end of traditional academic decision-making systems.

Another impact of the bargaining process has been the formation and development of the Faculty Association which many faculty members have come to view as their representative for certain issues. In fact, many faculty members who have not supported the concept of a union and who have not joined the association view it as the appropriate spokesman for their economic issues and interest. The active membership has grown to approximately two hundred members.

Collective bargaining has also been a factor in the development of an expanded role perception by the university administrators. It is inadequate to refer to this as management sensitivity. The very act of being required to negotiate to agreement has meant that the university has had to structure itself for thorough review of policies and practices. Participation in formal negotiations has forced administrators to analyze carefully and clarify their positions on matters which previously had not been faced up to. The fiscal impact of negotiations has made clear the necessity of a more sophisticated and responsible approach to the financial and program priorities of the university.

The faculty and administration of the university have concluded three years of a relationship new to university campuses. The results lead to guarded optimism. Traditional structures of governance and professional involvement by faculty have not disappeared; in fact, they have expanded. This may not have been caused by the presence of collective bargaining—but collective bargaining has not discouraged this development. The parties have learned that many issues are well-handled in the context of this new decision-making system. Faculty members have tended to develop the confidence and expectation that the bargaining agent will represent their interests well. The university administration has found that the process has brought clarity and definition to many fiscal and personnel issues. Although many questions remain unanswered and several basic fears remain, the experience has been productive.

9

Private University: St. John's

Frederick E. Hueppe

The third case study was chosen because of the earlier history of strife at St. John's University and the fact that the American Association of University Professors played an active role in resolving many of the issues which surfaced during the mid-1960s. Ultimately the local chapter of the American Association of University Professors in combination with a Faculty Association became the bargaining agent. This case presents the opportunity to examine the differences in style and content of an American Association of University Professors local chapter as contrasted with our two other models, which are representative of the National Education Association and state teachers association experiences.

175

As reported in this chapter there were major differences in the tone and substance of the negotiations process. The reader may wish to reflect upon the extent to which these emerged from a private campus setting as contrasted with a public one, the local desire not to reopen old wounds, or other factors.

It is interesting also to compare the relative importance of economic demands as opposed to those related to governance. Parallel to this contrast is the extent to which the polarization of earlier years colored the bargaining process. Finally, this chapter suggests precedents for a private campus of considerable size (since St. John's enrolls more than 13,000 students and employs 700 faculty members), and it leads to some hypotheses regarding the possible impact of the American Association of University Professors on the bargaining process.

Frederick E. Hueppe hold his doctorate in Germanic languages and literature. He has been president of the St. John's chapter of the American Association of University Professors since 1969 and currently is president of the New York State Conference of that organization. He has spoken widely on collective bargaining in higher education as well as being active in his discipline.

E. D. D. and R. S. F.

St. John's University is a private institution of higher learning under the sponsorship of the priests of the Congregation of the Mission, otherwise known as Vincentians. Founded in 1870, the university consists of the following schools or colleges, most of which offer both graduate and undergraduate degree programs: St. John's College of Liberal Arts and Sciences, School of Education, College of Business Administration, School of Law, College of Pharmacy and Allied Health Professions, St. Vincent's College, and St. John's University at Staten Island. The board of trustees, the administration, and the faculty are predominately lay. The student body numbers approximately 13,500 per year and the faculty, full and part time, about 700.

In 1966, after the board of trustees had summarily dismissed twenty-one faculty members without specific charges and hearings, the American Association of University Professors (AAUP) imposed a censure upon the administration in a case that gained national attention ("Academic Freedom and Tenure," 1966). In listing the names of censured administrations that year, the AAUP for the first time in its history admonished members not to accept appointments at St. John's University "owing to the extraordinary seriousness of the violation of academic freedom and tenure." Finally, in January 1966 a number of irate faculty members, some of whom had joined an industrial type of teachers' union, expressed their dissatisfaction with the administration by going out on strike, an action considered without precedent in private higher education.

Since 1966, through the persistence of national officers and the campus chapter of AAUP and because the administration and faculty willingly effected changes that would result in the removal of censure and the creation of a fine academic institution, a series of in-depth reforms have been undertaken to guarantee academic freedom and due process and to establish a new and effective governance structure that would ensure faculty and student participation ("College and University Government," 1968; "Report of the Survey Subcommittee," 1971). In January 1968 the board of trustees officially endorsed the 1940 AAUP *Statement of Principles on Academic Freedom and Tenure* (American Association of University Professors, 1971, pp. 1–4). Then, in May 1969, at the urging of the St. John's chapter, the board formally adopted the AAUP *Statement on the Government of Colleges and Universities* (American Association of University Professors, 1971, pp. 33–37), thereby making the institution one of the earliest to issue such an endorsement.

Motivated by the passage in April 1969 of an amendment to the New York State Labor Relations Act permitting collective bargaining at private, nonprofit institutions, the St. John's chapter of the AAUP initiated a campus poll in the fall of the same year to determine faculty sentiment on the question. St. John's University subsequently became the first private educational institution to utilize the new labor provision. In doing so it set a pattern which had an influence on negotiations at other institutions, especially those at which the AAUP represented the faculty.

The response of the faculty at large to the AAUP poll exceeded all expectations. Almost 50 percent of the full-time faculty replied, indicating a genuine interest in entering formally into collective negotiations. Undoubtedly, a major factor in this decision was an earlier resolution of the University Senate excluding the financial concerns of the faculty from its purview. This action was due to the fact that the senate structure includes students and administrators as well as faculty members. In retrospect, other significant contributory factors included the faculty's desire for genuine participation in budgetary matters and definite grievance procedures, particularly in view of what many considered arbitrary actions by administrators. Furthermore, the faculty sought a secure voice in determining its own destiny in the wake of ever-increasing national retrenchment in almost all areas of higher education.

Determination of Bargaining Unit

In the collective bargaining campaign that followed the local AAUP chapter stressed the need for a contract which would recognize academic as well as economic interests of the faculty. It placed great emphasis upon the principle of shared authority and thus upon a reinforcing of faculty participation in the university governance structure. Such principles had wide appeal among faculty members, many of whom had labored long and hard to achieve reforms. Furthermore, a contract of this type offered the possibility of contributing to the eventual elimination of the censure of the AAUP.[1]

Some faculty members, largely in the senior ranks, opposed the AAUP chapter's bid for exclusive bargaining agent, chiefly because they regarded the imposition of censure either as unwarranted from the outset or as unduly harsh in longevity; the added admonishment not to accept appointment at St. John's University seemed to impugn the integrity of the faculty as much as to chastise the administration. In addition, some opponents found little or no precedent for the AAUP's involvement in collective bargaining or disagreed strongly with the local chapter's position that all members

---

[1] The censure was removed by Committee A of the National AAUP in January 1972, after the university administration offered adequate redress to the interested faculty members involved ("Report of Committee A," 1971; "Developments Relating to Censure," 1972).

of the sponsoring Vincentian order (comprising only 5 percent of the faculty) with regular faculty rank and credentials be included in the bargaining unit. These adversaries formed a competing organization called The Faculty Association and subsequently filed a petition for consent election with the New York State Labor Relations Board (NYSLRB).[2] The AAUP chapter, after formally collecting designation cards, similarly petitioned the NYSLRB in January 1970.

At the initial hearing to determine the composition of the bargaining unit all parties agreed to include all full-time and regular part-time members of the faculty,[3] including professional librarians. Department chairmen were implicitly included as faculty. Representatives of the AAUP chapter and the Faculty Association acceded to the request of the university administration and the faculty representative of the St. John's School of Law to exclude that school from the unit and to the insistence of the administration that all athletic personnel also be excluded. The Faculty Association raised no further objections concerning the inclusion of the Vincentian clergy. At this point a new element entered the proceedings. A representative of the United Federation of College Teachers (UFCT) was present as a disinterested party, having been properly notified of the forthcoming election but having previously indicated no interest in participating. The representative unexpectedly reversed his position and entered the UFCT into the race as a midnight intervenor, without the usual submission of designation cards. He challenged the inclusion of the Vincentians in the bargaining unit. Although the meeting had been concluded following agreement on the composition of the unit, the NYSLRB upheld the UFCT challenge and thereby established a challenge also to the acceptance of the Vincentian faculty member ballots in the forthcoming election.

The campaign that followed was heated and acrimonious. Both the UFCT and the Faculty Association attacked the AAUP. The

[2] The National Labor Relations Board (NLRB) first announced in July 1971 that it would assume jurisdiction over private colleges and universities with income of a million dollars or more.

[3] In the subsequent contract, part-time or adjunct faculty members were designated as those teaching a maximum of six semester hours of credit on the graduate or undergraduate level; this was later widened to include a maximum of any two courses per semester.

former stressed the AAUP's lack of experience in collective bargaining; the latter waged an emotional grass roots campaign emphasizing the AAUP affiliation with a national organization responsible for the censure of St. John's. The AAUP chapter stressed the advantages of association with a national professional organization long associated with academic freedom and tenure. The university administration issued no real campaign literature and remained detached throughout, apparently resigned to the inevitability of collective bargaining.

Two campus elections for exclusive bargaining agent ensued. The first, on February 25–26, 1970, was indecisive with no group winning a majority of the votes cast (AAUP, 175; Faculty Association, 153; UFCT, 90; no agent, 19). The UFCT then threw its support to the Faculty Association in opposition to the AAUP in the run-off election of March 23 and 24. Again the outcome was inconclusive (Faculty Association, 225; AAUP, 215; challenged ballots, 23). In an unprecedented move, although the UFCT had no longer been a party to the second election and against the will of the parties involved, NYSLRB continued the challenge of the Vincentian votes which now proved to be crucial to the outcome.

This situation created a serious dilemma. The academic year was drawing to an end and still no bargaining agent had been designated. The faculty began to grow restless and disenchanted in the face of further legal entanglement. Although the strong possibility existed that successful litigation leading to the counting of the challenged ballots would throw the election to the AAUP, serious reflection regarding the additional loss of time and the lack of privacy afforded the Vincentian votes led the AAUP chapter and the Faculty Association to a unique solution. By a vote of the membership of both groups a coalition was formed for the sole purpose of collective bargaining, provided AAUP policy would be closely followed throughout the bargaining process. To that end, the Faculty Association signed a *Memorandum of Understanding* (American Association of University Professors, 1971) with the AAUP chapter on April 17, 1970. In this document, the Faculty Association agreed to espouse such basic tenets of the profession as the 1940 and the 1966 AAUP statements, as well as the 1958 *Statement on Procedural Standards in Faculty Dismissal Proceedings* (American Association of University Professors, 1971). Further, both groups unquestionably accepted the inclusion of the Vincentian faculty within the bargaining unit. On April 22 the NYSLRB certified the AAUP-FA as a joint venture, thereby ruling out any necessity to adjudicate the Vincentian ballots.

Preparing for Negotiations

Analyzing the needs of faculty members and obtaining their specific requests comprised the first order of business for the joint venture. Because of the late start in collective negotiations and the nature of a joint certification, both groups were forced to abandon prior plans for formally elected faculty advisory committees in favor of a more immediate informational approach. Hearings were arranged for various faculty interest groups (tenured, nontenured, superannuated, etc.); department representatives were consulted to determine specific wants; and all faculty members were urged to submit suggestions in writing without delay.

A faculty bargaining team was established jointly. It consisted of six members, three from each faculty group, with one alternate apiece. Special consultants such as economic advisors were to be brought into the negotiations as required. Each faculty group had its own counsel. The members of the team were nominated by the Executive Board of each association based upon competence and service and were elected by the general membership; a serious effort was made to include representatives from most faculty ranks and various divisions of the university.

The administration bargaining team consisted of four members from the administration—the university treasurer, the assistant to the president and dean of academic development, the administrative vice-president and university secretary, and the assistant to the president for community affairs—plus two attorneys—the outside legal counsel to the university, who served as spokesman, and the resident or in-house legal counsel.

The first hurdle for the faculty bargaining team was to obtain from the administration data essential for drafting an intelligent proposal. When the requested material followed only sporadically, an immediate reaction was to impugn the administration's good faith. After consideration, however, the faculty team realized that the administration had simply not kept the sophisticated records necessary for collective bargaining and consequently required more time to prepare the data. Both faculty and administrators later remarked, only half humorously, that if it accomplished nothing else, collective bargaining would usher in an era of better management and more precise record-keeping.

Fifty faculty demands were finally submitted. These ran the gamut from academic concerns such as the faculty selection of deans to mundane items such as improved faculty dining and parking facilities. Because not all the requested budgetary data had been made available, the faculty team decided to dramatize its salary needs with a demand of 35 percent across-the-board for one year. (The team members had decided on an across-the-board percentage increase rather than a set salary scale due to a desire to raise all salaries. A more detailed and costly salary scale was put aside for subsequent contract negotiations.)

The proposal for the salary increase was presented subsequently by the faculty team along with a detailed economic analysis prepared by a faculty economist with extensive corporation experience. His analysis included such factors as the AAUP salary scales, the cost of living increase in the New York City area compared with other parts of the country as reflected in the consumer price index, and related materials. While the faculty bargainers freely admitted that salaries at St. John's had drastically improved in the recent past, they also asserted that these increases did not yet raise the university to the level of other institutions of comparative standing and size. The administration, although it expressed a desire to maintain competitive salaries, stressed the severe limitation on spending dictated by the university's heavy dependence upon student tuition. The faculty team emphasized in contrast the fact that increased tuition rates over a four-year period had been announced in anticipation of the negotiations and that additional funds for salaries would be available as a result.

Bargaining

The first negotiating sessions brought out a contrast in attitudes across the table which is probably not unusual in such proceedings. The faculty group was convinced of its position as an equal in the bargaining process and imbued with the AAUP concepts of collegiality and shared authority, but it encountered a somewhat aloof and condescending attitude from the administrative side. The administration's initial chief spokesman was a distinguished counsel supremely expert in the techniques of collective bargaining in industry but seemingly without a thorough understanding of the day-to-day nuances of academic life. In contrast, most of the remaining members of the administration team were academicians with long classroom experience and a knowledge of educational and faculty problems. Not until the labor counsel dropped out of the negotiations and the Administrative Vice-President presided for the administration did a more relaxed, collegial, and productive atmosphere prevail.

For the faculty negotiators the situation initially presented the possibility of serious difficulties. Members of the team were drawn from many academic disciplines, but none were professional negotiators. Furthermore, they came from two different organizations which had only recently passed through a period of occasionally acrid competition. The potential difficulty proved minor, however. The team was able to handle its affairs with unanimity and to present a solid professional attitude at the table. Much of this achievement resulted from the manner in which the two spokesmen, representing each of the faculty groups, handled themselves and alternated responsibility for presenting the faculty point of view. Other team members passed information to the spokesman by means of written notes. After a short time, the faculty representatives acted increasingly as an entity rather than as representatives of two groups.

The administrative team followed a similar protocol. In contrast to the faculty its members had served together in the course of their regular responsibilities and knew each other reasonably well. While a smaller group, they did bring to the table valuable insights reflecting a variety of managerial backgrounds. Financial decisions were clearly in the hands of the University Treasurer, a man with considerable high-level corporate experience. He demonstrated a dedication to the university and firm yet fair convictions which gained the respect of negotiators on both sides of the process.

One factor of major importance for the faculty side was the

services of the two counsels, who provided a most essential combination of legal expertise and academic experience. This was a positive element during negotiations and in drafting the agreement which ensued. Both counsels were professors of law at the university. In addition, the faculty team had the benefit of further legal assistance from the director of the regional office of the AAUP.

The bargaining process commenced in late April and lasted throughout the summer. While the administration had hoped to negotiate academic and economic issues concurrently, the faculty took the position that substantial agreement on the monetary package would be the prerequisite for dealing with academic matters in subcommittee.

At the outset, the administration was clearly surprised by the formidable document of faculty demands amounting to over fifty pages, and it soon rejected most of the proposals out-of-hand. The University Treasurer estimated the cost of the faculty demands at a staggering sum. This was vigorously challenged by the faculty team who again cited the lack of sufficient available data. To raise substantially the university's initial monetary offer of $1,350,000, or approximately 20 percent in total compensation over a three-year period, the faculty negotiators did gradually sacrifice what they considered significant demands which would have added to institutional costs. These included reduced class size, credit-hour teaching maxima, a four-day work week, and reduced total student work load. When the administration countered with insufficient financial increases, the faculty refused to consider more than a one-year contract. The AAUP-FA regarded a longer term as especially inadvisable for an initial contract. Ultimately, to achieve a two-year contract and its primary goal of institutional stability, the administration raised the monetary offer to approximately 22 percent over a two-year period. It did reject, however, minima in salary according to rank and maintained a coolness toward allocations for merit which it felt various faculty committees had abused in the past.

A crucial point was reached in mid-August when the administration presented a final compensation package which not only fell short of the minimal faculty demand (approximately 26 percent for total compensation) but actually amounted to a slight reduction in its own previous offer. Immediately, the AAUP-FA broke off negotiations, prepared a letter to the faculty-at-large, and threatened to seek the assistance of the New York State Mediation Service. Undoubtedly troubled by the prospects of a disgruntled faculty and an unfavorable press, the administration consulted the board of Trustees and revised its offer to meet more closely the faculty demand.

From that time on, the subcommittee on academic items met regularly. Concurrently negotiators reviewed the principal question outstanding in the monetary area which was final agreement upon specific categories in the allocation of funds. With regard to the financial package, the administration exhibited generally a spirit of cooperation and flexibility, chiefly refusing to consider an adjustment fund to correct salary inequities which it considered almost impossible to implement and dental and eyeglass plans which it considered too costly and undesirable in establishing precedents. In the ordering of priorities, the faculty negotiators ultimately sacrificed increased compensation for chairmen and reduced teaching loads for mentors of doctoral dissertations, the latter because of the failure to agree upon a procedure for implementation. In a final trade-off for administrative concessions on the grievance machinery, the faculty team agreed to a no strike—no lockout clause which had been assiduously sought by the administration.

In the academic area, the faculty team realized basically all of its demands. This accomplishment was attributable in no small measure to the desire of the administrators to conform as far as possible to AAUP policy, with an unmistakable view to the ultimate removal of censure. The subcommittee on items of shared authority consisted of at least one negotiator from each side. It worked out with efficiency and cordiality the details of agreement related to the faculty demands for later submission to the full complement of bargainers at plenary sessions. A major item undertaken by this subcommittee was the restructuring of various college personnel committees as well as of the higher University Personnel Committee in order to ensure smoother, more equitable procedures and peer judgment. A Legal Subcommittee consisting of the three counsels concurrently hammered out the specifics of the grievance machinery and of other items requiring legal expertise.

Basic agreement was reached between the administrative and faculty negotiators on all major items, both financial and academic,

at the end of August 1970, barely one week before the commence-
ment of the fall semester. This necessitated the prompt drafting of
a lengthy letter by the faculty bargaining team to apprise colleagues
of the negotiated benefits. A faculty meeting was scheduled for early
September, at which time the bargaining team explained the contract provisions.

The faculty was pleased with the academic gains, notably
the provisions for faculty selection of deans, access to personnel files,
and formal grievance procedures. Some members were not content
with what they considered oversights in the monetary area. They
stressed the lack of provision for promotional increments, salary
inequities, and a save-harmless clause to protect existing compensation in the new pay rate for summer school which, while quite
favorable for the majority of faculty, inadvertently penalized the
lowest salary earners. At the request of the faculty team, both sides
returned to the bargaining table and the administration ultimately
accepted a faculty suggestion for a reallocation of money in several
categories to resolve these oversights.

In the last days of bargaining, the university released word
of the phasing-out of the Brooklyn campus and the acquisition of
an entire school, Notre Dame College of Staten Island, which would
merge with St. John's University. This announcement necessitated,
of course, a review of all the agreed upon provisions. The problem
was resolved with the insertion of a penultimate article into the
contract which constituted a mutual reopener clause applicable in
the future to any nonmonetary item affecting the Staten Island
campus. This reopener clause was never activated in the formal
sense, but the AAUP-FA did request and receive a briefing during the
following spring semester regarding the academic programs and
faculty working conditions at Notre Dame College of St. John's
University.

Agreement

A two-year contract covering the period from July 1, 1970
to June 5, 1972 finally emerged which contained excellent monetary
and academic provisions from the faculty point of view. In comparison with precollective bargaining settlements, the negotiated

financial package constituted an increase in total compensation of more than 25 percent. Besides a 21 percent across-the-board salary increase over two years for full-time faculty and a 10 percent increase for adjunct faculty (both amounts calculated upon the 1969–1970 salary base), the agreement established an adjustment fund with substantial minimum raises for each of the two years. This fund was designed particularly to alleviate the financial plight of younger faculty on the lower salary levels who had to cope with the high cost of living in the New York City area.

Fringe benefits included a sizable increase in the Teachers Insurance and Annuity Association and College Retirement Equities Fund (TIAA-CREF), culminating in a contribution of 5 percent by each faculty member and 10 percent by the university; an extended Blue Cross/Blue Shield coverage (completely underwritten by the university for the individual); major medical insurance to a $25,000 limit per individual; and group life insurance equal to the faculty member's annual contract salary in 1971–1972, with a minimum of $12,500.

In addition to research leaves which constituted a past practice and were based upon scholarly projects, sabbaticals awarded solely on the basis of seniority were introduced. The allocation of $25,000 for this provision was small but it set a precedent, and the reduction of this sum in the final contract to provide funds for such added categories as promotional increments and a summer rate adjustment was not considered detrimental.

A major breakthrough occurred with regard to summer compensation when the former flat rate of several years' standing was superseded by an on-going formula: one-thirty-sixth of the faculty member's annual contract salary per credit hour of summer teaching. This change raised considerably the summer income of the St. John's faculty and placed the university near the top in this category among institutions of comparative size in the surrounding area.

Of even greater and more lasting consequence, however, were provisions covering academic policies. Most noteworthy was the incorporation into the contract of the 1940 *Statement of Principles on Academic Freedom and Tenure* and the 1966 *Statement on Government of Colleges and Universities* (American Association of University Professors, 1971, pp. 1–4 and pp. 33–37), thus rendering them legal documents governing the university. Among other features, the 1940 statement ensured academic due process, while the 1966 statement gave to the faculty a "primary responsibility for such fundamental areas as curriculum, subject matter and methods of instruction, faculty status, and those aspects of student life which relate to the educational process" (American Association of University Professors, 1971, p. 36). In matters involving faculty status, peer judgment is guaranteed in the area of "appointments, reappointments, decisions not to reappoint, promotions, the granting of tenure, and dismissal." A faculty mandate thus gains immeasurable force: "The governing board and president should, on questions of faculty status, as in other matters where the faculty has primary responsibility, concur with the faculty judgment except for compelling reasons which should be stated in detail" (p. 36). In short, the 1966 statement laid the cornerstone of shared authority, which would require faculty consultation on all levels.

Thus, the faculty's judgment was to be heeded in the selection and appointment of deans. The agreement stipulated that whenever a vacancy occurred in the post of academic dean, a search committee composed of four tenured faculty members elected by the faculty of the school in question together with the chief academic officer of the university would submit to the president the names of no fewer than three candidates. If the president or the board of trustees should reject all the names submitted, reasons would have to be stated in writing and the committee would continue its search until a candidate acceptable to the president and the board of trustees was submitted.

Also, the faculty acquired an important voice in the reduction or elimination of academic programs and any concomitant reduction in faculty. The contract provided that if the administration sought at any time to abolish programs and consequently reduce the size of the faculty, it first had to consult the faculty in accordance with the 1966 statement. Once a financial exigency had been satisfactorily demonstrated, a definite order was to be followed in the reduction of faculty: first adjunct, then superannuated, then nontenured, and finally tenured members in the department affected. In all cases, the department personnel and budget committee had an initial voice in the process. The criteria for retention for the first three categories were to be worth to the department and the university and in the last category of tenured faculty a combination of seniority and worth to the department and the university. For tenured faculty, every effort had to be made to place the individual elsewhere within the university according to his academic competence. If this proved impossible, the tenured faculty member would be given preference in the order of seniority for reinstatement, should the program or position in question be reactivated during the life of the agreement.

Under the terms of the contract, department personnel and budget committees retained their existing structure and were granted extended power. No full-time faculty appointment could henceforth be made without the committee's approval. Furthermore, a school or college personnel committee would now be composed of elected faculty with the dean as chairman; the University Personnel Committee (its name changed to differentiate it from the former University Review Committee) would have an equal number of faculty and administrators with voting rights, whereas the former committee had consisted chiefly of administrators.

Most significantly, the agreement provided that all existing organizations within the university (the University Senate, faculty councils, departmental personnel and budget committees, etc.) or any other similar body composed in whole or in part of the faculty would continue to function as usual, provided that their actions did not repeal or modify the terms and conditions of the contract.

A related provision stated that nothing contained in the agreement would be construed to limit the freedom of the administration to recognize and deal with external educational associations, accrediting agencies, and professional organizations such as the national office of the AAUP, provided that such recognition or dealing would not repeal or modify the terms and conditions of the agreement. This article was inserted rather than a management rights clause which the administration had earnestly sought but to which the AAUP-FA could not accede, especially in light of the 1966 statement. The national AAUP was specifically mentioned because all parties acknowledged that its scope extended beyond collective bargaining to include such traditional functions as the investigatory role of Committee A into matters involving academic freedom and tenure.

Several other innovations won the special approbation of the faculty. First, faculty members gained access to their personnel files and were to be promptly notified of any material placed therein. Second, in accordance with recommended AAUP policy, the number of instructional preparations for different courses for each faculty member would not exceed three each semester, except that with his permission the number might be four, provided that there would not be more than a total of six preparations in any two successive semesters. Finally, the department chairman was obliged to consult each semester with the individual faculty members regarding their teaching schedule (the specific courses, course times, and campus location). The department personnel and budget committee then submitted the agreed-upon schedule to the dean for his approval. If the dean rejected any such recommendation, he was required to state his reasons in writing, and the department chairman, in conjunction with the personnel and budget committee, could submit further recommendations to the dean. Any reasonable change by the dean would be determining.

A major aspect of the contract was the detailed grievance procedure involving three possible steps: the department, school, or college level; the central or presidential level; and arbitration. The faculty member's right to grieve on his own was carefully preserved, but the AAUP-FA could be represented at any hearing and any adjustment of the grievance could not be inconsistent with the terms of the agreement. Grievances by or on behalf of a faculty member usually would be initiated in an informal way on the department level; grievances involving more than one school or college would commence on the central level. Matters explicitly excluded from the grievance procedure were complaints relating to the merits of the removal or suspension of faculty members, which concerns were treated exclusively in articles 35–40 of the university statutes; and complaints relating to the merits of appointment, reappointment, promotion, academic freedom, and tenure, which are also governed by the statutes. The rationale for these exclusions was that the provisions in the statutes cannot be unilaterally altered by the administration, and that they already provided ample protection for due process and peer judgment in consonance with AAUP guidelines.

Claims by either the AAUP-FA or the administration concerning a violation of Article XII (no strike-no lockout) or of article XV (which dealt with the university's center on Staten Island) could be submitted directly to arbitration with a hearing scheduled within seventy-two hours after receipt of notice by the American Arbitration Association.

The terms of the no strike-no lockout clause were precise and all-encompassing. The AAUP-FA agreed during the life of the contract not "to instigate, engage in, support, encourage or condone any strike, work stoppage, or other concerted refusal to perform work by any of the faculty." The administration agreed that it would "not lock out any or all of the faculty members covered by the agreement."

All in all, the faculty contract required a drafting period of almost two months on the part of four attorneys, including the Director of the Northeast Regional Office of the AAUP. Such painstaking care was employed to avoid any ambiguity in language and because of an awareness of the significance of the document not only as a basis for later St. John's contracts but also as a potential model for other institutions of higher learning.

The contract was finally submitted to the combined membership of the AAUP-FA for approval in late January 1971 by a mail ballot supervised by a national accounting firm. The faculty approved the agreement by a ratio of almost nine to one.

Contract Management and Implications

During its two-year life span, the initial agreement proved durable and effective. Faculty grievances were resolved on the lower levels without need for recourse to arbitration. Most of these grievances were minor in nature; for example, not fully aware of the contract's intent, some department chairmen failed to confer with individual faculty members prior to assigning class schedules. Both the faculty and the administration realized the positive value of the grievance machinery. The faculty was reassured that any legitimate complaint would have a full and fair hearing; the administration recognized the great saving of its time and energy in having many disputes resolved through the grievance process in conjunction with the AAUP-FA.

Only two grievances processed during the 1970–1972 contract had a major import. In June 1971 the board of trustees passed a resolution that amounted to the sudden imposition of a moratorium on the granting of tenure. The AAUP-FA immediately filed a grievance against the board citing this action as totally unfounded and as a direct violation of the 1966 AAUP statement which was incorporated into the contract. After considering the AAUP-FA objections, the board withdrew its resolution and granted tenure to those faculty members involved, all of whom had already been duly approved by their peers. The second serious grievance questioned the validity of procedures employed in arriving at a new undergraduate liberal arts core curriculum. The substance of the curriculum was not within the complaint of the AAUP-FA, since such matters of educational policy were outside its purview. The dean of the college, acting in his capacity as chairman of the Liberal Arts Faculty Council, however, was charged with violating the past-practices provision of the contract in that he had failed to observe a long-standing senate resolution requiring adequate public hearings and notice on important policy matters affecting the university. Concurrently, a majority of the liberal arts faculty, opposed not to the principle of curriculum revision, but rather to the specific plan proposed, petitioned the board of trustees to table the plan because of insufficient faculty consultation. Subsequently the Faculty Council recalled its controversial curriculum revision, meticulously culled faculty viewpoints, closely followed senate-mandated procedures, and ultimately passed an updated core curriculum acceptable to the majority of the liberal arts faculty.

Of primary significance in the St. John's collective bargaining experience was the fact that the predicted polarization creating a labor and management division within the university did not materialize. If anything, contact between the administrators and the faculty members became closer and more meaningful than before. The prompt appointment by the board of trustees of the former spokesman of the administration bargaining team as academic vice-president ensured the implementation of the principles of shared authority and faculty consultation as outlined in the 1966 AAUP statement. Representatives of the bargaining agent were briefed regularly on matters related to faculty welfare. A wide range of university problems were mutually resolved in a frank, congenial atmosphere. Memoranda of understanding were developed during the two-year contract period as a means to adjust existing procedures to the provisions of the agreement, including such matters as a revised university calendar for the submission of personnel items, the right of the faculty member to select any colleague of his choice to present his promotion or tenure case, the establishment of elected faculty bodies for the new Staten Island campus, and the granting of special waivers of limitations in class size, the number of class preparations, and so forth, because of extraordinary circumstances.

The collegial spirit which characterized relationships in the bargaining for the first contract carried over to the second round of negotiations. This relationship was enhanced in no small way by the fact that the majority of negotiators continued on for the second round of talks and thus were by then thoroughly seasoned. Also the first contract provided a firm point of reference.

The new contract in 1972 retained the academic gains made by the faculty in the first one and included minor refinements for clarity and effectiveness. It was a two-year agreement to expire in June 1974. Under its provisions, faculty members, including librarians, received a 5.8 percent salary increase across the board for each of the two years covered, with the stipulation that no one would receive less than $650 the first year and $600 the second. Other benefits included an increase in medical coverage, substantially increased promotional increments, and additional insurance benefits. A merit fund was set up to reward outstanding teaching and research. Chairmen were allotted an increased stipend for their administrative responsibilities.

A unique and especially significant aspect of the second contract was the designation of departmental chairmen as members of the bargaining unit. Under this agreement they were not to be viewed as supervisors, but rather as heads who derived their authority from the faculty members who nominated them for this position. To accentuate this collegial arrangement, the agreement provided for departmental committees on personnel and budget to share with chairmen the authority for recommendations on these crucial decisions.

Since the St. John's agreement provided that all elected faculty bodies would continue to exist as before, a period of adjustment was required to establish the jurisdiction of such bodies, notably of the University Senate, vis-a-vis the bargaining agent. At first, several standing committees of the senate, especially the faculty affairs and budget committees, were reticent to deal with any matters even remotely concerned with faculty working conditions. A senate committee was then appointed, with several officers of the bargaining agent among its members, to determine the role of the senate in light of the advent of collective bargaining. The committee recommended that the purview of the senate be defined as universitywide educational policy in the broadest sense of the term and that the senate should act freely in this area. However, whenever matters that involved faculty working conditions were passed by the senate, the bargaining agent retained the right to review them in terms of the existing agreement. One chief concern before the senate at this time is the formulation of universitywide criteria for tenure.

In its emphasis on collegiality and on the essentiality of elected faculty bodies, the St. John's agreement represents a marked departure from customary labor practice. It stands as a pioneering effort to shape the process of collective bargaining in higher education to the special circumstances of academic institutions.

Epilogue

Analysis and Perspective

Robert S. Fisk, E. D. Duryea

*This has been a volume of analysis and description of a new phe-
nomenon in higher education, one whose future is likely to be
problematical but which clearly warrants careful attention by all
who share our concern for the academic enterprise. To bring together the substance of the preceding chapters and to conjecture
about the basic nature of collective bargaining certainly strikes us as
requiring considerable temerity. Bargaining is entirely too new an
activity on college and university campuses to allow final judgments.
Thus, we submit our observations with a recognition of our brief
exposure to a very complicated development.*

We must await the tempering of further experience upon

*our observations and projections, perhaps with fingers crossed in
the hope they do not emerge naive or abortive. We submit, however, that to await further experience is undesirable when the need
for observations and insights, as well as suggestions and directions, is
so great.*

*What we have attempted is to portray the historical perspec-
tive, to examine the fundamental implications, and to identify
specific questions and issues associated with professional unionism
on campuses. We have confined our observations to the primary
concerns and future prospects. Thus we conclude the book with an
effort to describe the setting, to recognize past gains and future
hopes, and to project the immediate future for individuals, associations, and institutions contemplating or entering upon collective
negotiations.*

*Robert S. Fisk has been identified in the notes for Chapter
Seven. E. D. Duryea's career as administrator and scholar in higher
education includes posts as both dean and professor. He currently
is engaged in a study of the corporate status of universities and its
history which has led naturally to a concern over the implications of
bargaining.*

E. D. D. and R. S. F.

T he asking of the proper question is considered the first essential
step in determining a solution. For those who face decisions on
collective bargaining in higher education we have attempted to
solicit the right questions. They appear to be plentiful and relevant,
although the responses have proved sometimes tenuous, occasionally
contentious, and always subject to refinement as further empirical
data become available.

As we now turn to a summary and analysis to gain perspective on this new phenomenon we find that we must be less than
confident in many of the generalities we draw. Perhaps we should
be satisfied if the generalizations lead to a few working hypotheses.
We are agreed, however, that we should organize our comments
around three general dimensions. The first is the general milieu of
higher education and the nature of its culture; out of this unionism
is arising and into it unionism will intrude its particular set of

operatives. The second is institutional governance, which must undergo alteration most immediately as this new force enters affairs traditionally relegated to governing boards and their delegated recipients of authority—presidents and faculty governing bodies. Finally, we explore the broad impact of unionism on the total relationships of those associated with higher education.

Unionism and Academic Culture

Henry Steele Commager characterized the decade of the 1890s as the watershed of American history, one in which the topography is blurred, but in the perspective of a half century, the grand outlines emerge clearly. He referred to the maturing of the nation from a small-town, rural, self-centered society with values rooted in the seventeenth and eighteenth centuries, into an urban, industrial, technologically based country experiencing unsettling changes in its way of life. Concurrently, higher education expanded from a system of small colleges committed to teaching and a Protestant morality under the firm, personal hands of governing board members and presidents, to major, complex universities characterized by academic disciplines and professional schools and bolstered in academic standards by national associations. Graduate schools assumed a position of educational dominance, sending out faculty members imbued with a commitment to research and specialized knowledge. As professionals and experts in their substantive areas, since 1900 faculty members have slowly gained influence in the management of universities. The culture of the universities by the 1960s reflected the professionalization of higher education, with the faculty members both as participants and employees. While this frequently did not occur in many smaller institutions, which were dominated by their presidents and operated more like school systems or businesses, this culture set the standard to which all academicians in a general way aspired.

By the early 1960s, the trend to shared authority among faculty members and administrators seemed inevitable; it stamped with professional status the services of the professoriate, which made them inherently more than employees and strengthened the ancient ideal of the university as primarily an association of academicians.

The values were those which viewed the university as a body of scholars. As teacher-training institutions became state colleges, newer faculty members in the arts and sciences entered the ranks to bring a strong impetus in this direction. Research and scholarly contribution came to serve as the major criteria for evaluating achievement. The movement for faculty participation in academic government by the 1960s had gained the influence of a tradition respected by governing boards. It set the tone for the evolution of higher education. It had the continuing support of the influential American Association of University Professors (AAUP). It gained a formal statement in the 1967 report, *Faculty Participation in Academic Governance,* prepared by a special task force under the auspices of the American Association for Higher Education (AAHE). This report came out decisively for the concept of shared authority as the guiding principle for the development of the academic profession.

Yet, on the heels of the AAHE report, unionism appeared as a new and critical force. What had until then been associated with public schools and to a degree with two-year colleges—themselves viewed primarily as extensions of secondary education in many circles—spread to some four-year colleges and even into a few established large universities. As Garbarino noted in Chapter One, by 1970 tens of thousands of professionals in an expanding number of institutions had accepted bargaining agents, usually affiliated or associated with a national organization, to represent their interests. In effect, these individuals turned away from a primary dependence on shared authority to a more pragmatic reliance upon the power of organization outside the disciplinary and professional societies.

Whatever the causes of unionism, the consequence of a commitment to this form of organization poses a significant change in the academic milieu. Recognizing as it does a dichotomy of interests between those who manage and those who implement, collective bargaining accentuates the organizational role of faculty members as employees in contrast to the ideal of professionals who participate as partners in the academic enterprise. Perhaps this condition grows out of other factors such as the increase in size and complexity of colleges and universities and the emergence of state systems of higher education. Whatever the reasons, however, unionization will be associated with a changing campus scene in which professional personnel find their work far more regimented and conditioned by organizational arrangements than it now is. They face the possibility of finding themselves more like schoolteachers or business or public employees than the previous ideal of academic service portended.

The crux of this challenge to the traditional mode probably lies at the departmental level and in the relationship of the department to the administrative structure. If departments remain the centers for specialized study, much of the traditional context may remain. As the department loses its autonomous role through centralized administration or through loyalties to nondisciplinary bargaining associations, and even more fundamentally as research and scholarship based upon an extension of knowledge are forced to give way to additional teaching, one can anticipate a change in the professional role of faculty members in the organizational affairs of their institutions.

Such a change has further implications for the quality of life on campuses. It is logical that over time negotiated contracts will spell out far more distinctly the conditions of employment for faculty members. In one sense, such as the provision in the St. John's University agreement specifying maximum course preparations per semester, this will protect the burden on faculty members and the quality of their services. In another it will provide administrators with a mechanism for implementing efficiencies and achieving more effective or at least rational management. To this end they will support specifications for faculty productivity. To date, to judge from the Mortimer and Lozier report (Chapter Six), a trend in this direction has not surfaced.

What has appeared in campus relationships, however, is a greater formalization in the decision-making process. The discipline maintained by each side across the bargaining table necessitates a calculated interchange. This behavior and the attitudes it displays carries over into the grievance procedures and to meetings between union heads and campus presidents, which are required by contract to have formal agendas. Frank and informal administrative-faculty communications are placed under heavy strain. Formal, bureaucratic procedures combined with cautious, frequently written communication engender an uncomfortable climate to those accustomed to the more open give and take in which academic and administrative commitments had a much freer expression.

In many respects, the evolution viewed in this section will depend very much upon the governing structure of universities and colleges. The role of senates and other academic governing bodies and of departments as either autonomous academic units or as the outposts for effective administrative control of policy implementation may be important determinants. The analysis of unionization, in these terms, leads inevitably to a review of its impact upon governance.

Unionism and Governance

University and college governance refers to the formal structure and related activities which are used to make decisions affecting organizational relationships, procedures, and policies. In the college of yore, the president and board carried out this responsibility in a very direct and personal manner. Boards were authorized by formal grants of authority from public government to establish and manage colleges; presidents served as their administrators or executives.

The organizational history of higher education has been an account of the erosion of the personal influence of boards and presidents. As colleges became large and universities with complexities of size and expanded functions appeared, governing boards and presidents found themselves increasingly removed from the center of academic affairs. Board members, primarily noneducators, who met infrequently, could not keep in close touch with the on-going affairs of these increasingly complex institutions. Presidents had to spend more hours with a variety of essentially external relationships. More and more of the internal affairs shifted to administrative staff members such as vice-presidents, deans, office heads, and ultimately departments and their chairmen. At the same time faculty members perceived, or perhaps simply felt, what has been called a power vacuum, at least as far as academic affairs were concerned. They succeeded, particularly in the larger institutions, in bringing under the aegis of their own hierarchy of legislative bodies and councils control over academic policies. Out of the specialization and professionalization noted above, the departments emerged as the foundation stones of academic governance. In these units increasing numbers of faculty members gained professional security. Departments served as the crucible in which personal and professional values were fired, and they gained the toughness to enforce the criteria for appointments and promotions. As they were entwined with national associations, department-based faculty members achieved a kind of national self-governance.

Concurrently, over the past several decades, governing boards have experienced other intrusions which have eroded their power and influence despite the formal authority granted to them as private or public corporations. As higher education has become more available and consequently expanded, and as it has achieved an increasing importance for the society and its economy, public support has become increasingly a necessity and a prime source for funding. With this suport has come control, at least in public institutions, from budget offices, civil service commissions, and other offices of the executive branch of state government; an increasing legislative scrutiny of mounting budget requests; the overseeing by federal agencies of grants and allotments; and statewide coordinating and supervisory boards. The communications involved in nearly all of these bypass governing boards. Furthermore, state coordinating and supervisory boards, with their own executive bureaucracy, have added to the decision-making flow which passes by boards to presidents and even to members of their administrative staffs. The traditional autonomy of public colleges based upon the corporate status of their governing boards has been seriously eroded. It is likely that much of the same will happen to private institutions as they become dependent upon public financing.

It is in this kind of development that the movement to faculty unionism has taken place, and its impact requires evaluation within these terms of reference. For example, by negotiations with presidents and representatives of boards, unions may prove to be a force in support of the traditional corporate autonomy of public universities and colleges and a support for the autonomy of private ones. In contrast, as in the case of the Senate Professional Association (spa) in New York state, unions for public institutions may negotiate with representatives of the executive branch of state government and thus may reinforce the erosion of institutional autonomy and support the status of faculty members and professional personnel as employees of the state, parallel to civil service employees.

As one looks over the analyses presented in the preceding chapters, evidence of both tendencies appear. On the one hand, experience indicates that some bargaining efforts have enhanced the professional role of faculty members as participants in the academic enterprise. The analysis of Mortimer and Lozier demonstrates that contracts adapt their provisions in this regard to preexisting policies and thus serve as transmitters of past practices. They have supported to a degree the concept of a university as an enterprise in which at least the initiative for policies and procedures directing educational and scholarly affairs lies with the professionals and with governing bodies in which administrators and faculty members serve cooperatively. Other faculty associations, however, have accentuated the adversary relationship and stressed working conditions. The lines of divergence here are not clear. Conceivably unions can serve to support the trend to greater control by faculty members over institutional affairs and can bring into the established councils a greater strength in relationships with administrators on these matters. However, this may induce a change in faculty priorities. Evidence supports some tendencies to bring about a realignment of faculty commitments. The union can begin to hold the primary loyalty of professional personnel to the diminution of traditional attachments to disciplines and professions. This shift could stress conditions of employment, narrowly defined, to the denigration of concerns with academic affairs. Likewise, to the degree that unions negotiate directly with governing boards which have presidents as their agents, they accentuate the role of boards as the holders of corporate authority—the basis upon which the autonomy of institutions traditionally has rested. Yet, as unions gain strength they may erode further the responsibility of boards. The picture is not yet clearly focused. All we can do is examine some of the issues which have arisen.

One condition the foregoing analyses have brought out is that negotiations force into the open the question, as Wollett states it, of who is the employer. Conversely it forces into the negotiations and thus into the very administration of the institutions the individuals and agencies who must provide the support and approval essential to implement agreements. For private colleges and universities, members of governing boards have to involve themselves, if not directly at least in a very active consultative role. This proved to be the case at St. John's University, for example. In public universities and state systems, as in New York, the very fact that offices of employee relations handle negotiations conveys the message. They represent the governor who submits the budget and supports it to the legislature. Regents or trustees and chancellors or presidents, may have to step aside and accept an advisory role.

Such consequences generate two implications. One, they tell clearly whether an individual institution or system enjoys a degree of corporate autonomy. In Central Michigan University, despite public funding, such autonomy apparently exists, since the president represented the administrative interests of the institution, presumably for the board. For New York, it suggests either that the chancellor and his staff more appropriately belong on the union side of the table, or representatives of the governor and legislature must reconsider seriously their role. By assuming control of negotiations they relieve the university administrators of responsibility. Furthermore, they commit faculty members to the status of employees of the state rather than of the institutional corporation. The implications of these situations require careful deliberation in terms of the future welfare of higher education.

Another basic change accompanying collective bargaining concerns the formal nature of agreements which ensue. The written contract takes over as the fundamental law of the academic terrain. It provides legitimacy for administrative-faculty relationships in place of the policies and bylaws used in the past. Contracts may constitute an authority which transcends the board. To test this condition, the union of the City University of New York (CUNY) has instituted a case to force administrative compliance with contract provisions. The general use of external arbitration regarding points of disagreement moves internal affairs to bodies external to the corporation. Without question this will alter substantially the nature of participation in internal affairs. To the extent that contracts support a faculty role in decision-making, they give this role a far more secure basis than was ever possible previously. To the extent that boards concur in contractual arrangements through the exercise of their corporate authority, this authority is enhanced. In public institutions to the extent that state offices and centralized supervisory or coordinating agencies participate in negotiations, board authority diminishes. At stake is the nature of the university or college governance and concomitantly the nature of the academic enterprise.

A significant issue has emerged also over the role of the department chairman either as a kind of foreman or administrative supervisor responsible to the administration or as an elected representative of members of the department. As Mortimer and Lozier found, practice to date varies according to the local situation and existing function of these officers. But the issue must become crucial, since the traditional system of faculty government rests upon a foundation of departments whose representatives at the school or college level have exercised a major influence in academic and personnel affairs. As long as departments remain the major centers of academic power, the nature of their control must influence strongly the nature of institutional governance.

Closely related to the role of the chairman insofar as the professional versus employee role of faculty members is concerned is the question of participation in the determination of various personnel policies having to do with appointments, promotions, tenure, evaluation, and even personnel files. Mortimer and Lozier note that the evidence fails to support the contention that unions will bargain-off principles of participation for more immediate economic gains. They found provision for faculty participation in committees recommending the appointments of deans and presidents. Presumably, unions do not seek actively to replace by their own organization various faculty councils and senates and the associated committees where they exist. One gets the impression that the union press will be to maintain the status quo of faculty role in government where it exists but to supplement it with organized pressure in the areas heretofore subject to individual bargaining based upon criteria of disciplinary and professional associations. The experience in the State University of New York (SUNY) situation and the contract negotiated at St. John's certainly support this conclusion. Yet, it must be recognized in this fluid and uncertain situation that the evident acceptance of an adversary relationship may make the faculty-administration differences much sharper.

The adversary relationship supported by the intrusion into the academic realm of attitudes associated with unionism in industry and public departments may coerce academic unions into a similar mold. The statements and policies of the National Labor Relations Board (NLRB) and various state employment relations commissions support this prediction. It appears clearly in the case of Central Michigan University where the governing board and administration are designated as the "university," thus placing faculty members in an adversary or contending role against the institution rather than as a part of it. Within SUNY differences over the nature of this relationship have intruded into the councils of SPA, with the representatives of the major university centers viewing themselves as an integral part of the university and those from some of the other units perceiving administrators as their natural foes.

Illustrative points are many. The point of this analysis is that unions have come on the scene at a time when the basic autonomy of colleges and universities as corporate entities has suffered considerable erosion from a number of influences. The impact of unionism, therefore, looms as crucial for the evolution of higher education in this and subsequent decades. If one feels a concern for the autonomy of higher institutions, then one of necessity must consider this impact. To date, how it will affect university and college government, and its related autonomy, remains uncertain. Yet one thing is quite clear. Unions will establish, where they obtain contracts, a new legal basis for the nature of faculty participation and for many of the policies which direct institutional affairs. They will open up to a broader swath of the professional personnel the opportunity for greater control over their working conditions. At the same time, as the contracts studied by Mortimer and Lozier confirm, one can anticipate a clarification of administrative powers. Evidence of this appears in the common insertion of management rights clauses in these early agreements. Unions require one more bureaucracy which will impose a new set of relationships for individuals to contend with. Furthermore, they set up a new focus for

professional loyalty which must inevitably interfere with commitments to disciplinary and professional associations. In this sense they
turn the professionals toward a much more local orientation, and
they may threaten seriously established criteria associated with
scholarly production as a basis for advancement. Above all, unions
will, as they have in factories and government offices, reduce distinctions based upon individual achievement or administrative preference to the end of what is called the common good.

These considerations are largely of the long-range variety.
In the more immediate future unionism on campuses is likely to
have other impacts.

Impact of Collective Bargaining

As noted above, it is too soon to arrive at firm generalizations
about collective negotiations in higher education. Yet, it is possible
to propose a number of central tendencies and specific conditions
which begin to surface and which constitute important signposts for
those actively concerned about this phenomenon from a more immediate, operational point of view.

First, we may anticipate increased political activities on
behalf of higher education by the employee organizations that
emerge. States without enabling legislation for such organizations in
public higher education will be pressured toward the appropriate
statutes unless the need should disappear because of superior federal
legislation. The states already providing the necessary sanctions will
undoubtedly experience formal pressure on their own behalf by the
new unions. Whether the new alliances between higher education
organizations and their counterparts in the public schools will prove
as politically potent as their advocates predict remains to be seen.
There is still much latent suspicion within the ranks of each category concerning the motives of the other. Also, legitimate differences
exist, from the point of view of society in general, in the perceptions
of what should be given the higher priority when choices must be
made. But either in combination or unilaterally the new organizations may constitute a significant force for causing society to rethink
its priorities. They certainly will exert major efforts toward a financing which will continue to provide what professors regard as an

adequate economic return for their labors. As persons possessing well-developed social consciences combined with disciplined minds, faculty and professional staff can also be expected to make a strong case for continuing development of higher education.

Closely related to the commitment to political activity or lobbying on the part of unions will be the assumption of much of the responsibility for translating to the general public the nature and importance of the academic function. Heretofore, the public relations effort to interpret the importance of a university or colleges has rested with presidents and board members. However, as bargaining associations press for greater benefits and thus a larger share of financial resources, they will have to defend the value of the services of their members for the general society.

While we may anticipate a political challenge from the stronger base the unions provide and from their growth in political sophistication, there may be a serious question as to the ultimate impact within higher education itself. Some freely predict that unions will become essentially conservative forces, resistant to innovations directly affecting their working conditions or compensation and instead becoming walls of protection for the academician to continue to be academic. Their reaction to Buckminster Fuller's demand for the abolition of tenure is predictable. They can be expected to use the unions to bulwark their definition of academic freedom, concepts of work load, requirements for library and research facilities, and needs as contrasted with those of students (which are seldom mentioned in existing contracts). For professors to behave otherwise is to expect them to be more than human.

In other areas, however, such as that of peer judgment, the horizon is far less clear. The customary union structure suggests that its membership must always unite in advocacy of the interests of the membership, individual as well as collective. Thus union officials must assume that the grievance of any member, if it possesses any perceivable merit, should be processed aggressively. The thrust of the AAUP, however, and of tradition in prestige universities has been toward a high degree of involvement of one's peers in the process of review of a grievance and recommendation for administrative action. Where peer judgment is maintained contractually, the first test to be passed by the grievant is set by those who are or will be members of the bargaining unit and who may be governed by strong institutional considerations. It may be a far more severe test than whether the grievance will stand up in arbitration or with management. Can the two concepts, peer judgment, based upon rigorous concepts of institutional professional principles, and peer support, based upon the normal requirements for organizational development, exist side-by-side?

As noted above, what may prove to be a most significant development can emerge from the contractual relationship an agreement sets and the contrast in the power it generates for the union with that power formerly held by faculty members protected only by trustee policy and administrative benevolence. Under the protection of the NLRB and state employment relations statutes, plus what may be anticipated in judicial rulings, administrators and trustees should have a critical constituency, namely, the faculty, to whom they shall be highly accountable in matters dealt with in the agreement. Out of this should ultimately emerge a much more predictable basis for internal governance in higher education, one less subject to drastic change because of a new administration or a trustee directive.

Also, one can speculate about the relationship between a faculty union and existing faculty governance bodies. Will the union foster, weaken but still endorse, or totally substitute itself for the traditional faculty senate or council? Initially, and particularly where there has been a tradition of self-governance in many aspects of academic decision-making, unions will probably assume the posture of support for the other organizations out of genuine conviction or for political and organizational purposes or both. But as unions grow in strength, particularly with the support of agency shop legislation, and when the chips are down on a matter which the union views as within its territory of terms and conditions of employment, it is hard to conclude that the traditional bodies will not surrender many prerogatives. Just as the standards-setting function of AAUP may assume quite a different character and perception under collective bargaining, so may self-governance change in form and content with serious implications for previously highly regarded bodies and their procedures.

Finally, we can anticipate much troubled speculation about

the ultimate impact of unionism upon the sanctity and purity of a discipline as viewed by its constituents and from the point of view of social need. Presumably rigorous scholarship and objectivity in research and teaching have mandated the development of unique criteria for admission to and continuing sanction within a given discipline or area of inquiry. To this extent a discipline may have taken on much of the nature of the craft among skilled workers. On the other hand, the words and implications of due process constitute a battle cry within increasing numbers of employee organizations. While the Supreme Court in its two decisions in June 1972 failed to give sanction to due process for teachers, unions will certainly continue their battle for it except where their efforts may be qualified by the anxieties of the disciplines themselves and those of their members in academic settings which place a high premium on research and scholarship. Here it may be felt that the greater social need is for academic excellence and that this must prevail over protection of the individual. Faculty apprehension in this area may deter union development as much as any other single factor.

Some have said that the great universities and colleges represent the final bastion of true entrepreneurial activity, competition in the Adam Smith sense of it, unshackled by externally imposed limitations or encouragement such as that most business today enjoys. Such value may be attached to the continued progress of research and scholarship in this kind of competition and the nature of the setting which permits it that it limits the growth of unions in many institutions and qualifies it in others. To predict this as a pervasive hold on the unionization of faculty and professional staff in colleges and universities would be folly. The rate of development may be unpredictable, but the fact of future union growth seems undeniable. What remains is the task of shaping the form so as to continue to meet the changing needs of our society as well as to provide adequate safeguards for a constituency which is largely in need of them.

In addition to the above generalized tendencies associated with the advent of collective bargaining, a number of specific considerations will warrant attention. Briefly, a review of the following aspects of the process is essential for those who desire a better understanding of it: Most fundamental from our point of view has been the almost complete absence in the negotiation process and in the agreements ensuing of references to students and to institutional obligations for their clientele, both student and community. The most obvious reaction voiced on campuses has been the proposal of unions for students as a separate entity. The myopia of faculty members and administrators and of boards and state officials in this area will have to be broken down in the negotiations of the future, or serious repercussions will follow.

Another issue which may have been either pushed aside or viewed as no longer viable is that of the concept of merit or discretionary salary adjustments. It is still alive although it appears that SUNY is the only major institution to make mandatory provision for such, and it is too soon to determine whether the effort there will gain acceptance on both sides of the table. In SUNY most administrators throughout the system and many of the faculty and the professional staff in the university centers support the concept. Elsewhere the greater priority would appear to be improvement of salary minima and reduction of inequities between similar ranks and titles among different categories of unit. Speculation has it that the central administration of SUNY will need to press hard for the concept to maintain it in future contracts. Yet there are models in other unions, such as some of those in the arts and in professional sports, where substantial differentials are anticipated in the reward structure. It may be that the ultimate response in complex systems will lie in a measure of campus preference which is locally determined and consistent with the mores and value structures of the personnel on that campus. Those who place a high premium on the viability of the marketplace approach to faculty procurement and retention will continue to support merit reward systems. Those who view these as conflicting with other and more important values may seek the uniformity of the salary schedules which predominate in the public schools and other public enterprises. The empirical data would suggest that the more creative minds and productive scholars will seek the campuses which make some semblance of material reward for these qualities. To eliminate the potential for this is to suggest there are other, more important rewards possible and available or to deny the importance to a college or university of this kind of contribution.

Other problems should be contemplated by both sides before

moving too far down the road of the new relationship. The process is costly. It calls for much essentially nonproductive effort that will add significant financial burden to both sides. It requires additional bureaucracies to carry on negotiations, pursue grievances, and meet the requests for consultation and information. It relies heavily on faculty volunteer effort and must therefore supplant other activities. Many administrations have added to their staffs special officers to handle this activity. Union officers, on their side, already have begun to seek extra time on load, office space, and various secretarial or administrative services and facilities.

Not unrelated to the question of productivity is the need for precise language in contracts, a time-consuming effort at best. Although many urge that contracts should not attempt to spell out arrangements in detail, the contract stands as a document which must be referred to constantly and which at times must serve as the determining factor in legal disputes. Contract language should be sufficiently general to permit flexibility and adaptability in this new definition of staff and administrative relationships. No contract will be able to anticipate all exigencies. Presumably the more general the language the greater will be the dominance of the administration in the bargaining process or the mutual trust between the two sides. If the language should emerge from the latter circumstance, the administration will probably require careful attention to the communications processes which will best preserve the trust which has been demonstrated. The use at Central Michigan University of regular faculty-administrative committees stands out as a constructive effort to gain mutual understanding without detailing arrangements. This provision may serve as one facet of a new model for collective bargaining that can take advantage of the strong tradition of open communications found in some institutions.

Another fundamental consideration has been the composition of the bargaining unit. Within state systems it sharpens the functional contrasts between major universities and state colleges, both in terms of their academic endeavors and in their traditional administrative relationships. Where both are included in the same unit the differences among them will doubtless remain a pressing and divisive concern within the union itself. Concurrently, efforts to bring into one unit both academic and nonacademic professionals raise other problems related to the definition and interpretation of a community of interest essential to organizational strength. The effort on the part of central administration and state officials to limit their burden by supporting the concept of one major association could lead to undermining the academic stature of the complex university centers, for example. Joining teaching and nonteaching professionals in one unit may support efforts to spell out faculty work loads in a manner that challenges established and cherished customs for academic self-direction, which is deemed critical for scholarly efforts as well as for effective teaching. Overall, bargaining may contain an inherent tendency toward commonality and uniformity, at odds with the essentially individualistic role of teachers and researchers. Before making these initial decisions in terms of the advantages of single rather than separate bargaining units, from the point of view of the convenience of administrators and state executive staffs, it would seem most important to consider them in the frame of reference of the nature of the academic enterprise.

A parallel injection of external interests into the academic realm has appeared in the attitudes and values held by national associations such as the National Education Association (NEA) and American Federation of Teachers (AFT). These organizations are conditioned to public schools and to success and influence in gaining benefits for their members from the schools. Officers from such associations may bring to unionism in higher education a new tone or quality that, like other bargaining influences, rates deliberate review before allowing it to pervade the academic enterprise.

In many respects the grievance procedure constitutes one of the most vital aspects of academic unionism. As Finkin (Chapter Four) has mentioned, a broad spectrum in approach is apparent among agreements reached to date. There are at least two major considerations. First, formal grievance procedures give faculty members and professional staff members a far greater assurance of equity in their relationships with administration. The access to personnel files customarily agreed upon, the establishment of a formal review process on personnel decisions which are grieved, and the frequent availability of arbitration should lead to an ordering of administrative personnel procedures long overdue on many campuses. However, the place of peer review in these processes is far from clearly established. Where it is retained or established it lays the union open to the problem of grievances by members which are, in reality, against other members. Again referring to Chapter Four, this aspect of negotiations probably represents the phase most in the process of evolution. How practice evolves will depend to a high degree on the climate of relationships which begins to characterize collective bargaining in higher education generally.

For grievances and for bargaining in general one can discern rather clearly that a great restraint will be imposed upon capriciousness on the part of both the administration and the faculty. The opening general purview of a variety of decisions and actions very likely will have a healthy impact. Faculty members should find it to their advantage to clarify the nature of their contributions. Administrators will find it difficult, and at times embarrassing, to resort to under-the-table practices by which decisions affecting the interests and welfare of others only too frequently have been made. What could result is a reaching of some kind of balance which imposes accountability and yet provides for the exercise of responsibility on the part of both sides. Teaching is a personal activity not easily forced into neat patterns; yet it carries responsibility to students and to the public. Administration has a responsibility for good institutional management which rests upon forms of authority and power; yet this responsibility retains its social effectiveness over the long run when exercised in a manner that is accountable to students, faculty members, and the general public.

Essentially, unions have to protect the economic interests of their members. So self-evident is this that one tends to neglect it in an examination of the overall implications of the bargaining movement. But present it is and must remain. To a high degree, as Angell documents in his survey of the community colleges (Chapter Five), unions have contributed substantially to the economic welfare of their constituencies. The significant raises gained at St. John's University, the upper limit of well over thirty thousand dollars a year at CUNY, the more than 10 percent total over two years in SUNY during a time of budget retrenchment, and numerous other examples testify to this achievement. Fringe benefits of various sorts regularly have accompanied contracts and added to faculty accrual of indirect income.

In a real sense, however, economic gains more than any others fertilize unions and give them the strength with their constituency that is necessary for their organizational survival—an element, as noted before, inevitable in a movement of this sort. Such thinking carries us clearly to the final fillip of this summary, namely, the use of strikes. It would serve no purpose here to go over the substance of Wollett's excellent analysis in Chapter Two. For unions in general, strikes constitute the final force—the ultimate weapon. Whether this will be true in higher education must at this writing remain moot. One historian contemplated a major strike on the part of the faculty of SUNY and concluded there would be dire consequences—including the ruin of the academic enterprise, overwhelmed as it would be in a vigorous, retaliatory response by state government backed by strong public opinion. At this time the strike does not proffer itself as a viable weapon for the academic unions. Academic unions lack a tradition in their constituency and the logistical support of organization and funds to carry through with several months of enforced unemployment without pay within institutions that simply do not face a parallel loss of income and need but wait for support from students and parents fearful of the loss of an education for themselves or their offspring.

Thus it seems inevitable that faculty associations will look to legal supports and authority and to public criticism when administrators and boards, or even state executive officers, fail to bargain genuinely or to implement contracts which have been signed. They will turn to the NLRB and to parallel state employee relations boards for support and ultimately will rely on legal action and court injunctions. How this will work out remains to be seen. But the strike as a weapon of unionism will not leave the horizon easily and will remain at least a conjectural action, if a somewhat remote one.

Need for a New Model

It must be granted that the spread of unionism reflects a kind of symptomatic response to conditions of the late 1960s growing out of the many uncertainties and threats which have beset faculty members in these years. This condition was accentuated by student violence on one side and by the societal reaction leading into a recession of support on the other. An era of academic prestige and prosperity appeared terminated. A new, uncertain future of different relationships and restricted opportunities loomed. As this uncertain future settles into the more customary present and a stable if not affluent situation shapes up, the thrust to unionism may lose much of its force. Collective bargaining may gain only a partial success, to become one form of administrative-faculty relationship and be limited largely to the smaller institutions. Yet, this prospect does not fit the history of unionism over the past few decades. Far more likely, collective bargaining will continue to spread, even if it does so much more slowly than first anticipated.

Thus, it is probable that collective negotiations will replace individual bargaining as the basis for the professionals' relationships with their institutions. All concerned about the welfare of higher education and the maintenance of its significant role in our society will do well to give heed. To this end several considerations grow out of the foregoing discussion.

First, a union is an organization, a bureaucracy. As such it has the will to survive associated with all organizations. One cannot expect from it a dedication which would place a commitment to the higher principles of education ahead of its existence. One can expect realistically many of the same kind of self-aggrandizements which characterize other associations, both those related to organizational success and those related to the advancement of individuals who serve within it. One can expect all the petty foibles and failures which seem eternally a part of human associations.

Second, one can hope that faculty members and their non-teaching associates will hold values associated with professionals in the sense of a high degree of commitment to teaching, scholarship, and educational allegiance generally. One ought to expect also that a repugnance to the status of employees, narrowly defined, of an institution or a state government will be felt more deeply than in other enterprises. One would hope to see among faculty members a sense of the professional nature of the university enterprise in terms of the educational development of citizens and the ability of society to maintain itself in an increasingly complex knowledge-based world civilization. Similarly one would anticipate that administrators would exhibit this kind of professional commitment. In

sum, one can believe that professional and administrative staff members should find a professional commitment very much in common,
a basis for mutual interest and endeavors stronger than that for un-
ending and pervasive adversarial conflict.

Finally, one may even project that an enlightened realism
might ultimately begin to characterize collective negotiations by
unions in which short-range concerns having to do with the security
and standard of living of members in the competition for society's
resources would be balanced with a dedication to professional responsibilities. Likewise, it would seem at least possible for administrators to balance their managerial responsibilities with a recognition
of the primary circumstances related to the academic endeavor. The
short-range commitment constitutes short-sighted self-interest; the
broader view alone amounts to an ineffectual idealism. The two
combined, however, suggest that both union negotiators and their
counterparts across the table avoid sliding unthinkingly into a model
for bargaining which has served for a different kind of enterprise.
More positively this line of thinking urges the immediate, thoughtful
examination of academic unions as professional organizations holding a potential for a professional relationship over the bargaining
table and in the administration of contracts that would be based
upon a new model, unique to the academic scene. The alternative
for both professionals and administrators poses an employee-man-
agement relationship which can hardly serve an enterprise so inti-
mately concerned with humanity's intellectual welfare and possible
survival.

Selected
Bibliography

William C. Puffer

The following references are appended to the book as a convenience to readers who may wish to push further into the discussions of collective bargaining. As in any selected bibliography, judgment has had to be made as to what should be included or excluded. The criterion used here is the degree to which a work complements the foregoing discussions. Thus, many references have been omitted which nevertheless make a positive contribution to the understanding of collective negotiations in higher education. For comprehensive listings several bibliographies are now in print, such as the annotated listings by Schulman, North, and Marks.

Collective bargaining in higher education has two major

characteristics: its recency, or "newness," and its dramatic development over a very few years. The literature reflects both. Since 1966 it has grown from a handful of works to a burgeoning list of books, reports, and journal articles. Most of these tend to be more speculative than empirical (since operating experience has been limited) even though the implications of this new mode for faculty-administrative relations are quite dramatic. More recent publications have tended to draw more heavily upon experience in the field and upon related conditions such as precedents and legal opinions.

Despite the lack of hard data, most of the early articles prove to be quite insightful; they constitute a body of analysis which focuses on the major issues, discusses the potential implications, and formulates and articulates positions on the issues. One example is Elam and Moskow's *Employment Relations in Higher Education,* which is a report of a symposium sponsored by Phi Delta Kappa and Temple University in 1967. It contains a number of excellent papers, and the discussion is both informative and spirited. A second example is the American Association for Higher Education's *Faculty Participation in Academic Governance,* which contains an insightful discussion of the relationship between academic governance and collective bargaining.

A number of articulate position papers approach the issue of collective bargaining from an essentially ideological perspective, addressing themselves to the pros and cons. Three representative papers expressing various faculty positions are Kugler's "The Union Speaks for Itself," Marmion's "Unions and Higher Education," and Davis' "Unions and Higher Education: Another View."

In terms of the number of institutions involved, the types of institutions affected, and the amount of time institutions have been negotiating or living under their second or third contract, it is now feasible to conduct empirically oriented studies and collect corroborative data. The appearance of a number of case studies reflects this trend. These include reports of the Michigan community colleges, the California state colleges, the University of Wisconsin, and the City University of New York. A number of others are in the research stage. It is also now possible to state the implications of contract provisions, as in Mortimer and Lozier's *Collective Bargaining: Implications for Governance.* This trend is also reflected in the studies by Garbarino for the Carnegie Commission and by the various contributors, such as Wollett and McHugh, in the 1971 *Wisconsin Law Review.*

While much of the literature is rapidly filling in some of the gaps in our knowledge, much remains to be done, particularly in terms of precisely how the collective bargaining process affects established modes of academic governance and degrees of institutional autonomy.

General

American Association for Higher Education. *Faculty Participation in Academic Governance.* Washington, D.C., 1967.

BEATTY, D. L., AND ENCINIO, P. A. "Professional Negotiations on the Higher Education Scene." *Illinois Education,* February 1971, *59,* 108–10.

BOYD, W. B. "Collective Bargaining in Academe: Causes and Consequences." *Liberal Education,* October 1971, *57,* 306–318.

BROWN, M. A. "Collective Bargaining on the Campus: Professors, Associations and Unions." *Labor Law Journal,* March 1970, *21,* 167–181.

BROWN, R. S., JR., "Collective Bargaining in Higher Education." *Michigan Law Review,* February 1969, *67,* 1067–1082.

BROWN, R. C. "Professors and Unions: The Faculty Senate: An Effective Alternative to Collective Bargaining in Higher Education?" *William and Mary Law Review,* Winter 1970, *12,* 252–332.

BUCKLEW, N. S. "Employment Relations of Staff Employees in Institutions of Higher Learning." *Journal of the College and University Personnel Association,* December 1970, *22,* 74–107.

BUCKLEW, N. S. "Collective Bargaining in Higher Education: Its Fiscal Implications." *Liberal Education,* May 1971, *57,* 255–260.

"Colleges and Universities Where Faculties Have Chosen Collective Bargaining Agents," *Chronicle of Higher Education,* May 15, 1972, p. 2.

DAVIS, B. M. "Unions and Higher Education: Another View." *Educational Record,* Spring 1968, *49,* 139–144.

"Developments in the Law—Academic Freedom." *Harvard Law Review,* March 1968, *81,* 1045–1159, especially Part II, Section D, "Regulations by Professional Associations," and Section E, "Collective Bargaining," 1105–1121, 1121–1128.

DURYEA, E. D., AND FISK, R. S. "Collective Bargaining: What Does It Mean for Public Higher Education." *Compact,* June 1972, *6,* 40–43.

ELAM, S., AND MOSKOW, M. H. (Eds.) *Employment Relations in Higher Education.* Bloomington, Ind.: Phi Delta Kappa, 1969.

FERGUSON, T. H. "Collective Bargaining in Universities and Colleges." *Labor Law Journal,* December 1968, *19,* 778–804.

FINKIN, M. W. "Collective Bargaining and University Government." *AAUP Bulletin,* Summer 1971, *57,* 149–162.

GARBARINO, J. W. "Precarious Professors: New Patterns of Representation." *Industrial Relations,* February 1971, *10,* 1–20.

GARBARINO, J. W. "Faculty Unionism: From Theory to Practice." *Industrial Relations,* February 1972, *11,* 1–17.

GIANOPULOS, J. "Collective Bargaining: What Part Should College Presidents Play?" *College and University Business,* September 1970, *49,* 71–72. 102.

GILLIS, J. W. "Academic Collective Bargaining." *Liberal Education,* December 1970, *56,* 594–604.

GILLIS, J. W. "Continuing Development of Academic Collective Bargaining." *Liberal Education,* December 1971, *57,* 529–540.

GOODWIN, H. I., AND ANDES, J. O. *Collective Bargaining in Higher Education: Contract Content 1972.* Morgantown: College of Human Resources and Education, West Virginia University, 1972.

HAUG, M. R., AND SUSSMAN, M. B. "Professionalization and Unionism: A Jurisdictional Dispute?" *American Behavioral Scientist,* March 1971, *14,* 525–540.

HANLEY, D. L. "Issues and Models for Collective Bargaining in Higher Education." *Liberal Education,* March 1971, *57,* 5–14.

HEALEY, T. S. "The Future of Tenure." *Bulletin of the Association of Departments of English,* May 1972, pp. 3–7.

HOWE, R. A. "Bloody Business of Bargaining." *College and University Business,* March 1970, *48,* 63–67.

KENNELLY, J. R. "Collective Bargaining in the Community College." *Educational Record,* Winter 1971, *52,* 87–92.

KUGLER, I. "The Union Speaks for Itself," *Educational Record,* Fall 1968, *49,* 414–418.

LIEBERMAN, M. "Representational Systems in Higher Education." In S. Elam and M. H. Moskow (Eds.), *Employment Relations in Higher Education.* Bloomington, Ind.: Phi Delta Kappa, 1969.

LIEBERMAN, M. "Professors United!" *Harper's Magazine,* October 1971, pp. 61–70.

MC CONNELL, T. R. "Faculty Unionism and Faculty Senates." In T. R. McConnell (Ed.), *The Redistribution of Power in Higher Education.* Berkeley: Center for Research and Development in Higher Education, University of California, 1971.

MC HUGH, W. F. "Collective Bargaining with Professionals in Higher Education: Problems in Unit Determination." *Wisconsin Law Review,* 1971, *1,* 55–90.

MARKS, K. E. *Collective Bargaining in United States Higher Education, 1970–71.* Ames: Library, Iowa State University, 1972.

MARMION, H. A. "Unions and Higher Education." *Educational Record,* Winter 1968, *49,* 41–48.

MORTIMER, K. P., AND LOZIER, G. G. *Collective Bargaining: Implications for Governance.* University Park: Center for the Study of Higher Education, Pennsylvania State University, 1972.

MOSKOW, M. H. "The Scope of Collective Bargaining in Higher Education." *Wisconsin Law Review,* 1971, *1,* 33–54.

National Education Association. *Sample Master Contract for Colleges and Universities.* Washington, D.C., 1970.

"The National Labor Relations Board and Faculty Representation Cases: A Report from Committee N." *AAUP Bulletin,* Autumn 1971, *57,* 433–438.

NORTH, J. *Collective Bargaining in Higher Education.* University, Ala.: Manpower and Industrial Relations Institute, University of Alabama, 1972.

SABOL, G. G. "NLRB's Assertion of Jurisdiction over Universities." *University of Pittsburgh Law Review,* Spring 1971, *32,* 416–429.

SANDS, C. D. "The Role of Collective Bargaining in Higher Education." *Wisconsin Law Review,* 1971, *1,* 150–176.

SHULMAN, C. H. *Collective Bargaining on Campus.* Washington, D.C.: American Association for Higher Education, 1972.

SPARVERO, L. J. "The Impact of Labor Legislation in Colleges and Universities—State Labor Legislation Jurisdiction." *The College Counsel,* June 1967, *2,* 185–194.

TICE, T. N. (Ed.) *Faculty Power: Collective Bargaining on Campus.* Ann Arbor, Mich.: Institute for Continuing Legal Education, 1972.

VAN ALSTYNE, W. W. "Tenure and Collective Bargaining." In G. K. Smith (Ed.), *New Teaching, New Learning: Current Issues in Higher Education 1971.* San Francisco: Jossey-Bass, 1971.

WOLLETT, D. H. "The Status and Trends of Collective Negotiations for Faculty in Higher Education." *Wisconsin Law Review,* 1971, *1,* 2–32.

Case Studies

Analysis of Faculty Contract Information at Public Community Colleges in Michigan 1969–70. Lansing, Mich.: Michigan Community College Association, 1970.

ANGELL, G. W. "Collective Negotiations in Upstate New York," *Junior College Journal,* October 1971, *42,* 9–11.

BERUBE, M. R. "Strike at St. John's: Why the Professors Picket." *Nation,* February 14, 1966, pp. 172–174.

BUCKLEW, N. S. "Administering a Faculty Agreement." *Journal of the College and University Personnel Association,* May 1971, *22,* 46–51.

BUNZEL, J. H. "Faculty Strike at San Francisco State College." *AAUP Bulletin,* September 1971, *57,* 341–351.

CHRISTENSON, A. "Collective Bargaining in a University: The University of Wisconsin and the Teaching Assistants Association." *Wisconsin Law Review,* 1971, *1,* 210–228.

FEINSINGER, N. P. "The University of Wisconsin, Madison Campus—TAA Dispute of 1969–70, A Case Study." *Wisconsin Law Review,* 1971, *1,* 229–274.

HAAK, H. H. *Collective Bargaining and Academic Governance: The Case of the California State Colleges.* San Diego: Public Affairs Research Institute, San Diego State College, 1968.

HAEHN, J. O. *Collective Bargaining in Higher Education: An Empirical Analysis in the California State Colleges.* Chico, Calif.: Chico State College, 1971.

HEPLER, J. C. "Timetable for a Takeover." *Journal of Higher Education,* February 1971, *42,* 103–115.

MC HUGH, W. F. "Collective Negotiations in Public Higher Education: Experience Under the Taylor Law." *College and University Business,* December 1969, *47,* 41–44.

MINTZ, B. "The CUNY Experience." *Wisconsin Law Review,* 1971, *1,* 112–124.

MOORE, J. W. *Pennsylvania Community College Faculty: Attitudes Toward Collective Negotiations.* University Park: Center for the Study of Higher Education, Pennsylvania State University, 1971.

POLISHOOK, S. S. "Collective Bargaining and the City University of New York." *Journal of Higher Education,* May 1970, *41,* 377–386.

SHERMAN, F. E., AND LOEFFLER, D. "Universities, Unions and the Rule of Law: Teaching Assistants at Wisconsin." *Wisconsin Law Review,* 1971, *1,* 187–209.

References

AARON, B. *Some Painful Realities*. Unpublished paper delivered to the First Annual Conference of California Higher Education Association. December 1971.

"Academic Freedom and Tenure: St. John's University (N. Y.)." *AAUP Bulletin*, Spring 1966, *52*, 12–19.

American Association for Higher Education. *Faculty Participation in Academic Governance*. Report of the Task Force on Faculty Representation and Academic Negotiations. Washington D.C., 1967.

American Association of University Professors. "Academic Freedom and Tenure, 1940 Statement of Principles and Interpretive Comments." *AAUP Bulletin*, Autumn 1970, *56*, 323–326.

American Association of University Professors. *AAUP Policy Documents and Reports*. Washington, D.C., 1971.

ANGELL, G. W. "Grievance Procedures Under Collective Bargaining: Boon or Burden?" *Phi Delta Kappan*, April 1972, 501–505.

Board of Higher Education of the City of New York v. *Legislative Conference*, AAA Case 1339-0706-70 (December 1, 1970).

Board of Higher Education of the City of New York v. *United Federa-*

tion of College Teachers. AFL-CIO, Local 1460, AAA Case 1330-0282-70 (June 24, 1972).

Board of Trustees of Schoolcraft College v. Schoolcraft College Faculty Forum, AAA Case 5440-0177-69 (August 22, 1969).

BOYD, W. B. "Collective Bargaining in Academe: Causes and Consequences." *Liberal Education,* 1971, *57,* 306–318.

BUCKLEW, N. S. "Employment Relations of Staff Employees in Institutions of Higher Education." *The Journal of the College and University Personnel Association,* March 1971, 44–78.

Central Michigan University. *Agreement, 1970–1971.* Mt. Pleasant, Michigan, 1970.

Central Michigan University. *Agreement, 1971–1974.* Mt. Pleasant, Michigan, 1971.

City University of New York v. United Federation of College Teachers, Local 1460, AFL-CIO, AAA Case 1330-0286-70 (May 26, 1971).

"Colleges and Universities Where Faculties Have Chosen Collective Bargaining Agents." *Chronicle of Higher Education,* May 15, 1972, p. 2.

"College and University Government: St. John's University (N. Y.)." *AAUP Bulletin, Autumn* 1968, *54,* 325–361.

"Developments Relating to Censure by the Association." *AAUP Bulletin,* Spring 1972, *58* 78–82.

FINKIN, M. W. "Collective Bargaining and University Government." *Wisconsin Law Review,* 1971, *1971* (1), 125–149.

GARBARINO, J. W. "Creeping Unionism and the Faculty Labor Market." Mimeographed. 1971.

HAEHN, J. O. *A Survey of Faculty and Administrator Attitudes on Collective Bargaining.* Academic Senate of the California State Colleges, May 1970. Mimeographed.

HEALEY, T. S. "The Future of Tenure." *Bulletin of the Association of Departments of English* May 1972, 3–7.

HEPLER, J. C. "Time Table for a Take Over." *Journal of Higher Education,* February 1971, *42,* 103–115.

HOGAN, J. B. "Arbitrating a Grievance." *Journal of Collective Negotiations in the Public Sector,* February 1972.

Legislative Conference v. Board of Higher Education, 330 NYS 2d 688 (App. Div. 1st Dept., 1972).

LIEBERMAN, M. "Professors Unite!" *Harper's Magazine,* October 1971, 61–70.

MC HUGH, W. F. *New York Community College Collective Negotiation Contract Survey.* January 1971.

MORTIMER, K. P., AND G. G. LOZIER. *Collective Bargaining: Implications for Governance.* University Park, Pa.: Center for the Study of Higher Education, 1972.

National Education Association. *Salaries in Higher Education, 1969–70.* Research report 1970–R6. Washington, D. C., 1970a.

National Education Association. *Sample Master Contract for Colleges and Universities,* Washington, D.C.: June 1970b.

"Report of Committee A, 1970–71." *AAUP Bulletin,* Summer 1971, *57,* 191–205.

Report of Special Subcommittee on Faculty Organization for Collective Action of the Academic Senate, Berkeley Division. Berkeley, California, University of California, May 20, 1972.

"Report of the Survey Subcommittee of Committee T." *AAUP Bulletin,* Spring 1971, *57,* 68–124.

St. Clair County Community College v. *St. Clair County Community College District of Michigan Association for Higher Education,* AAA Case 5439-0307-71 (September 7, 1971).

SANDS, C. D. "The Role of Collective Bargaining in Higher Education." *Wisconsin Law Review,* 1971, *1971* (1), 150–176.

SHERWIG, J. *Collective Negotiations: Is This the Answer?* Unpublished paper delivered to the First Annual Conference of California Higher Education Association. December 1971.

SHOUP, C. A. *A Study of Faculty Collective Bargaining in Michigan Community Colleges.* Unpublished dissertation. Michigan State University, 1969.

SLICHTER, S. H. "The Changing Character of American Industrial Relations." In J. T. Dunlop (Ed.), *Potentials of the American Economy: Selected Essays of Sumner H. Slichter.* Cambridge, Mass.: Harvard University Press, 1961.

SLICHTER, S. H., HEALY, J. AND LIVERNASH, R. *The Impact of Collective Bargaining on Management.* Washington, D.C.: Brookings Institute, 1960.

SMU Faculty Federation Chapter 1845 AFT v. *Board of Trustees, SMU,* AAA Case 1139-049-70 (March 10, 1971).

STEVENS, C. "The Professor and Collective Action: Which Kind?" Paper presented at University of Minnesota Industrial Relations Center. May 18, 1971.

United Federation of College Teachers, Local 1460, AFT, AFL-CIO

v. *City University of New York,* AAA Case 1339-0284-70 (June 23, 1970).

U.S. Department of Health, Education, and Welfare, National Center for Educational Statistics. *Projections of Educational Statistics to 1979–80.* Washington D.C., 1970.

VAN ALSTYNE, W. W. "Tenure and Collective Bargaining." In G. K. Smith (Ed.), *New Teaching, New Learning.* San Francisco: Jossey-Bass, 1971, 201–217.

WOLLETT, D. H. "Trends in the Law of Collective Negotiations in Education." *Popular Government,* 1970, *36*(7).

WOLLETT, D. H. "The Status and Trends of Collective Negotiations for Faculty in Higher Education." *Wisconsin Law Review,* 1971, *1971*(1), 2–32.

Index